T0387161

'INNOCENT WOMEN AND CHILDREN'

Gender in a Global/Local World

Series Editors: Jane Parpart, Pauline Gardiner Barber
and Marianne H. Marchand

Gender in a Global/Local World critically explores the uneven and often contradictory ways in which global processes and local identities come together. Much has been and is being written about globalization and responses to it but rarely from a critical, historical, gendered perspective. Yet, these processes are profoundly gendered albeit in different ways in particular contexts and times. The changes in social, cultural, economic and political institutions and practices alter the conditions under which women and men make and remake their lives. New spaces have been created – economic, political, social – and previously silent voices are being heard. North-South dichotomies are being undermined as increasing numbers of people and communities are exposed to international processes through migration, travel, and communication, even as marginalization and poverty intensify for many in all parts of the world. The series features monographs and collections which explore the tensions in a 'global/local world', and includes contributions from all disciplines in recognition that no single approach can capture these complex processes.

Also in the series

(En)Gendering the War on Terror
War Stories and Camouflaged Politics
Edited by
Krista Hunt and Kim Rygiel
ISBN 0 7546 4481 2

Women, Migration and Citizenship
Edited by
Evangelia Tastsoglou and Alexandra Dobrowolsky
ISBN 0 7546 4379 4

Transnational Ruptures
Gender and Forced Migration
Catherine Nolin
ISBN 0 7546 3805 7

The Gender Question in Globalization
Changing Perspectives and Practices
Edited by
Tine Davids and Francien van Driel
ISBN 0 7546 3923 1

'Innocent Women and Children'
Gender, Norms and the Protection of Civilians

R. CHARLI CARPENTER
University of Pittsburgh, USA

ASHGATE

© R. Charli Carpenter 2006

All rights reserved. No part of this publication may be reproduced, stored in a retrieval system or transmitted in any form or by any means, electronic, mechanical, photocopying, recording or otherwise without the prior permission of the publisher.

R. Charli Carpenter has asserted her moral right under the Copyright, Designs and Patents Act, 1988, to be identified as the author of this work.

Published by
Ashgate Publishing Limited
Gower House
Croft Road
Aldershot
Hampshire GU11 3HR
England

Ashgate Publishing Company
Suite 420
101 Cherry Street
Burlington, VT 05401-4405
USA

Ashgate website: http://www.ashgate.com

British Library Cataloguing in Publication Data
Carpenter, R. Charli
  'Innocent women and children' : gender, norms and the
  protection of civilians. - (Gender in a global/local world)
  1. Combatants and noncombatants (International law) 2. War
  victims - Legal status, laws, etc. 3. Intervention
  (International law)
  I. Title
  341.6'7

Library of Congress Cataloging-in-Publication Data
Carpenter, R. Charli.
  'Innocent women and children' : gender, norms and the protection of
  civilians / by R. Charli Carpenter.
      p. cm. -- (Gender in a global/local world)
  Includes bibliographical references and index
  ISBN 0-7546-4745-5
  1. War--Protection of civilians. 2. War victims--Legal status, laws,
  etc. 3. Combatants and noncombatants (International law) 4. Women
  and war. 5. Children and war. I. Title. II. Series.

KZ6515.C37 2006
341.6'7--dc22

2005034914

ISBN 0 7546 4745 5

Printed and bound in Great Britain by Antony Rowe Ltd, Chippenham, Wiltshire.

Contents

List of Figures and Tables	*vi*
Preface and Acknowledgements	*vii*
List of Abbreviations	*x*

1	Introduction: Gender, Norms and the Protection of Civilians	1
2	Gendered Innocence: The Concept of the "Civilian" in International Society	25
3	Implementing the Civilian Immunity Norm: Three "Gender Sub-Norm" Effects	55
4	Advocating for Civilians: Gender Discourse in Transnational Human Rights Networks	91
5	Protecting Civilians in Conflict Zones: Evacuation Operations in the Former Yugoslavia	131
6	"Un-Gendering" Civilian Protection, Engendering Change	163

Bibliography	*175*
Index	*211*

List of Figures and Tables

Table 2.1	Frequency of rhetorical references incorporating sex according to context, PoC documents 1999-2003	39
Figure 4.1	Agenda-setting in world politics	105
Table 4.1	Change in number of references to vulnerability, peace, and decision-making, as a percentage of total number of references to women, PoC documents 1999-2003	124
Table 5.1	Hypotheses	147
Table 5.2	Belligerents' policy-preference structures regarding evacuation	153
Table 5.3	Protection agencies' policy-preference structures regarding evacuation: counterfactual v. actual	155

Preface and Acknowledgements

Throughout the 1990s, it was commonplace in international security and human rights discourse to argue that women and children constitute the primary civilian victims in armed conflict. In October 2005, the Liu Institute launched a report providing a wealth of epidemiological data debunking this claim, but the argument that women and children are disproportionately affected by war continues to be reiterated in many policy circles concerned with the protection of war-affected civilians. The point of *'Innocent Women and Children'* is not simply to unpack this view and examine it as the deeply gendered construct that it is, but also to explore how the association of "women and children" with the concept of the "innocent civilian" affects and undermines the protection of civilians in international society.

Many individuals and institutions contributed to the genesis and evolution of this project. My greatest debt is owed to Ron Mitchell, who taught me how to ask good "why" questions, encouraged my unorthodox approach and always took the project seriously. Yosef Lapid was the first to expose me to the writings of Cynthia Enloe and the radical idea (to me, back then) that gender could matter independently of other considerations in shaping world politics. Robert Keohane's work inspired me to talk about gender as if it should matter to mainstream IR theorists, and he has provided necessary feedback and mentorship along the way. Helen Kinsella's genealogy of the "civilian" got me thinking about knowledge claims in IR theory, and she has been a helpful source of critique as I've developed and refined my own explanatory claims. Robert Darst opened my eyes to the study of humanitarian affairs, schooled me in the use of irony as an emotional bulwark, and provided the catalyst to change direction at a number of critical junctures. Adam Jones's work on sex-selective massacre sparked the insight that led to this empirical study, and I will never forget his thoughtful reply to a curious graduate student's email: this letter sparked a friendship and intellectual engagement for which I am deeply appreciative. Julie Mertus critiqued several versions of the Srebrenica case study and gave me clues about the fine art of communicating across epistemological divides (though I still don't have it down pat, and any ongoing traces of ineptitude are due entirely to my own stubborn Sagittarian lack of tact). Julie also continues to provide tremendous inspiration as a teacher, practitioner, activist and theorist.

The methodology for this project involved collecting narratives from humanitarian practitioners who routinely put their lives on the line to do some of the most difficult, dangerous and important work on this planet.

viii   *'Innocent Women and Children'*

These conversations left me in awe of this profession, and I hope that this book honors these individuals' experiences and stories while providing useful critical insights that may shape best practices for the future. I thank all those who gave precious time and emotional energy participating in or aiding this research, at the International Committee of the Red Cross (ICRC), the United Nations High Commissioner for Refugees (UNHCR), and United Nations Children's Emergency Fund (UNICEF), for their availability, openness and insight. A particularly warm thanks to David Harland for being thoughtful, frank and amazingly reflective; to Mark Cutts and Iain Levine for time, encouragement and invaluable contacts; and to Charlotte Lindsey for shaping, refining and engaging with my ideas as they have developed.

The University of Oregon supported the data-gathering for this project with a research grant and a Jane Grant Fellowship through the Center for the Study of Women in Society, and with two Stephen Wasby research grants through the Department of Political Science. The University of Pittsburgh's Graduate School of Public and International Affairs supported research-related travel as well, and faculty and staff at the University of Pittsburgh provided invaluable guidance as the final version of this book took shape: particular thanks go to Carolyn Ban, Simon Reich, William Keller, Martin Staniland, Nita Rudra, Michael Goodhart, Sandra Monteverde, Karen Chervenick, Betsy Jose-Thota, Robyn Wheeler and Marianne Nichols.

Numerous individuals provided input on drafts of the manuscript as it developed. I am very grateful to Lars Skalnes, Dennis Galvan, Anita Weiss, Jeremy Schiffman, Jaroslav Tir, Maurits van der Veen, Judith Steihm, Elisabeth Prugl, Peregrine Shwartz-Shea, Jeffrey Legro, Ann Tickner, Michael Barnett, Lisa Martin, Josh Goldstein, Bruce Russett, Terrell Carver, Kristin Williams, Stathis Kalyvas, Craig Parsons, Alyson Smith, Debra DeLaet, David Skidmore, Joel Oestreich and Jordan Salberg for feedback on earlier versions of the project. In addition, various anonymous reviewers provided constructive advice both on several incarnations of the book manuscript and, earlier, on article versions of chapters 4 and 5.

Finally, some thanks to the family whose thirty years of support and encouragement made it possible to pull this off. Dr. Carey Carpenter put a word-processor in my nine-year-old hands before most people had heard of word processors, taught me to respect the title "Dr." and spent almost thirty years egging me on to disprove his politically incorrect theories about world affairs. Renee Hyman Carpenter taught me about the Holocaust early in life and sparked my awareness of transnational women's activism and of events in the Balkans. I gratefully acknowledge her contributions to my awareness of how gender suffuses interpersonal power relations as well. Other members of my family have helped craft my thinking about this topic over thirty years of road trips, holiday dinners and late-night coffee chats. I have been particularly influenced by intellectual exchanges with Captain

Preface and Acknowledgements

Edward Haley Carpenter of the US Marines, who continues to help me (sometimes unwittingly) to think about war and about gender. Ami, Richard and Joseph Carpenter have also at various times provided helpful feedback on various portions of the manuscript and/or played devil's advocate with my ideas.

Early in the data collection phase for this project, I married Stuart Shulman, a fellow political scientist, cultural critic and Jon Stewart fan. Shifting gears from single mothering a daughter to this experiment in co-habitating and co-parenting taught me much about gender relations, kinship ties, power, identity, negotiations, global political economy and international relations generally. Stuart has been my closest intellectual ally during this period, and as noted above, his dedication to our children and our household gave me the mobility required to complete the shoe-string budget fieldwork on which the empirical chapters were based.

Finally, my (many unsuccessful) social engineering efforts as a mother over the past ten years have been an additional source of critical insight into how people become socialized into gendered and militarized normative structures. I deeply appreciate my children Haley and Liam for their patience when Mama had to write, for dragging me out of my office often enough to keep me whole, for following me into the field when necessary, and for teaching me about both the innocence and agency of children. But mostly, I thank them for inspiring me every day to craft a better world for them to live in. I hope this book contributes modestly toward that end.

R. Charli Carpenter

List of Abbreviations

BSA	Bosnian Serb Army
CARE	Committee for Aid and Relief Everywhere
CSCE	Commission on Security and Cooperation in Europe
ECOSOC	Economic and Social Council
ECOWAS	Economic Community of West African States
FARC	Revolutionary Armed Forces of Columbia
GBV	gender-based violence
IASC	Inter-Agency Standing Committee
ICRC	International Committee of the Red Cross
IR	international relations
JNA	Yugoslav National Army
KLA	Kosovo Liberation Army
MSF	Medecins sans Frontières
NATO	North Atlantic Treaty Organization
NGO	non-governmental organization
OCHA	Office for the Coordination of Humanitarian Affairs
OHCHR	Office of the High Commissioner for Human Rights
OSCE	Organization for Security and Cooperation in Europe
PoC	Protection of Civilians
UN	United Nations
UNAMIR	United Nations Assistance Mission in Rwanda
UNHCR	United Nations High Commissioner for Refugees
UNICEF	United Nations Children's Emergency Fund
UNITAR	United Nations Institute for Training and Research
UNPROFOR	United Nations Protection Force
UNSC	United Nations Security Council
US	United States
USCR	United States Committee for Refugees
WCRWC	Women's Commission for Refugee Women and Children
WHO	World Health Organization

Chapter 1

Introduction:
Gender, Norms and the Protection of Civilians

Children, women and the elderly are innocent victims
who deserve and demand vigorous protection.
– Costa Rican Delegate to the UN Security Council, February 22, 1999

In early July, 1995, the Bosnian Serb Army (BSA) overran the city of Srebrenica in eastern Bosnia-Herzegovina. After forcing the civilian women, children and elderly onto buses, BSA fighters systematically slaughtered nearly 8,000 adult men and older boys (Rhode 1998). Two years before the massacre, the United Nations High Commissioner for Refugees (UNHCR) had evacuated several thousand civilians from the besieged city. Women, children, the elderly and the sick were allowed on the convoys; adult civilian men were told to stay behind (Hollingworth 1996). Four years after the fall of Srebrenica, the United Nations (UN) Security Council met to discuss its obligation to protect war-affected civilians. While military-age males were being massacred in Kosovo (Danner 2000), delegates to the meeting asserted that "civilians, particularly women, children, the elderly and the sick have been victimized" and that "civilians, in particular women and children, have the right to receive humanitarian assistance" (United Nations 1999a, 9 and 1999b, 8).

This book examines the influence of gender ideas on the international regime protecting war-affected civilians. It asks: why did BSA fighters execute civilian males while allowing women and children to flee Srebrenica, and then claim to have complied with the civilian immunity norm? Why did international agencies mandated with the protection of civilians in the former Yugoslavia leave civilian men and older boys in the enclaves, while evacuating besieged women and younger children? Why, while the international community still agonized over Srebrenica, did delegates to the Security Council invoke the protection of every category of civilian except "adult male" in their moral discourse? I argue that to understand the way in which the laws of war are implemented and promoted in international society, we must understand how gender ideas affect and, I argue, ultimately undermine the principle of civilian immunity.

2   *'Innocent Women and Children'*

Most commentators claim that civilian immunity forms the bedrock of the laws regulating war (Sandoz et al. 1987, 586). Although the targeting of civilian populations has been a feature of international politics throughout history (Carr 2002; Chalk and Jonassohn 1990; Rummel 1994), international actors have long agreed that, in principle, the uninvolved should be shielded from the effects of armed conflict (McKeogh 2002). Only in the post-Cold War period, however, has the "protection of civilians" emerged as a prominent issue on the global security agenda (Roberts 2001). In recent years, the international community has aimed to protect civilians through a variety of pro-active means: advocacy groups lobby warring parties; states condemn atrocity and refine international agreements; and international organizations attempt to feed, safeguard, and prevent the massacre of non-combatants in armed conflicts worldwide (Jones and Cater 2001).

In the chapters that follow, I demonstrate that the "innocent civilian" is invoked through the use of *gender essentialisms* (Smith 2001): political actors typically associate women and children, but not adult men, with civilian status. This practice contradicts the spirit and letter of the very norm such actors intend to strengthen. According to the laws of war, "civilians" whose lives must be spared are to be distinguished from "combatants," who may legitimately be killed, according to whether or not they participate directly in hostilities (McKeogh 2002; Palmer-Fernandez 1998). In other words, fighters are to distinguish civilians from combatants according to an assessment of what they are actually doing, rather than assuming their "innocence" based on *who* they are (AP 1 1977, 51:3; AP 2 1977, 13:3).[1] In reality, however, "distinction" is often accomplished instead through the use of sex and age as proxy variables for "civilian/combatant."

This makes a difference because the category "women and children" is not empirically interchangeable with "the civilian population," nor are all men "combatants." Although a majority of women and children are civilians, this is also true of most men in contemporary wars, many of which are fought by fringe nationalist elements rather than through mass mobilization (Mueller 2000). Moreover, both women and older children may also be combatants and perpetrators in armed conflict (Dombrowski 1999; Goodwin-Gill and Cohn 1994; Moser and Clark 2001; Turshen and Twagiramariya 1998). The category "women and children" conflates infants, who are indeed both innocent and vulnerable, with adult women and adolescents who may be neither (Bennett, Bexley and Warnock 1995; Enloe 1993; Hamilton 2002;

---

1   Article 50:1 of Additional Protocol I to the 1949 Geneva Conventions also states that "in case of doubt whether a person is a civilian, that person shall be considered to be a civilian." A number of political theorists have problematized the concept of moral innocence as a basis for the civilian/combatant distinction. See Anscombe 1970; Fullenwider 1985; Johnson 1999; McKeogh 2002; Norman 1995.

Introduction: Gender, Norms and the Protection of Civilians 3

Lindsey 2001).[2] It also suggests that battle-age men are neither vulnerable nor innocent, whether or not they are actually combatants (Jones 2000).

Insofar as these essentialist assumptions are incorrect, they undermine the moral logic of the civilian immunity norm itself. Using sex and age as proxies for civilian/combatant involves doing precisely the opposite of what the doctrine of "distinction" requires: that legitimate targets be identified by an objective assessment of who actually poses an immediate and direct military threat in a given situation. In short, gender beliefs can trump the regime's broader normative principles. This has important implications for the protection of civilian populations, as well as for theories about the role of morality in world politics. In the following chapters, I make this case by demonstrating how gender influences the activities of three sets of actors with respect to civilian protection: states and belligerent forces, transnational advocacy networks, and humanitarian practitioners.

First, gender beliefs are embedded in the principles of the civilian protection regime and directly affect belligerents' compliance with the key regime norm, protecting some civilians but putting others at greater risk. Belligerents are less likely to target women than men in armed conflict, and they are less likely to attempt to justify their behavior when they do so. Moreover, third parties' condemnations of atrocity or justifications for intervention on behalf of civilians are related to the age and sex of civilian victims.

Second, these gender constructions affect and are reproduced in the representations that transnational advocacy networks use to frame atrocity and draw attention to war-affected civilians. These actors seek to align their metaphors of persuasion with the imagery most resonant to the transnational publics and statespersons on whom they rely for resources and whose views and behaviors they hope to affect. They draw strategically on gender constructs in pre-existing cultural discourses to press their claims. Insofar as they have been successful at placing the issue of civilians on the UN agenda, it has emerged as a profoundly gendered discourse: essentialist assumptions are embedded in both the category "innocent civilian" and the category "especially vulnerable."

Third, this construction of innocence and vulnerability according to gender essentialisms has affected the actual "protection of civilians" by humanitarian organizations. I show how this turned out to be tragically true during the war in Bosnia-Herzegovina. Emphasizing humanitarian evacuation as a protection mechanism, and looking at the 1993 evacuation of Srebrenica in depth, I argue that gender assumptions exerted regulative

---

2   The stereotype is problematic in other ways with which I do not deal fully here. For example, it assumes a harmony of interests between women and children that may not exist, and it fails to treat fathering as central to the protection of children's human rights in armed conflict.

4 *'Innocent Women and Children'*

effects on the behavior of humanitarian actors as well as constitutive effects on the language they use. Moreover, these effects operated so as to leave adult male civilians at grave risk of humanitarian law violations.

These chapters demonstrate that international norms are not simple, static constructs but may be buttressed or distorted by implicit moral frames that "piggy-back" on or "stow-away" inside the norm in question, often contradicting it. Actors engaged in norm emergence, dissemination, implementation and change in world politics must negotiate these contradictions. And self-proclaimed social constructivist international relations (IR) scholars, exploring the effects of ideas on world politics, must pay close attention to these implicit schemas – such as gender – in order to understand the dynamics of the broader normative landscape in which they are interested.

Gender, Social Constructivism and International Relations Theory

The main explanatory argument made in this book is that *gender* – "interpretations of behavior culturally associated with sex differences" (Peterson 1992, 17) – shapes the implementation of international *norms* – "collective expectations for actors with a given identity" (Jepperson, Wendt and Katzenstein 1996). From this follows the conclusion that international relations scholarship, particularly that dealing with international norms, is impoverished without an understanding of such gender effects.

Of course, this argument is nothing new: IR feminist literature has demonstrated the causal and constitutive effects of gender on a wide variety of international phenomena including armed conflict (Elshtain 1987; Enloe 2000; Zalewski 1995), nationalism (Mertus 1994; True 1993; Yuval-Davis 1997), international political economy (Enloe 1989; Marchand and Runyan 2000), globalization (Hooper 2001; Kelly et al. 2001; Turpin and Lorentzen 1996) and international organizations (Meyer and Prugl, 1999; Steinstra 1994; Whitworth 1994 and 2004; Baines 2004). Moreover, many of these scholars have been encouraging the wider discipline to engage with gender as a mode of analysis for over a decade (Grant and Newland 1991; Hooper 2001; Peterson, 1992a; Prugl 1999; Sylvester, 2002; Tickner 1997; Zalewski 1996).

Unfortunately conventional constructivism, like most other mainstream theories of international relations, has been slow to explore the effects of gender ideas on the norms and identities that they claim structure and shape political outcomes. For example, scholarship on international security norms has proliferated (Barnett 2002; Finnemore 1996b and 1999; Katzenstein 1996; Nadelmann 1990; Price 1998; Tannenwald 1999; Thomas 2001; Wendt 1992; Zacher 2001), but this literature has very seldom incorporated the insights of the vast feminist literature on how gender hierarchies affect international security in theory (Cooke and Woolacott 1993; Tickner 2001; Zalewski 1995)

Introduction: Gender, Norms and the Protection of Civilians 5

and in practice (Cohn 1993; Elshtain 1987; Enloe 2000; Orford 1996; Steihm 1982; Whitworth, 2004). Constructivist scholars thus miss an important element regarding how the norms they discuss are constituted, as well as the ways in which they are implemented and enacted. In particular, conventional constructivists have trouble accounting for gaps between theory and practice that are often naturalized by gender, because without conducting a gender analysis they are unlikely to even identify these gaps (Prugl 1999).

Yet as I have argued elsewhere (Carpenter 2002a; 2003b), one reason for the mainstream neglect is precisely the fact that gender analyses in international relations have traditionally been associated with IR feminism, itself a discourse archetypically defined in relation to, rather than as part of, the conventional discipline of IR (Caprioli 2004; Keohane 1991, 45; Peterson 1992b, 1; Whitworth 1994, 39; Zalewski 1995, 341).[3] Driven by a concern with overcoming gender inequality on a global scale, a major contribution of "IR feminism" has been to problematize the traditional research agenda of international relations in the interest of recovering women's concerns and promoting a politics of emancipation (Enloe 2000; Peterson 1992b; Steans 1998, 26).[4] Additionally, IR feminism has historically been skeptical of conventional epistemologies and methodologies in IR because they accept existing power structures. While not all feminist theory is post-positivist (see Caprioli 2004 and Marchand 1998), many "IR feminists" consider the neo-positivist methods associated with mainstream international relations theory to be inherently masculinist, and claim that critique is an important aspect of any truly feminist epistemology (Cockburn 2001, 16; Kinsella 2003, 297; Locher and Prugl 2001b; Steans 1998, 15; Whitworth 1994, 2; Tickner 2005).[5] This framing of IR feminism as substantively and epistemologically distinct from the "mainstream IR," while it enables certain strands of feminist

---

3 Equating gender theory with feminism, Cynthia Cockburn writes: "a gender analysis generates demands for change, for the satisfaction of women's needs" (Cockburn 2001, 15). Analyses of gender that do not adopt a feminist perspective are, in Carver's words, "virtually an oxymoron" (Carver 2003, 290); and it is precisely this "difference from the mainstream" that characterizes IR feminism, according to Tickner (2001, 126).

4 As Tickner writes (2001, 29): "A key task of feminist analysis is to extend the scope of the agenda rather than to answer questions about what is already on the agenda."

5 To put it in Tickner's words, "conventional IR usually employs theory as a tool. IR feminists, along with other critical theorists, have generally used theory as critique for emancipatory purposes" (2001, 136-137; see also Zalewski 1996). This formulation situates gender not primarily as an explanatory framework but instead as a lens for uncovering "hidden power relations" (Whitworth 1994, 267), presumably for the goal of overcoming gender oppression (Carver 2003). While these are worthwhile goals, it is my view that gender analysis is valuable for policy-makers and scholars concerned with more traditional topics as well.

theory to avoid the risk of "cooptation," inadvertently lets mainstream IR scholars off the hook with respect to gender analysis, allowing them to brush aside questions of gender if their work does not explicitly involve women or feminist concerns.[6]

As Caprioli (2004) has argued, however, gender analysis in IR theory need not be an all or nothing enterprise, and the analysis of the civilian immunity norm that follows will make this point precisely. This book contributes to a small but growing literature in IR that seeks to "take gender seriously" within the context of the substantive agenda that has long defined the study of world politics. For example, Tessler et al. (1997) have analyzed linkages between individuals' gender ideologies and their foreign policy preferences, advancing theories of the "democratic peace." Wilmer (2002) uses psychoanalytic theories of gender identity formation to explain the social mobilization of ethnic violence in the former Yugoslavia. With respect to national security issues, Kier (1998) has examined the extent to which homosexuality in the armed forces presents a risk to combat effectiveness; Hudson and den Boer (2002) track the security ramifications of demographic trends related to China's one-child population policy; Miller and Moskos (1995) employ social theories of race and gender to explain variation in US servicemen and women's performance during Operation Restore Hope in Somalia. What connects these authors is not necessarily a commitment to overcoming gender hierarchies (though that may also obtain) or a repudiation of neo-positivist epistemologies, or the rejection of conventional IR questions, but simply a desire to better understand the way the world "hangs together" (Ruggie, 1998), and a recognition that understanding gendered social relations is an important piece of that puzzle.

To this end, the following study integrates a very basic form of gender analysis into existing constructivist models for understanding how actors behave in situations of armed conflict. Such analysis involves demonstrating that a set of inter-subjective beliefs regarding gender relations is socially constructed rather than biologically given; demonstrating that socio-political outcomes are different than would be expected in the absence of those beliefs and the norms constituted by them; and providing a convincing empirical

---

6 For example, Keohane has posited that it is up to IR feminists to "deliver" convincing scientific analysis on terms mainstream IR will understand: "Feminists will need to supply answers that will convince others" (Keohane 1998, 197). Similarly, Jones (1996, 420) argues that in order to be persuasive, feminist frameworks must be "expanded and to some extent reworked." Not surprisingly, this is a position to which a number of feminists have reacted negatively (Brown 1988; Carver, Cochran and Squires 1998; Weber 1994), because it asks feminists to adapt to existing disciplinary norms rather than requiring the mainstream to master the burgeoning literature on gender (Smith 1998).

Introduction: Gender, Norms and the Protection of Civilians   7

account of the ways in which these beliefs and norms operate to constrain, enable or constitute the outcomes in question.[7]

This minimalist approach to gender is similar to what Carver (2002, 88) calls "Type 1" gender analysis. According to Carver, this form of analysis simply starts from the assumption that "gender is socially learnt and culturally variable behavior expressing sex." Carver distinguishes this from more sophisticated Type 2 and 3 gender theories (many of which are more popular with IR feminists), which incorporate critiques of gender as a set of power relations "producing advantage and oppression in terms of sex and sexuality." By contrast, Type 1 analysis simply begins with the assumption that gender is socially constructed and examines the effects of these constructions on social and political outcomes.[8]

The incorporation of such an analysis into existing models for explaining the effects of armed conflict norms on actors' military behavior advances the social constructivist literature on norms. As explained at greater length below, constructivists look for two kinds of explanatory effects exerted by actors' identities and the norms they agree to abide by (Wendt 1999). *Constitutive* effects occur when actors share a set of identities, beliefs and norms that define the parameters of a particular set of social arrangements (Onuf 1998; Ruggie 1998); *causal* effects occur when such inter-subjective beliefs and norms produce variation in political discourse or behavior (Goldstein and Keohane 1993; Yee 1996). An analysis of the particular significance of gender constructs can and should be incorporated into both kinds of explanatory framework by social constructivists trying to understand how nations and individuals think about ethical standards regulating armed conflict.

In addition, this book contributes substantively to the literature on gender and international relations by emphasizing the way that gender constructs adversely affect men and boys. There has been far too little systematic work in international relations theory on this topic: mainstream scholars talk about men as if they were unaffected by gender, and feminist literature on

---

7   This is different, however, from research on norms and identities that happens to deal with women's issues without explicitly investigating the influence of gender as a set of ideas (see Tickner 2001, 134 on gender as a "descriptive" v. "analytical" category). For example, Finnemore and Sikkink's (1998) study of norms relating to women's suffrage is a constructivist analysis on an issue relevant to women, not a gender analysis per se. This sort of literature is appearing more often in the pages of major international relations journals such as International Studies Quarterly, while gender analyses are still largely absent. See also Joachim 2003; and True and Minstrom 2001.

8   Thus, while Kinsella (2003, 297) claims that "gender analysis necessarily requires an exploration of disciplinary and productive power," in fact this is true only for Type 2 and 3 analyses: as feminist empiricists have been well aware for many years, Type 1 gender analysis is quite amenable to conventional explanatory science (Caprioli 2003).

8   *'Innocent Women and Children'*

gender in world politics tends to emphasize the negative effects of gender hierarchies on women (Jones 1996; Meyer and Prugl 1999; Tickner 2001, 10).[9] While recognizing the impact of gendered assumptions on women, this project systematically explores the ways in which adult men are rendered vulnerable by gendered institutions and norms.

This is particularly true with respect to armed conflict, perhaps the most gendered of all human activities (Goldstein 2001). A number of scholars have recently demonstrated that the gendering of international humanitarian law has had important consequences for women's human rights in armed conflict, as well as for the priority attached to the protection of civilians in general compared to prisoners or wounded soldiers (Askin 1997; Charlesworth and Chinkin 2000; Gardam and Jervis 2001; Kinsella 2005; Zalewski 1995). I accept these claims and add little to them here. Instead, I want to pay closer attention to what gender analyses of war have generally overlooked: the invisibility of the *civilian* male in the construction, dissemination and enactment of the laws of war. This topic has largely been neglected by scholars studying war-affected civilians (rare exceptions include Goldstein 2001; Jones 2002a; Lentin 1997b; Lindsey 2001; Zarkov 2001), as well as by the burgeoning literature on gender and armed conflict, which generally takes as its starting point the experiences of women (Barstow 2000a; Bennett, Bexley and Warnock 1995; Jacobs, Jacobson and Marchbank 2000; Lorentzen and Turpin 1998; Meintjes, Pillay and Turshen 2001; Moser and Clark 2001; Turshen and Twagiramariya 1998). Here, I hope to generate more substantive and theoretical interest in how gender structures the fate of men and boys in armed conflict, to complement the significant work in this area that has already been developed on women and war.

Finally, this book also seeks to inform humanitarian policy-making. Stakeholders interested in securing the "protection of civilians" in war-affected areas must reverse the current trend to normalize wartime violence against civilian males. This argument can be made on two grounds. As members of the civilian population, men and boys have the right to benefit from the legal and humanitarian protections afforded by the civilian protection regime. While feminist scholars have correctly pointed out that most of human rights and humanitarian law is designed to protect the interests of men rather than women or children (Bunch 1990; Charlesworth 1995; Deutz 1993; Gardam and Jervis 2001), in time of war I argue this is the

---

9   Although more feminist literature is appearing that addresses men and masculinity in world politics (Enloe 2000; Hooper 2001; Zalewski and Parpart 1998), the fact that feminism predominantly focuses on women "is hardly a surprise" (Carver, Cochran and Squires 1998, 29) given women's historical marginalization from the discipline. That Charlotte Hooper (2000, 59) would need to justify her chapter on masculinity in a recent feminist volume, and would do so in terms of "know[ing] thine enemy," is indicative of the disciplinary norm to focus on women.

case only with respect to male combatants.[10] *Civilian* males remain, in the words of an International Committee of the Red Cross (ICRC) official, "the big forgotten ones, the ones nobody talks about" (Respondent #1, Personal Interview, Geneva, May 2002).

A case can also be made that the protection of adult civilian men is crucial to the successful protection of the civilian population itself. One of the insights of the literature on women and armed conflict is that the absence of adult men due to conscription, detention or massacre is an important factor in civilian children's and women's vulnerability in wartime (Lindsey 2001). While women may benefit from the shifts in conventional roles that accompany the upheaval of war (Meertens 2001; Skjelsbaek 2001; Turshen 1998), and while women are vulnerable to gender-based violence from their own men when they are present (Aafjes and Goldstein 1998; Enloe 1993), the separation of men from their families increases women's and children's hardship in a number of ways. It can affect their ability to receive assistance, cause acute psycho-social trauma in children and their mothers, and increase women's and girls' risk of sexual violence (Barstow 2000a; Bennett, Bexley and Warnock 1995; Lentin 1997a; Mertus 2000). Moreover, to the extent that the civilian immunity norm is weakened by its gendered application, this may put all civilians at greater risk in wartime, a point to which I return in the final chapter.

A potential misinterpretation of this approach warrants heading off at the pass. Some might argue that by emphasizing only which civilians are more likely to be *directly killed*, I inadvertently imply a hierarchy of atrocity that ranks civilian deaths above other forms of wartime violence in a way that would fail to acknowledge women's experience of armed conflict. Gardam and Jervis (2001) have cautioned that the immunity norm itself is open to critique on this basis, since it requires that civilians not be directly targeted, but does not protect them against the long-term side effects of war which, as Ghobarah et al. (2003) detail, disproportionately affect children and women. Other feminist writers have pointed out that the emphasis on lives spared as a benchmark for civilized behavior tacitly legitimizes the non-lethal atrocities to which women and girls are often exposed at rates greater than are males, including sexual torture, exploitation and slavery (Askin 1997). These concerns are valid and it is not my goal to overlook them.

This book, however, focuses on the boundary between legitimate and illegitimate killing rather than other forms of atrocity. I limit my analysis to the principle of distinction, which divides the enemy population into the categories of civilian and combatant, because I am interested in how

---

10 In fact, assuming that the extensive protection for combatants and prisoners in humanitarian law constitutes effective protection for men as such reifies the gendered construction of the civilian/combatant distinction. This logic is particularly evident in Gardam and Jervis (2001, 118).

10   *'Innocent Women and Children'*

international norms shape actors' ability to kill with sanction. Rape, torture, slavery and other forms of inhumane treatment never involve invoking the principle of distinction. (The laws of war do not specify that civilians should be protected from rape but that combatants may be raped. They specify that it is wrong to rape or torture *anyone*: a person's legal protection from such acts does not depend on their status as civilian or combatant.)

Thus, while this project substantively demonstrates that men and boys too may be harmed by gender constructions that distort actors' interpretations of a particular international norm, it is not my intent to place men per se at center stage to the exclusion of women in all discussions of the laws of war. Rather I attempt to place *gender* at center stage, understood as a set of social beliefs that can affect political practice in unexpected ways.

Gender, Norms and the Protection of Civilians

When I write about the "civilian protection regime," I am using the word "regime" as it is discussed by political scientists, to denote a process of international cooperation around a given substantive issue area (Scott 2004, 161). I draw on Krasner's (et al.'s) classic distinction between *regime principles* ("beliefs of fact, causation and rectitude"), *norms* ("standards of behavior defined in terms of rights and obligations,") and more specific *rules* ("prescriptions or proscriptions for action") (Krasner 1983, 2). Principles constitute the inter-subjective empirical and moral context for addressing an issue. Norms provide a set of standards by which discourse and behavior are interpreted and either condoned or condemned by third parties (Kratochwil and Ruggie 1986). As general standards, norms are then codified and (sometimes) implemented in the form of specific rules, which actors then choose to obey, break or redefine (Onuf 1998).

The civilian protection regime can be understood in terms of these categories, as can the manner in which gender operates to distort its principles and norms, producing rules that run counter to the moral logic of the regime itself. The civilian immunity *principle* is expressed in Article 51 of the 1st Additional Protocol to the Geneva Conventions (AP 1 1977, Article 51:1): "The civilian population and individual civilians shall enjoy general protection against the dangers arising from military operations." The twin ideas that civilians a) exist as a meaningful category and b) ought not to suffer give rise to the civilian immunity *norm*, which requires belligerents to distinguish between civilians and combatants and direct their attacks only at the latter: "The civilian population as such, as well as individual civilians, shall not be the object of attack" (AP 1 1977, Article 51:2). This general set of rights and obligations has generated numerous specific *rules* including a requirement that belligerents distinguish themselves from the civilian population, limitations on indiscriminate attacks, and an obligation

Introduction: Gender, Norms and the Protection of Civilians 11

of civilians to refrain from hostilities or forfeit their right to immunity (Kalshoven and Zegveld 2001).[11]

As noted briefly above, social constructivists have identified a range of explanatory effects exerted by norms such as these, often defined (more amorphously than in Krasner's formulation) as "collective expectations for actors with a given identity" (Jepperson, Wendt and Katzenstein 1996). One sort of effect is to actually regulate behavior. In such a case, bad deeds will be avoided and good ones enacted: civilians will not be slaughtered or otherwise assaulted, and will indeed be fed, sheltered and in general treated humanely. Norms can be evaluated for their robustness based on whether actors actually comply with them, but as Kratochwil and Ruggie remind us (1986), norm violations do not invalidate the existence of the norm. What matters then is whether and how norm violators justify their actions (Shannon 2000), whether third parties feel entitled to react to the violations, and how strong these reactions are (Coleman 1990). Early literature on norms, seeking to prove that norms "mattered" independently of material interests, aimed at demonstrating these kinds of regulative and discursive effects (Finnemore 1996a; Katzenstein 1996; Klotz 1996).

Other scholars have emphasized the constitutive rather than regulative effects of norms. The norm of sovereignty not only provides road-maps for legitimate state behavior, but also defines which actors count as states (Wendt 1992). Much of the social constructivist literature on norms has emphasized the ways in which they interact with actor identities to constitute preferences (Jepperson, Wendt and Katzenstein 1996; Ruggie 1998). Other constructivists have looked at the construction of social categories such as "terrorism," "anarchy" and "threat." Each of these concepts is constituted by particular sets of inter-subjective meanings, without which the concepts themselves, and the practices that stem from them, become meaningless. When Finnemore (1999, 163) writes that "war is its rules" she means that organized warfare, much like Ruggie's game of chess (1998), cannot be understood apart from the enactment of the social norms that distinguish it from crime and give the activity meaning.

The chapters that follow describe both constitutive and causal effects. I examine first what the concept of "civilian" *means* to actors engaged in the protection of civilians. I also demonstrate how these particular meanings affect the ways in which civilian protection is carried out in practice, by

---

11 Kalshoven and Zegveld 2001. The regime is considerably more complex than the specific prohibition on attacking civilians that is the topic of this study. It also limits indiscriminate attacks and the use of non-lethal forms of terror (including rape), specifies protection of civilian "objects" as well as civilians per se, and details specific rules for treatment of civilian detainees and those under occupation from enemy forces. I am most interested in the boundary between legitimate and illegitimate killing, hence my emphasis on the immunity norm specifically.

different kinds of international actors. In particular the empirical chapters examine the way *warring parties* comply with, justify violations of, and enforce the regime norms; how *norm advocates* frame civilian protection as a transnational issue; and how *international organizations* mandated with the "protection of civilians" go about achieving this in practice.

What is gender and how does it relate to social norms? I follow IR feminists such as Peterson (1992b) and Tickner (2001) in distinguishing gender (social beliefs) from sex (biological characteristics). Here, sex is understood as the roughly dichotomous coding of human individuals according to their differentiation in reproductive capacity. Gender refers to the culturally constructed beliefs that regulate relations between and among men and women, manifest at various levels of social organization (Carpenter 2002b; Cockburn 2001). "Gender rests not on biological sex differences but on *interpretations* of behavior that are culturally associated with sex differences" (Peterson 1992b, 17).

Other scholars of gender sometimes conflate sex and gender, either through linguistic inconsistency (the "gender" gap to describe sex-differentiated attitudes or "gendered" to describe sex-specific distributions) or for ontological reasons. Some believe the distinction is untenable because gender helps to constitute sex-distinctions in the first place (Butler 1993; West and Fenstermaker 1993). For others, biology and culture are mutually constitutive and must be treated as aspects of the same thing (Goldstein 2001). For some postmodernists, there is no meaningful distinction between the material and the ideational because it is only through ideas and discourses that objects gain relevance, only through collective understandings that subjects recognize material reality (Kinsella 2003; Sylvester 1994; Zehfuss 2002).

In my view, the sex/gender distinction clarifies more than it distorts, and maps usefully onto the conventional constructivist distinction between "brute" facts (such as death, tanks, or people with uteruses, which exist whether or not people agree they do) and "social" facts (such as marriage, money or manliness, which require inter-subjective agreement for their existence) (Searle 1995, 2; Wendt 1999, 96). It is particularly useful in the context of this study, which seeks to illuminate the inconsistency of ascriptive gender assumptions with the social location and experiences of embodied actors. Thus, I aim to use the terms "sex" and "gender" consistently, the former to code males v. females, the latter to describe ideational constructs pertaining to gender roles and relations. For example, I call the singling out of men for execution "sex-selective" massacre while I call the innocent civilian a "gendered" concept.

Norms as understood by social constructivists may relate to configurations of gender in several ways. "Gender norms" explicitly define appropriate relations between and among men and women: for example, the norm that men should protect rather than harm women translates into the rule for boys

Introduction: Gender, Norms and the Protection of Civilians　　　13

"don't hit girls." Other norms may be ostensibly sex-neutral but possess a gender bias, applying to men and women differently. For example, the norm "dress appropriately" applies to everyone, but what it means in a specific cultural setting will typically vary according to sex. Moreover, in addition to their directive aspect, norms also contain *parameters*, which define the conditions under which the norm's prescriptions or proscriptions are expected to be upheld (Shannon 2000). Seemingly sex-neutral norms may encode gender if the conditions under which they are held to apply vary according to the sex of those in question. For example, norms against sexual promiscuity are routinely criticized as exhibiting such a double standard.

The distinction between "gender norms" and "gendered" norms is important because I argue gender beliefs exert a *constitutive* effect only on the former. According to Wendt, "ideas… have constitutive effects when they create phenomena that are conceptually or logically dependent on them" (Wendt 1999, 88). Norms regulating gender relations are *constituted* by the gender beliefs that underlie them. However, the norm "dress appropriately" is not itself logically dependent on a gender bias existing within the norm. Such gender beliefs might, however, exert a constitutive effect on the *practices* (such as sex-differences in appropriate dress) that then perpetuate and normalize such bias. As I argue below, the use of language is such a practice whose form may be constituted by embedded gender beliefs (Fierke 1996).

Such bias perpetuated by language and practice can produce a third kind of norm effect: what I call a *warping effect*. Ideas embedded in broader normative understandings can generate an application of a broader norm that is inconsistent with its own internal logic. The implicit beliefs (or *sub-norms*) are not constitutive of the broader norm, nor do they by themselves cause the norm to be implemented. Rather, they distort the way in which norm effects are manifest, while masquerading as a proper application of the norm.

This latter effect is evident here. The civilian immunity norm is not a "gender norm." Rather it is a sex-neutral norm protecting those not taking a direct part in hostilities at a given time. The civilian protection regime regulates not gender relations per se but relations between combatants and civilians.[12] However, the immunity norm is *gendered* insofar as women and children are more likely than men to be associated with civilian status. While in principle all civilians are to be protected on the basis of their actions and social roles, in practice only certain categories of the population (women, children, elderly, sick and disabled) are *presumed* to be civilians regardless of the context (Carpenter 2003a). There is, in effect, a gender *sub-norm* hidden

---

12 In fact, the immunity norm originally developed as a means of providing protection not to gender/age groups but to clerics. The concept of "women and children" as a protected category arose later and became grafted onto the immunity norm.

14 *'Innocent Women and Children'*

inside the immunity norm. This sub-norm distorts the application of the broader regime prescriptions.

Accordingly, while Kinsella (2005) has argued that gender is constitutive of the very civilian/combatant distinction, I make a more limited claim. Gender constitutes not these concepts themselves but the socio-linguistic practices through which the concepts are deployed in international society. These language practices, generated by the gender sub-norm, naturalize the adoption of specific rules such as "spare the women and children" or "women and children first" that do not accurately correspond to regime principles. Thus, the sub-norm warps the way that the "civilian" is understood and the way the norm is enacted. Moreover, the gender discourse that causes this distortion also hides it: most actors do not readily notice that there is a disconnect at all.

Methodology

Before proceeding, a few words on method are in order. How do we know that norms exist and how do we measure their effects? Or, in this case, how does one make the case that an international norm is gendered and how does one demonstrate that this gender sub-norm affects the way in which the norm is implemented?

The first and sometimes overlooked task for a student of international norms is to figure out whether they are evident at all. As Lake and Powell have observed (1999, 33), it is all too easy for constructivists to take norms as a given when conducting research. Thus I first evaluate whether gender beliefs indeed are embedded within the two concepts most central to the moral language of the civilian protection network: the "innocent civilian" and the "especially vulnerable." Steinstra (1998, 265) writes that evidence of the existence of norms (or in this case, of gender beliefs embedded within norms) is "often difficult to pin down but [is] reflected in the language of interstate agreements, the agendas of international conferences and their resulting documents, the priorities of international organizations, and the areas where no work is done and silence is maintained." To this could be added the content of the Internet web pages of the actors in question, as the Internet now serves as a critical medium for the promulgation of norms, articulation of actor identities, and mobilization of issue network constituencies (Warkentin 2001; Price 2003).

I gathered data on the deployment of gender essentialisms in civilian protection discourse from a variety of such sources. Historical literature, the writings of prominent early international legal jurists, and texts and commentaries of relevant international legal instruments provided evidence for the ways in which the civilian immunity norm emerged as a gendered construct, related in Chapter 2. A detailed content analysis of the 1999 and

Introduction: Gender, Norms and the Protection of Civilians 15

2000 Security Council debates on the Protection of Civilians enabled me to gauge the extent to which contemporary protection discourse invokes these gendered understandings. This involved an analysis of the frequency and context of references to "men", "women" and "children" in the verbatim minutes of the meetings. I found that while it is clearly *civilians* at issue in this discourse, rather than women or children, the category "women and children" was often used as a rhetorical flourish to communicate a sense of moral urgency regarding civilians. There were almost no similar references to adult male civilians. Nor did the Security Council (or other major international forums) emphasize the particular kinds of vulnerabilities to which adult civilian men are exposed in wartime.

So the discourse is gendered. But so what? To many conventional IR scholars, ideas are primarily interesting to the extent that they affect outcomes (Goldstein and Keohane 1993). Does the fact that the "civilian" is a gendered concept matter in terms of actually protecting civilians? There are a number of ways to investigate whether this language has political consequences. First, we can look at whether actors actually treat civilians differently depending on sex and age, and if they do, we can look for clues as to why this is the case. Are male civilians more likely to be killed? Even where civilians are killed indiscriminately, it is relevant to compare the ways that belligerents account for their actions (in war crimes trials, interviews, commentaries or public statements) depending on the age and sex of the victims. As I elaborate in Chapter 3, there is a continuum by which we can judge the relative strength of a norm, as evident not in compliance rates, but in the social strategies deployed by norm violators to avoid censure for their actions. The historical record from Vietnam, Rwanda and the former Yugoslavia provide evidence of the way that gender has long informed belligerents' understandings of their responsibilities toward civilians, and continues to regulate their actual patterns of restraint.

I also investigate how third parties react to the killing of civilians. As Coleman writes, a norm is evident not merely to the extent that people comply with it or feel compelled to justify their violations of it, but to the extent that third parties feel empowered to react to norm violations (Coleman 1990). We can measure differentials in norm strength according to how strongly third parties react. How do bystander states, the Security Council, human rights groups, and the media recognize and rank atrocity? By looking both at which killings attract condemnation and the wording used to draw attention to particular victims, researchers can make empirical claims about whose deaths are considered more or less constitutive of atrocity. These sorts of statements are evident in media reports of specific killings, appeals for money, intervention or attention by human rights NGOs, and the language used in the Security Council to frame civilian protection as a moral issue, or to debate the atrocity threshold required to justify humanitarian intervention (Cohen 2001; Wheeler 2000).

With small children at home and funding for only short trips to the field, it was not feasible for me to collect primary data on the decision-making processes of belligerents, so the conclusions drawn in Chapter 3 regarding compliance rates are based on what is known of the historical cases in question. With respect to the behavior of the civilian protection advocates in particular, however (Chapters 3 and 4), I supplemented content analysis of these sources with 34 semi-structured in-depth interviews with humanitarian practitioners. Those interviewed included headquarters staff in the UNHCR, the ICRC, the UN Children's Emergency Fund (UNICEF), and the UN Office for the Coordination of Humanitarian Affairs (OCHA). For the humanitarian evacuation case study (Chapter 5), I also spoke with protection workers formerly engaged in field operations in the Balkans between 1991 and 1995, including most of those present for the 1993 evacuation of Srebrenica. While this does not represent a cross-section of the organizations involved, the data gathered provides a useful supplement to the picture that emerges from written accounts. Quotations of individuals by name are used only with their permission.

I used the interview process as a source both on the "empirical reality" (as a means of verifying reports from other sources) and on the ways in which civilian protection workers make narrative sense of the events in which they are involved. These encounters were more like interactive conversations than "objective" question-and-answer sessions where my own opinions were kept carefully distanced from those of my subject. We were both informants in these conversations and the authorial voice I use when describing the interview process will reflect my sense of being "situated in" the protection discourse rather than observing it "objectively" from the outside.

Typically, I began by asking respondents to articulate what was meant by "protection of civilians"; what is a "civilian"; and how protection workers assess which civilians are more vulnerable and why. Later in an interview, I would look for opportunities to pose open-ended questions about gender disparities in protection. The ability of respondents to reflect on the questions, rather than to assume the answer was obvious, was taken as an important indicator of whether a logic of appropriateness or an instrumental reaction to particular constraints appear to account for the language and practice of the civilian protection community.

Since my own ideas interacted with those of the respondents, this approach does not meet strict positivist standards of scientific objectivity, though it does meet Keohane's (1998, 197) more minimal definition of scientific validity involving observation, replicability and falsifiability. I used this approach rather than more rigorously consistent survey methods because it seemed appropriate for qualitative work of this type, and useful for eliciting primary data not so much on protection operations per se but on the narratives through which regime actors make sense of the work they do. By "trying out" my hypotheses on actors with the field experience I lacked, I was able to identify areas in which I was clearly mistaken and areas where their narratives mapped onto those I had culled from other sources of protection discourse.

A method aimed at reducing the distance between researcher and subject also seemed particularly appropriate for interview settings where the topic is sensitive or might implicate the respondent (Cockburn 1998, 2-3). I found that by providing a context in which we are just "trying to think this through together" I was able to engage field workers in conversation about how precisely these ideas operated, witness them thinking through their assumptions, and also speak frankly about potential gaps in the discourse, while gauging their reaction to these suggestions. A number of respondents remained engaged with the project long after the interview, reviewing drafts and corresponding with ideas, suggestions or anecdotes.

Participant-observation data-gathering at conferences proceeded in much the same way. I negotiated carefully the terms of my presence at the ICRC's Seminar on the Protection of Special Categories of Civilian as an explicit participant-observer: I was allowed to take field notes but not to record on audio; the workshop officials asked to approve my field notes before they were used; and I was encouraged not to generalize the remarks from the seminar to the organizations whose members were present or quote anyone by name without explicit permission. At the seminar I was interested in what would be on the agenda, and how the issues would be framed, discussed or challenged. What would happen when I threw in questions subtly challenging the use of gender essentialisms, if they were evident (indeed, to what extent would I feel it appropriate to do so?) If I waited, would someone else do so first, and how? This experience gave me a rich data set on the use of these constructs and the ways protection workers actively think around and contest them, as well as (through participation in role-playing games) a deeper insight into the nature of protection operations in the field.

In all these sources – literature, public documents, web content, interviews, seminars – evidence of gender essentialisms in these norms was gleaned by comparing the language used by regime actors to what is known about civilian women's and men's actual experience of war. By demonstrating the discrepancy between essentialist assumptions used in language and empirical realities, a strong argument can be made that the language used is idea-based rather than simply descriptive of reality.[13] This enables me to respond to the obvious counterpoint, beloved of polemics on the job circuit and at conferences where I have presented my findings: "well, there really

---

13 The idea that there is any "reality" that can be posited as prior to a discourse constituting it is a controversial one (see Zehfuss 2002) but I believe it is crucial for this argument and justifiable. I am fully cognizant, however, that I am also participating in a political act by drawing attention to these gaps, both through writing and through the conversational process with regime actors.

18   'Innocent Women and Children'

are more women civilians than men, and most men really are mobilized, so these references are simply statements of fact rather than gender essentialisms." By demonstrating that this language persists despite the presence of many female fighters or of adult civilian males in the population, I aim to problematize this language as a prelude to evaluating its effects. It is then important to reconstruct the particular way in which these gender beliefs influence actual policy-making in situations of armed conflict.

There are a number of effects one could look for. In each case, we want to know whether actors (belligerents, norm advocates or humanitarian workers) act differently than would be expected in the absence of gender beliefs. We might try to measure whether female combatants are more likely to be given immunity than male combatants in different contexts and what this means in terms of military strategy. Such an approach would require looking at cases where there were too many female combatants for the "innocent women and children" assumption to be sustainable on empirical grounds, and then look for evidence that it still exerted effects. Heather Hamilton (2002) has adopted this approach in her analysis of UNHCR's failure to effectively separate armed elements from bona fide refugees after the genocide in Rwanda.

I am less interested in the policy implications of sparing female combatants who arguably could be killed under the civilian immunity norm than of killing male civilians who definitely should be spared under that norm. My substantive focus on policy gaps with respect to civilian males in particular has driven my regional emphasis on the former Yugoslavia. This is not a great case in terms of female combatancy, for while some women fought in the wars of secession, particularly as snipers, their numbers were relatively small compared to theaters such as Eritrea and Sri Lanka (Kesic 1999; Lindsey 2001). With respect to civilian men, however, the former Yugoslavia is a case in which the disjunction between the experience of male civilians on the ground and the international discourse and practice of civilian protection was profound.

From the onset of the wars, adult men were detained, tortured, sexually mutilated, forcibly conscripted and singled out for massacre (Helsinki Watch, 1992/1993). Combatants and prisoners of war also suffered abuse in violation of the laws of war, but numerous adult men in the Balkans were civilians avoiding conscription, were too old or too young to have been drafted, or occupied non-combatant professions (Wilmer 2002). While thousands of women were systematically raped and hundreds of thousands of people displaced (Ball 1999; Stigalmeyer 1994), it is the bodies of unarmed men and boys that fill most of the mass graves in Bosnia and Croatia (Jones 1994). This is a significant political outcome that I argue only a gendered understanding of the immunity norm can adequately explain. More paradoxically, despite these trends, depictions of Bosnia's war victims have tended to portray the victims as "women and children" (Council of Europe, 1993; UNHCR 1992c). This is another outcome that both reflects the gender beliefs underpinning

Introduction: Gender, Norms and the Protection of Civilians 19

discourse on civilians and reproduces those beliefs in a most unlikely arena: human rights advocacy.

I want to understand how inattention to adult male civilians has been normalized during this period through a convergence of rhetoric between warring parties, humanitarian practitioners and human rights advocates. The former Yugoslavia provides important evidence of all these trends. Thus while I draw on global data from the post-war period, each empirical chapter emphasizes the post-Cold War Balkans in particular.

The book is organized as follows. I first delineate the parameters of the civilian protection regime and the way in which it is gendered. Scholarship on norms sometimes makes vague references to the ways in which multiple norms may be "nested" (for example, Kowert and Legro 1996, 490), but the specific character of these ideational relationships is often left under-specified in constructivist literature. I want to explicitly understand the parameters both of the immunity norm and its gender sub-norm, and the specific ways in which they interact with one another to generate specific outcomes. Thus, the focus in Chapter 2 is less on complicity with specific rules than it is on what the concept of the "innocent civilian" *means* to actors engaged in the protection of war-affected populations and how and why gender essentialisms infuse these meanings. To make the claim that the principles and norms are gendered, I must demonstrate that actors associate "women and children" with the civilian population to an extent disproportionate to their actual numbers.

Chapter 2 examines three interrelated *principles* on which the protection regime rests: 1) that a meaningful distinction can be drawn between combatants and civilians; 2) that persons not taking part in hostilities ought not to suffer as a result of them; and 3) that belligerents and third parties have an obligation to ensure such suffering is indeed avoided or minimized. It then traces the process by which gender categories have become associated with these principles. While gender is not constitutive of regime principles as such, the regime has developed in conjunction with a gender discourse that positions women as mothers, as non-combatants, and as physically inferior to adult men. This convergence of gender with the protection regime is explained by both the gender beliefs of early norm entrepreneurs and the institutional climate of the early modern state-system. In short gender beliefs "piggy-backed" on or "stowed away" within the idea of civilian immunity, affecting the linguistic practices by which immunity discourse is deployed in international society, as exemplified by the debates over civilians in the UN Security Council.[14]

---

14 Chapter 2 details the prolific use of the "women and children" trope in the 1999 Security Council meetings on the "Protection of Civilians" subsequent to the Secretary-General's report. Relatedly, Security Council Resolution 1325 on Women

20   'Innocent Women and Children'

The three empirical chapters then trace the effect of this gendered discourse on the implementation efforts of belligerents, of norm advocates, and of humanitarian practitioners. If gender beliefs create no "warping" effect on the broader norm, we would expect implementation rates to vary in a way consistent with regime principles: that is, based on who is actually fighting at a given time. But if gender beliefs warp the application of the immunity norm, we would expect to find that norm strength varies according to the sex and age composition of the target population. We would see actors use sex and age as proxy variables for civilian/combatant, bypassing the actual act of "distinction" as codified in regime norms.

In Chapter 3, I analyze a specific norm stemming from the second principle that civilians should be spared: the proscription on killing civilians intentionally. This chapter argues that gender influences the way in which the immunity norm is implemented by warring parties. In essence, the civilian immunity norm has two sets of *parameters* (Shannon 2000) – conditions under which it is understood to apply – that vary according to the age and sex of the victims in a particular case. This gives belligerents far greater latitude to disregard the norm when the "civilians" in question are adult males. This chapter builds on the above-mentioned social constructivist methods for gauging the effects of norms on behavior, drawing on evidence from Bosnia, Vietnam and Rwanda. I examine patterns of non-compliance, the language used by belligerents to avoid social censure for norm violations, and the reaction of third parties to norm violations, including the propensity to "intervene" for humanitarian reasons.

These gendered patterns within the civilian protection regime are then illustrated through a case study of the 1999 war in Kosovo. I compare patterns of atrocity against the Kosovar Albanians to the political rhetoric with which atrocity was framed in the Western media, and the language used in the Security Council to debate the legitimacy of NATO's military campaign. Although military age men were the primary civilian targets, the intervention was justified as necessary to protect "innocent women and children." The gendered construction of the "innocent civilian" explains both.

The language of what I call the *civilian protection network* in the 1990s has mirrored these gender constructs. Chapter 4 traces gender representations in the rhetoric used by actors in the network. It asks why the civilian protection network has become a site for the reproduction of this discourse, rather than aiming to transform it so as to strengthen the immunity norm. This analysis is situated in the literature on transnational advocacy networks (Florini 2000; Keck and Sikkink 1998; Khagram, Riker and Sikkink 2002; Smith, Chatfield and Pagnucco 1997) and draws on social movement theorists' work on the

---

and Armed Conflict defines women nearly exclusively as civilians. See Kinsella 2002.

use of strategic frames in agenda-setting (McAdam, McCarthy and Zald 1996; Snow et al. 1986; Tarrow 1994). Although much of the IR constructivist literature looks at frames as causal mechanisms explaining the influence of ideas on politics (Barnett 1999; see, however, Payne 2001), I am more interested in how particular frames promote or inhibit the placement of certain issues – like the protection of adult civilian males – on the international agenda, and why those frames are chosen despite the fact that they may be inimical to the moral purpose of an advocacy network.

An initial hypothesis was that network actors use this language unreflexively, as "cultural dupes" (Barnett 1999), but the interview process convinced me that to the contrary, these actors are well aware of the way gender tropes distort their moral claims. However, many of them claim that it is strategic to employ this discourse because they believe attention to civilians in general outweighs the gender bias perpetuated by the language they use. In this sense, pre-existing gender discourses constitute cultural resources through which they press their agenda in world politics, which confirms a central insight of literature on advocacy networks: that ideas can be tools as well as constraints or roadmaps, and the most successful norm advocates are those that use ideas most strategically (Barnett 1999).

But such ideas also ensnare network actors (Finnemore and Barnett 1999). The choice to reproduce these gender discourses results from pre-existing gender beliefs converging with the specific strategic-institutional context. Once embedded in the moral language of protection, gender has become difficult to disentangle from that language. It remains part of the international moral landscape even as individuals within the network become aware of its limitations and unwanted side-effects. Inter-subjective gendered understandings, hidden within a seemingly sex-neutral norm, again matter greatly in shaping the discourses through which norm advocates can succeed in international politics.

How does this matter in concrete terms? In Chapter 5, I investigate the extent to which these gendered meanings have impacted protection operations themselves in complex emergencies. According to explanatory theorists, ideas may exert a causal effect if they generate political outcomes that would have looked different in their absence (King, Keohane and Verba 1994, 191-192). My case study on humanitarian action in the Balkans begins with a puzzle. If humanitarian protection workers know that adult men are most likely to be summarily executed when a town falls, why evacuate women, children and the elderly, but not adult males, from besieged enclaves? The analysis accounts for this seemingly irrational behavior by examining the pathways by which gender beliefs impacted evacuation operations.

Writing on this topic previously, Adam Jones has suggested that humanitarian practitioners themselves subscribe to a "women and children first" norm. Given a mandate to evacuate "especially vulnerable populations," adult men, traditionally perceived as invulnerable, do not count and are left behind (Jones 2002a). I tested his hypothesis by conducting in-depth interviews with ICRC, UNHCR and United Nations Protection Force (UNPROFOR) staff formerly stationed in Bosnia and Croatia. The interview data support a more complicated argument than Jones offers. Although aid workers shared the belligerents' perceptions to some extent, evacuation procedures were shaped more by the constraints imposed by belligerents and donors than by aid workers' adherence to such gender rules. When explaining why aid workers went along with such discriminatory evacuation schemes, however, a logic of appropriateness consistent with the influence of gender ideas on perceptions of civilian status and "vulnerability" appears to have some explanatory value.

Put together, these case studies demonstrate that gender has influenced the implementation of the immunity norm with respect to several sets of actors. It affects compliance by belligerents as well as the meanings they attach to different patterns of atrocity. It affects the normative strategies by which transnational human rights advocates make moral claims on behalf of war-affected civilians. And it affects the actual operations by which humanitarian practitioners attempt to provide practical protection for civilians in complex emergencies.

In each case, it is not that a gender norm overtly operates to produce these effects: practitioners do not necessarily see themselves as singling out "women and children" for protection. Rather, ascriptive gender beliefs are embedded within the sex-neutral categories "civilians," "combatants" and "vulnerable." This enables actors to see themselves as operating in a gender-neutral way – "protecting the innocent," "prioritizing the most vulnerable" – while perpetuating a serious gender bias in the implementation of the norm.

These findings are significant both for theory and policy. It is now well known how gender norms operate to constrain the opportunities and life chances available to women. But mainstream IR scholars studying norms have historically assumed that unless the topic is women or women's issues, gender is irrelevant to their analyses. These case studies demonstrate that even norms that nominally have little to do with gender relations can be mis-applied by actors responding inadvertently to cultural interpretations of gender. Scholars of norms in world politics should be alert to the effects of such implicit norm schemas and the way that they can work to undermine the moral logic of a given norm.

In terms of policy, these case studies identify consequences for the way in which the "civilian" is conceptualized, which affects the implementation of the immunity norm in practice as well as the way in which third parties carry out humanitarian operations to "protect civilians" in situations of armed conflict. As I will demonstrate, while this gender rhetoric serves the political purposes of interventionist states, belligerents and humanitarian actors, it carries unmentioned side-effects for civilians, particularly for adult civilian men and adolescent boys. In short, both civilian males and (by extension) civilian protection itself are casualties of this gender discourse.

Chapter 2

Gendered Innocence:
The Concept of the "Civilian" in
International Society

Our pity is structured by history and culture.
– Michael Ignatieff 1998, 287

Although the formal laws of war do not distinguish civilians from combatants on the basis of sex, the innocent civilian is a gendered concept.[1] Subsequent chapters will demonstrate that a gender sub-norm's "warping effect" shapes and distorts the implementation of the immunity norm itself. Here, I am concerned with situating the immunity norm within the broader "civilian protection regime" and demonstrating the ways in which it is gendered by reference to the principles underlying the norm. I do so in this chapter by reviewing both the historical emergence of the immunity norm now codified in international law, and the socio-normative meanings associated with the "innocent civilian" as evident in international moral discourse.

The chapter is in three main sections. The first section below sketches the parameters of the civilian protection regime, appropriating Krasner's (1983) typology of ideational regime components. On the basis of existing law and discourse, I identify three key regime principles: the distinction principle, the immunity principle and the protection principle. I then discuss the specific ways in which gender interacts with these social ideas, and provide an explanation for how these ideas came to be so interrelated during the historical emergence of the laws of war.

The immunity and protection principles are based on the idea that some people are incidental to armed conflict, as they do not participate directly in hostilities. Therefore, by virtue of their material "innocence" (in the sense of non-participation) and "vulnerability" they deserve not to be harmed and in

---

1   Aspects of the Geneva Conventions do specify particular protections on the basis of sex, but the concept of the "civilian" per se is not articulated in these terms. See de Preux 1985. Some scholars have critiqued formal international humanitarian law for its implicit reproduction of gender assumptions (Gardam and Jervis 2001; Kinsella 2001), but I focus here on the informal understandings reproduced in actor practice.

fact should be protected from harm. The distinction principle specifies how to identify who those people are. Because women, along with children, the sick and the aged, have been positioned as innocent and vulnerable, sex has emerged, along with age categories, as a central means by which "distinction" is to be accomplished in practice. Simply put, women and children, but not adult men, have been historically perceived as having civilian status and associated with the material innocence and vulnerability that underpin the principle that civilians should be spared the effects of war.

A seemingly obvious counterpoint to my argument is that "most civilians *are* women and children" or "most men *are* soldiers," therefore we do not need "gender assumptions" to explain why women, but not men, are perceived as civilians in wartime. But sex-disaggregated data on mobilization rates contradicts this view. According to available statistics, only 20 per cent of military-age men were mobilized in formal armies and paramilitaries at the start of the post-Cold War period (Kidron and Smith 1991, 33). On the other hand, some 500,000 women are under arms worldwide (Smith 1997, 64); in some contexts the percentage of female combatants is 25-30 per cent (Lindsey 2001, 23). By illuminating the gap between the "empirical vs. the narrative realities of war" (Sylvester 2002, 4), the gender essentialisms embedded in immunity discourse are exposed as ideational constructs, rather than as signifiers of wartime realities.

This begs the question of the exact relationship between what I describe as a "gender sub-norm" and the immunity norm in which it is embedded. Drawing on Wendt's understanding of constitutive effects, I conclude that these gender discourses are embedded in, but do not *constitute* the immunity norm, as suggested by some scholars (for example Kinsella 2005). I make this case by demonstrating that the immunity norm and the gender sub-norm I describe are rooted in very different sets of normative understandings historically. Prohibitions on killing women in ancient times were related to their status as property to be appropriated rather than any sense of their moral "innocence"; and antecedents to the immunity norm extended immunity not to women or children but to certain categories of men. Since both sets of norms can exist and have existed independently of the other, one cannot be said to constitute the other.

Moreover, the moral logic of the immunity norm itself is not logically contingent on or even, I argue, compatible with these gender essentialisms. The concept of civilian immunity is based on distinguishing between those people actually participating in combat and therefore posing a military threat, and those who choose not to participate. Nothing about biological sex necessarily determines that a particular man or woman will be channeled into either group. It is the social construction of gender role differences that accounts for the disparities that do exist, but only if these were absolute would sex be an adequate proxy variable for civilian/combatant. Rather than *constituting* civilian immunity, the gender sub-norm actually *distorts* the

Gendered Innocence 27

immunity norm. It does so by directing belligerents' attention to the age/ sex of potential targets as the basis for whether or not to shoot, rather than the question of whether or not they are participating directly in hostilities, which forms the moral/legal basis for the distinction principle as codified in the Geneva Conventions and Additional Protocols.

The third task of this chapter, then, is to provide an explanation for how the gender sub-norm became grafted onto the immunity norm, as a prelude to considering its effects and persistence in the following chapters. I claim the emergence of "gendered innocence" took place as part of a particular, though not an inevitable, historical process. Specifically, the consolidation of the tradition of civilian immunity in the early Westphalian period corresponded to ongoing shifts in gender relations characteristic of early modern state-building. I highlight two changes in particular: the emergence of modern militaries along with mass male conscription; and the emergence of national narratives associating "women and children" with the protected, civilian, domestic space of the newly territorialized nation-state. These factors produced institutional and normative conditions favorable for *gender essentialisms* – the association of biological characteristics (male/female) with assumed social attributes – to be reproduced in the context of the civilian immunity norm.

The Civilian Protection Regime: Three Principles

When I use the term *civilian protection regime* I draw on the much-cited definition of "implicit or explicit principles, norms, rules and decision-making procedures around which actors' expectations converge in a given area of international relations" (Krasner 1983, 2). The actors in question include state and non-state *belligerent groups* bound by the relevant laws of war; a *transnational advocacy network* of citizens, journalists, global bureaucrats, humanitarian workers and statespersons who work to disseminate and encourage compliance with regime norms; and certain *international organizations* whose mandate is to actively ensure the practical implementation of these norms.[2]

What Krasner and the contributors to his 1983 edited volume call "decision-making procedures" are beyond the scope of this analysis. The distinction between principles, norms and rules is more useful because it enables us to map out the moral characteristics of a regime and examine how the social ideas of which it is composed fit together. For example, the moral *principle* "civilians should be protected" underpins the *norm* "don't target

---

2 Although I do not analyze them firsthand in this study, to the extent that they share the intersubjective understandings of the regime and are constituted as actors by its principles and norms, war-affected civilians themselves might also be considered regime actors.

28 *'Innocent Women and Children'*

civilians" which requires *rules* such as "combatants must carry arms openly" that constitute the social context in which complicity with the distinction principle is possible.

In this chapter and the next two, I highlight the connection between principles and norms, excluding rules as Krasner defines them, because the emphasis here is less on compliance with specific rules as it is on the broader normative meanings within the regime. These meanings are codified formally in international law but also reproduced implicitly through the actual practices of relevant actors (the formal and implicit rules do not always look alike, though they derive from the same principles). I return to a consideration of specific rules in Chapter 5, when I analyze civilian protection operations in practice.

According to Krasner, principles include "beliefs of fact, causation and rectitude" (Krasner 1983, 2). I amend and expand this description as follows. Principles may be composed of two sorts of beliefs: *descriptive* beliefs that answer constitutive questions of how or what and causal questions of why; and *principled* beliefs that answer questions of ought.[3]

Descriptive beliefs include both Krasner's beliefs of fact and of causation: they define social ideas and contexts and shape expectations of causal relationships. It is important that descriptive beliefs may concern material facts, such as the existence of chemical weapons, but also *social* facts, such as the existence of soccer or war criminals (Searle 1995, 2). The difference between brute and social facts is that the former exist independently of whether anyone believes they do, but social facts – such as the "innocent civilian" – require inter-subjective agreement for their existence (Ruggie 1998, 856).

Principled beliefs contain moral claims about how actors *should* behave given a configuration of social arrangements. In short, regime principles can be both constitutive, defining the social context in which actors exercise agency and the identities of the actors themselves, and regulative, specifying the legitimate range of actions available to actors in a particular situation (Florini 1996, 366; Onuf 1998, 68; Ruggie 1998, 871). The principles of the civilian protection regime explain *what* civilians are, *why* they presumably require protection, and why actors *should* therefore protect them.

The distinction between descriptive and principled beliefs is important for my analysis because I purposely avoid engaging with questions of ought. To do so would require normative analysis. Rather, I am interested in how the descriptive beliefs underlying these principles are constructed and the effects they have on policy. Because descriptive beliefs deal with questions of *is* (as actors see it), they can be subjected to empirical scrutiny in a way that *ought* questions cannot. One can compare the social perception of what

---

3   Goldstein and Keohane (1993) also distinguish between principled and causal beliefs.

Gendered Innocence 29

is to the empirical reality in order to make arguments about how ideas about that reality influence actors' perceptions irrespective of brute facts. One can then explore the origins and effects of these ideas on a particular area of moral discourse. This is different from questioning the moral content of the discourse itself. While valid critiques of the whole concept of civilian immunity have been broached by feminist and post-colonial authors (Gardam and Jervis, 2001; Thakur 2001), I will start from the assumption that the norm itself is a moral good – that is, the world would be a measurably better place if it were consistently implemented – and seek to understand and elucidate some particular sources of trouble with respect to its implementation.

Currently, the civilian protection regime can be regarded as resting upon three broad principles: the distinction principle, the immunity principle and the protection principle. Most fundamental is the principle that it is possible to draw a conceptual and practical distinction between those persons who take part in hostilities and those who do not. Civilians do not exist apart from a set of arrangements that define the parameters of their existence: the "innocent civilian" is a *social* fact. The civilian protection regime rests partly on the shared descriptive belief that civilians exist as a category distinct and distinguishable from those directly engaged in hostilities. This *distinction principle* defines what a civilian is and how to recognize one when you see one.[4] If civilians did not exist in some sense, there would be little sense in regulating their treatment in times of war.[5]

The second principle contends that persons not taking part in or responsible for hostilities ought not to suffer as a result of them. This is based on both a descriptive and a principled belief. The descriptive belief is that civilians, as both innocent and vulnerable, are not a threat to those conducting military operations (Nagel 1985, 69; Norman 1995, 168). The principled belief, derived from the humanitarian principle of military necessity (Hampson 1999), is that those persons not posing a threat should not be harmed (Fullenwider 1985, 94). Thus, belligerents are enjoined both to respect civilian immunity and to actively protect civilians against violations of that immunity (Sandvik-Nylund 1998, 14).

Despite popular usage, this *immunity principle* is not ultimately based on a claim that civilians are innocent in a moral sense; rather that they are

---

4 The definition of a "civilian" is laid out in the 1977 Additional Protocols to the 1949 Geneva Conventions, in relation to the category "combatant." See Articles 43, 50 and 51.

5 When civilian protection officials or international lawyers describe the "principle of distinction," they are describing what Krasner would call a norm: the requirement that belligerents endeavor to distinguish between civilians and combatants by following certain rules, such as carrying arms openly and only attacking military targets (Ipsen 1995). By contrast, when I use the term "distinction principle" I am referring to the belief that this conceptual distinction is possible or meaningful in the first place.

30   *'Innocent Women and Children'*

materially innocent, that is, not engaged in immediate, direct participation in hostilities (Fullenwider 1985, 94; Mavrodes 1985, 80-81; Norman 1995, 188). The equation of civilian status with moral innocence is frequently refuted by the fact that some civilians, notably politicians, are generally guiltier of initiating and enacting armed conflict than the combatants, who are often coerced into serving (McKeogh 2002, 8; Norman 1995, 167). Instead, most scholars and historians agree that the contemporary civilian immunity principle comes down in theory to whether or not an individual is engaged in an act of combatancy at a given moment in time (Johnson 1999, 239-240; McKeogh 2002, 140; Nagel 1985, 69; Walzer 1977, 146-51).[6] This explains why it is no longer *always* legitimate to kill soldiers (when they are off duty, sick, captured or wounded), and why a non-uniformed person not formally occupying the role of "soldier" may give up their immunity as soon as they begin engaging directly in hostilities. "The distinction is between civilians who are 'harmless' and combatants who are engaged in the activity of 'harming' others" (Norman 1995, 168). As I will argue, however, this distinction is in practice somewhat muddier, as gendered perceptions of moral innocence are often conflated with gendered assumptions of who is doing what.

The third *protection principle* states that third parties, as well as belligerents themselves, have a responsibility to prevent or deter the targeting, and alleviate the suffering, of war-affected civilians. This principle contains a descriptive belief that the targeting of civilians is endemic and the principled belief that this state of affairs is unacceptable, involving moral obligations of onlookers to take an active role in its rectification.[7] Kofi Annan captured the spirit of this principle with the following words, quoted on the Office for the Coordination of Humanitarian Affairs Protection of Civilians Homepage (Protection of Civilians 2003): "As human beings we cannot be neutral, or at least have no right to be, when other human beings are suffering." Unlike the principle of civilian immunity, this principle is much more emergent (Finnemore 1996b). Indeed, the current emphasis on the rights and obligations of outside parties to intervene is what sets the contemporary "civilian protection regime" apart from its earlier manifestation, which had been limited to regulating the behavior of belligerents themselves. Today, citizens in donor countries (at least, sometimes) demand that their governments "do

---

6   McKeogh (2002, 140) argues that until the 1977 Additional Protocols to the Geneva Conventions, the consistent basis for the non-combatant immunity principle was the distinction between professional soldiers, who formally occupied a role in which they could be treated as a means to an end, and those not in such a role. Now, he writes, "the reason for killing them is that they are engaged in harming or killing others. This is a very significant alteration to the justification of killing combatants in war."

7   For a critique of the descriptive claim, see Frohardt, Paul and Minear (1999, 17) and Smith (1997, 24).

Gendered Innocence   31

something" and delegates to the UN Security Council debate whether and how far it is legitimate to take action on behalf of civilians in other lands (Wheeler 2000).

In the sections below, I make the case that each of these principles, while in theory sex-neutral, has been articulated in international society through the use of gender dichotomies. This analysis deals less with the formal law itself and more with the inter-subjective meanings attached to the *idea* of the "innocent civilian," as evident in scholarly writings on the laws of war, field manuals, international documents, and speeches in transnational public fora. The distinction principle is gendered because sex, along with age and disability, has historically been described as a proxy variable for "civilian/combatant": in cases where it is difficult to tell who is who, women are presumed civilians, men are not. This is related to the immunity principle that specifies why civilians should not be targeted. Through their association with children, women, but not men, have been constructed as possessing the attributes associated with a claim to immunity: innocence and vulnerability. Correspondingly, the emergent protection principle also reproduces these gendered assumptions. If women can be assumed to be civilians, and are innocent and vulnerable, it is they in particular (along with children, the elderly and the disabled) who must be protected. I provide evidence of these connections below and illustrate their present-day salience through an analysis of diplomatic discourse at the UN Security Council, before turning in the next chapter to an explanation of *how* gender essentialisms came to be "stowed away" inside the concept of the "civilian."

Gender Discourses Within the Civilian Protection Regime

> The U.S. will have to accept the moral responsibility to intervene where innocent women and children are being slaughtered in the name of ethnic cleansing. (US Rep. Coleman, quoted by Garnett News Service 1993)

> The failure of the warring parties to cease hostilities has led to the massive destruction of property and the massacre by all the parties of thousands of innocent civilians, including foreign nationals, women and children...(ECOWAS 1990, quoted in Cain 1999, 290)

> Our argument is not with the women and children of Iraq. It's with the dictator. (President Bush 1991)

As a number of authors have described at greater length, women as a group, but not adult men, have historically been more frequently accorded the protection offered by the distinction, immunity and protection principles (Carr 2002; Hartigan 1983; Jones 2000). While women's treatment as civilians can to some extent be empirically explained by the fact that women have tended to in fact experience war as civilians, this correlation is not absolute.

32 *'Innocent Women and Children'*

Moreover, this cannot explain the corresponding assumption that all men are armed. While most women are civilians, most men are not combatants (Lindsey 2001). The discrepancy between the discourse of war and the empirical sex-gender structure of war has been exacerbated by technological and social changes that increased the number of women under arms while reducing the number of men conscripted into the armed forces during times of war (Goldstein 2001).

As the quotes above demonstrate, the gendered nature of this discourse is still evident today in the way that international players discuss the protection of civilians. This section unpacks the overlapping gender essentialisms within civilian protection rhetoric before offering an explanation of how this configuration of ideas has emerged and persisted in international society.

Images of Women in Immunity Discourse

Two distinct but interrelated discourses relating to women underpin this gendered construction of the innocent civilian. In both, women are positioned in relation to small children, the social category most indisputably innocent in both a moral and material sense. First, women are constructed as indispensable to children's protection, and receive respect and rights on the basis of their reproductive and child-rearing roles (Gardam and Charlesworth 2000). The special protections afforded to women in the Geneva Conventions accrue specifically to mothers in their capacity as caretakers of young children (de Preux 1985; Krill 1985). This construction does not require the assumption that women themselves are "innocent" or "vulnerable" but that their labor is crucial to the protection of small children (whose possession of both attributes is typically viewed as indisputable).[8] As Finnis puts it, non-combatants include "those who cannot take care of themselves, together with those whose full-time occupation is caring for the helpless" (Finnis 1996, 27).[9] This assumption constructs women as mothers and privileges actual mothers over other women, while distancing fathers and fathering from the care and protection of children (Gardam and Jervis 2001).

---

8   For example, the idea that children are innately innocent and vulnerable is expressed in the following quotations: "Why do we care about children, it's because of their innocence, because they are deemed to be free of the guilt associated with those who perpetrated the conflict." (Respondent #30, Phone Interview, October 2002.) Some respondents made this case to a stronger degree than with respect to adult women: "Children are innocent, they shouldn't be in a position where they are forced to participate, whereas women can participate if they like." (Respondent #5, Personal Interview, August 2002, Geneva.)

9   In humanitarian law, the category "non-combatant" encompasses, in addition to civilians, those no longer able to take part in the fighting, including the sick and wounded.

Gendered Innocence

Secondly, women are conceptualized as *analogous* to children in terms of their perceived *vulnerability*, and their perceived *innocence*. With respect to vulnerability, women have been and still are constructed as inherently weaker and more delicate than men biologically:

> Women and children... are the most vulnerable members of the population. (Declaration on the Protection of Women and Children in Emergency and Armed Conflict, 1974)

> Women are more vulnerable than men for physical reasons and these kinds of factors. (Respondent #25, Personal Interview, September, 2002, Geneva)

> The weaker and vulnerable groups of society become easy victims of conflict. Abuses of the rights of women and children are most common. (United Nations 1999b, 12)

The perception of women as the "weaker sex" underpinned the chivalric prohibition on killing women during the Middle Ages (Johnson 1981, 131-50; Stacey 1994) through their association with other "vulnerable" groups. Despite much empirical evidence that there are not significant physical differences between adult men and adult women (for a summary see Goldstein 2001, 132-134) many actors today persist in the belief that women as such are more vulnerable than men because they are physically weaker. The belief that women, like children, are therefore physically incapable of combat constitutes them as civilian non-combatants; the belief that they, like children, are a "vulnerable" group physically, thus deserving protection and even "special" treatment, constitutes assaults upon them as dishonorable. As Lindsey notes (2001, 29) this perception stems in part from a problematic conflation of *all women* with "pregnant or lactating women with infants" who indeed possess intrinsic physical vulnerabilities that men and other women do not.

In addition to being seen as the protectors of children, women are viewed as child*like* insofar as they are seen as less likely to be culpable agents of social forces and should thus be shielded from them (Kinsella 2005). According to an ICRC Official associated with the Women and War Project, women are "often perceive[d as] having more innocence attached to them than a man, in the sense of not having participated in hostilities... less likely to have been perpetrators or less likely to have asked for what happened to them or less likely to have been in a position to have changed anything because they're not at the negotiating table, they're not part of the debate, they couldn't have stopped anything" (Respondent #5, 2002).

Despite these views, it is not true that women have always been innocent of war-making or passive objects in the face of militarization within their societies. Throughout history women (particularly healthy ones without children) have engaged in war-making activities alongside men (Goldstein

2001; Lindsey 2001). In addition to their myriad support roles, women have participated in war directly: in female combat units, mixed-gender units, as individual fighters and military leaders. They are increasingly serving as combatants in large numbers (Bennett, Bexley and Warnock 1995; Seager 1997). Although women have often been described as naturally incapable of bearing arms, it has rather been societies' socially constructed disinclination for them to do so which accounts for disparity between male and female fighters, and this disparity, although striking, is rarely absolute.

Additionally, an extensive feminist literature has documented the diverse ways in which women participate both in supporting and resisting militarization (Elshtain 1987; Elshtain and Tobias 1990; Enloe 2000; Lorentzen and Turpin 1998; Moser and Clark 2001). The ICRC's 2001 global study on women and war found that women are neither helpless in the face of war (mobilizing many sources of strength in the face of adversity) nor always inactive (participating as spies, combatants, agitators and perpetrators as well as supporting troops, inciting violence and indoctrinating their sons into warrior masculinity). Moreover, to the extent that civilian women are incapable of affecting socio-political events in which they are caught up, the same is true for the majority of civilian men (Respondent #5, 2002).

Images of Men in Immunity Discourse

Yet by contrast, adult men have typically been positioned as presumed combatants in civilian immunity discourse, through a reversal of precisely these discourses of innocence and vulnerability. In the same way that women are accorded special protection by virtue of their responsibility for children, men are marginalized conceptually from parenting as a valued social activity.[10] This is reflected in the codified laws of war: while the Geneva Conventions provide that women who are convicted of a crime in a situation of armed conflict cannot receive the death penalty *if* they are pregnant or have a child under five years old, the father of the same small child may be executed as long as he has first received a fair trial (Additional Protocol I 1977, Article 76.3; Additional Protocol II 1977, Article 6.4). The woman's life is spared on the basis that the child would be adversely affected by the loss of its mother, but no such assumption is made in terms of the child's relationship to her father.

---

10 This does not necessarily mean that fathers have been "distant" throughout modernity or that their role is insignificant for children's development. Some sociologists have identified a typology of fathering relationships (Jain, Belsky and Crnic 1996). But it is to say that the cultural value associated with fathering as a male role has been low in the modern period as a result of the capitalist division of labor (di Stefano 1991), although this may be gradually changing (Russell 2001).

Gendered Innocence 35

Likewise, while women are defined in terms of their vulnerability, men are typically not cast as vulnerable in this discourse. The Security Council debates on protection of civilians contain no references to the vulnerabilities of adult men, and the ICRC's definition of "vulnerable groups" at a Civilian Protection Seminar in May 2002 included every category except able-bodied adult men. "It's really not in the general definition of being vulnerable, when you're a healthy, strong, 20-year-old male," one humanitarian official told me (Respondent #29, Phone Interview, October 2002).

Similarly, while women are defined in terms of their innocence with respect to the political events leading up to the conflict, men are treated as agents responsible both for political reality and for their own fate (Jones 2002a). "For the same reason that women are seen as vulnerable, men are seen as able to protect themselves (Respondent #18, Personal Interview, August 2002). This follows from a gender discourse in which men are "separated from the boys" in the process of maturity (Connell 2000), in which military service is seen as a proving ground for civic manhood, and in which being a man is associated with autonomy, reason and the ability to protect not only oneself but one's family and, by association, one's nation (Elshtain 1987).

Just as these beliefs essentialize complex realities when applied to women, so too the construction of adult men as soldier/citizens (and thus combatants) is explained only by the power of ideas, rather than the actual sex-gender structure. It is not the case that most adult men are mobilized most of the time in most conflicts: despite lingering traditions of universal conscription, "almost all soldiers are men, but most men are not soldiers" (Connell 2000, 215). The ICRC's women and war study describes male absenteeism as a key factor in women's vulnerability during armed conflict (Lindsey 2001, 32), but rather than being off fighting, as is commonly supposed (for example Cockburn 2001, 21; Mertus 2000, 27) men are as likely to be fleeing or hiding to avoid recruitment (Enloe, 2000). Generalizing from a variety of other sources, Kidron and Smith (1991, 33) claimed in 1991 that only 20 per cent of battle-age men are mobilized in formal armies and paramilitaries worldwide. If these statistics are to be trusted, this left some 80 per cent of adult males in the civilian sector at the start of the post-Cold War period.

While global statistics such as the above are always to be taken with a grain of salt, the lengths to which states go to prevent or punish desertion give an indication of the scale at which adult men attempt or manage to remain in the civilian sector (Levi 1997; Mjoset and van Holde 2002a). The use of press gangs to terrorize draft dodgers into serving is common (Jones 1999-2002). In Northern Afghanistan, a system of extortion was reported in 2002, by which families desperate to keep their sons out of the military were forced to make cash payments to local commanders (HRW 2002); in Iraq, the problem of desertion became so severe after the Gulf War that the Hussein regime implemented a policy of mutilating captured deserters by removing ears, feet or hands in hospitals (Erdem 1994). In the former Yugoslavia, contrary

36 *'Innocent Women and Children'*

to the notion shared by belligerents and the international community that most of the adult men were eagerly participating in hostilities, approximately 700,000 people had fled to avoid conscription at the war's onset, and over 9,000 charges of desertion were initiated in 1992 alone (Wilmer 2002, 157).

Just as women, like men, sometimes participate in violence, men, like women, often make the choice to avoid such participation; and like many women, men's efforts often do not serve to protect them or their families or to avert war. According to one interviewee, the perception that women lack agency "gives an enormous amount of responsibility to the vast majority of civilian men who also weren't in a position to change anything. So it's a stereotype that I don't believe should be one that the ICRC portrays because we see the reverse of that so often" (Respondent #5, 2002).

The Protection of Civilians at the United Nations

Recent debates over the protection of civilians within various United Nations machinery, particularly the Security Council, provides a useful illustration of the way in which gender essentialisms infuse contemporary diplomatic discourse on civilian protection. Just prior to the air war over Kosovo in early 1999, the UN Security Council undertook a series of meetings to discuss its responsibility with respect to the protection of civilian populations in times of war (Goldberg and Hubert 2001). These discussions were in response to an April 1998 report by the Secretary-General that identified the protection of civilians as a "humanitarian imperative" (UN 1998). After the Kosovo intervention, these discussions continued and gathered momentum. The Secretary-General has presented three additional reports on the subject to the Security Council; the Security Council has issued two resolutions and two presidential statements. Since October 2002, the UN Office for the Coordination of Humanitarian Affairs (OCHA) has organized a series of regional workshops on the protection of civilians, bringing together policy-makers from governments, international organizations and NGOs.[11]

The language used in these discussions, the resulting documents, and the United Nations web portal on "protection of civilians" tells us a great deal about how the concept of the "innocent civilian" is deployed in international society as well as the basis for the shared meanings embedded in the emerging "civilian protection principle." I analyzed all documents available on the OCHA website, including reports to, speeches at and resolutions by major United Nations organs, web content on the site itself, and the verbatim minutes of the Security Council thematic debates over the issue, held in February 1999, September 1999, April 2001, December 2002 and December

---

11 Data and pertinent documents on the "protection of civilians" within the United Nations is available from the OCHA website. See Protection of Civilians 2003.

Gendered Innocence 37

2003. Passages that referred to women, men, girls or boys were identified and coded according to whether they invoked gender essentialisms, and if so which ones.[12]

As the content analysis indicates, the "innocent civilian" is often signified by ascriptive categories rather than behavioral non-combatancy, and women (but not men) are typically included as one of the presumptive civilian groups. Consider the following passages from the minutes of the Security Council discussions in early 1999 (see UN 1999a, 1999b, 1999c, 1999h and 1999i):

ZAMBIA: Civilians, including women, children and the elderly, are today the deliberate targets in the current wave of internal conflicts.

SWITZERLAND: Crises which have recently broken out in various parts of the world have inflicted great suffering on the civilian populations, particularly the most vulnerable groups such as children, women, the elderly, refugees and displaced persons.

UN EMERGENCY RELIEF COORDINATOR: If sanctions can be used to prevent war criminals from enjoying the fruits of their evil, without harming innocent women and children, we have given ourselves a potent new tool for good.

AZERBAIJAN: ...having razed the town to the ground, the [Armenian armed forces] killed hundreds of innocent people, not even sparing women, children or the elderly.

UKRAINE: We strongly support the idea that [sanctions] must be used appropriately to target those responsible and not to increase the suffering of women, elderly and children who are the prime victims in times of war.

CHINA: Women and children in particular, as one of the most vulnerable social groups, are most gravely affected in conflict situations.

COSTA RICA: We are witness to the death of civilians, especially women, the elderly and children, dragged by harsh reality into armed conflicts that they had simply and unwittingly inherited.

ICRC PRESIDENT: I look forward to working very closely with you to try to translate some of these ideas into concrete measures on the ground that might

---

12 I operationalized essentialisms by comparing the contextual deployment of these references in civilian protection discourse to what is known about the actual vulnerabilities of war-affected populations. For example, I wanted to know how often "women" were associated primarily with children, with civilian status, with peace-making, or with vulnerability, and whether or not the existence and particular vulnerabilities of draft-age men were also highlighted in the transnational discourse framing "protection of civilians" as an issue. The frequency distributions for gender references and to references by context are summarized in Table 2.1.

make a small difference to the protection of civilians, especially women and children.

These examples from the Security Council thematic debates demonstrate the connections between the gender discourses of vulnerability, innocence and the equation of "civilians" with "women and children." The association of women with children is frequent, although not always as blatant as China's description of women and children as "one" social group. In other passages, women's and children's specific needs are broken into separate categories, but they nearly always appear juxtaposed.

In a few cases (seven times during the discussions), the category "women and children" is used as a signifier for "civilian" (Undersecretary). More frequently, the category is used to articulate the gravity of the problem, the sense that "not even" women and children are spared (Azerbaijan). The claim that civilians are being increasingly attacked (different delegates list the statistics as 75, 80 or 90 per cent of casualties) is repeatedly buttressed by claims that women and children constitute the majority of these victims (Zambia, Ukraine). Despite the Secretary-General's specific statement in his 1999 report that "men have been the major victims of summary mass executions," the statement that women and children are the main victims of armed conflict is made 20 times in the text of these discussions. Similarly, the term "including women and children," (appearing five times) attached to broad references to civilians, acknowledges the existence of other groups within the civilian population but underscores the relative gravity of women's and children's suffering. The term "especially women and children" (used 20 times) is employed both in descriptive statements (Switzerland) claiming that women and children's suffering is more acute, and in principled statements (ICRC), claiming that the protection of women and children is the first and greatest imperative.

Women are designated a particularly vulnerable group ten times in the verbatim text, alongside children, the elderly, sick and displaced (China, Switzerland); vulnerable men are mentioned zero times. The innocence of women and children is underscored by statements (Costa Rica, Ukraine) about their powerlessness, which correspondingly associate culpability for the conflict with adult men as a group. Missing from the discussion is a sense that women play a role in armed conflict other than that of passive victims and mothers, or that adult male civilians possess specific protection needs or vulnerabilities in war-affected regions.

Gendered Innocence   39

Table 2.1 Frequency of rhetorical references incorporating sex according to context, PoC documents 1999-2003

Context of Sex Reference	Frequency
Women and children	163
Women and children to signify civilian	44
Especially or including women and children	60
Women as vulnerable	56
Women as parents or peacemakers	29
Special protection needs of women and children	33
Women and children as victims	79
Women and children as deliberate targets	42
Women and children as primary victims/targets	27
Women as combatants	6
Men as victims/targets	6
Men, women and children	9
Men specifically mentioned as civilians	3
Men as vulnerable	1
Men as parents	1
Men as perpetrators/combatants	7

The construction of women alongside children and the elderly as innocent, vulnerable and "hapless," coupled with an absence of attention to civilian men as a specific group, suggests that the "innocent civilian" has emerged on the UN agenda as a deeply gendered construction, although it is sex-neutral in law. As Table 2.1 demonstrates, this pattern is consistent with that in the verbatim records of later meetings, as well as other UN documents available on OCHA's Protection of Civilians (PoC) web pages. In December 2003, the recently disseminated "Aide Memoire on PoC," updated to "reflect the latest concerns pertaining to the protection of civilians in armed conflict, including new trends and measures to address them," identifies the need for "special measures to protect women and girls from gender-based discrimination and violence," but makes no such mention of the special protection needs of civilian men and boys.

In short, while international humanitarian law defines the civilian/ combatant distinction in terms of a sex-neutral assessment of who is participating in hostilities, the two concepts that give the principle of civilian immunity its moral force – material innocence and vulnerability – are gendered, both historically and in contemporary discourse. This is true insofar as actors perceive that these attributes are more closely associated with women than with men. To the extent that this perception ill-describes

40   *'Innocent Women and Children'*

reality – to the extent that some women fight and many men do not – then using sex as a means of distinguishing civilians from combatants warps inter-subjective understandings of the distinction principle, and can distort its implementation and enforcement in practice.

Gender and the Civilian: Constitutive v. Warping Effects

But what does it mean to say that an international norm is "gendered"? What kind of norm effect does gender actually exert on the principles of distinction and immunity themselves, and what are the implications for changing this so as to bring the behavior and discourse of international actors more in line with the spirit of the norm?

In a recent essay, Helen Kinsella has argued that "discourses of gender" literally make the principle of distinction possible; that is, they exert a constitutive effect on actors' ability to identify civilians: "the very distinction of combatant and civilian is dependent upon, not merely described by, discourses of gender" (Kinsella 2005, 251). Kinsella argues that gender is constitutive of the civilian/combatant distinction insofar as it is the "natural" civilian status of women that "stabilizes the otherwise indeterminate distinction between those who may and may not be killed" (Kinsella 2005, 261). Although she points out that three distinct categories of individuals – children, women and the elderly – function as "synechdotes" for the "civilian," she claims that only women are said to "already possess the… attributes [of] not bearing arms, [being] outside the fighting, weak, suffering or in distress as a matter of sex… [as opposed to] temporally or chronologically" (Kinsella 2005, 268). The implication of Kinsella's argument is that without this use of gender essentialism to stabilize the distinction principle, no concept of civilian immunity is possible.

Kinsella is right to say that both the principles of distinction and immunity, which together underpin the proscriptive "civilian immunity norm," are sites for the articulation of specific gender dichotomies. However, I disagree that the civilian immunity norm itself is contingent upon and directly constituted by these discourses. This is an important distinction to make for two reasons. First, at stake for social scientists is the question of what comprises a valid constitutive claim in constructivist research. It has become commonplace to talk about constitutive effects in IR scholarship on norms, but as Wendt argues (1999, 78), "constitutive theories must be judged against empirical evidence just like causal ones."

Second, Kinsella's argument has important normative implications for the protection of civilians and the promotion of the norm in international society, as she recognizes in her concluding paragraph. If she is correct, then attempts to "ungender" the civilian protection regime, such as encouraging actors to avoid gender essentialist language in their appeals on behalf of

Gendered Innocence 41

civilians, will "overturn the foundation of the distinction of combatant and civilian... upon which lives depend" (Kinsella 2005, 272). My case studies demonstrate, however, that precisely the opposite is true: lives depend on ungendering the principle, because gender does not so much *constitute* the norm of civilian immunity itself as it constitutes a gender sub-norm, temporally linked to the immunity norm, and which exerts a *warping* effect on civilian protection regime norms and principles.

So how do we judge a "constitutive" claim such as Kinsella's, and if gender does not directly *constitute* the principles of distinction and immunity then what does it mean to say that these principles are gendered? In the remainder of this chapter, I begin by making the case that the immunity norm and the gender sub-norm are distinct rather than mutually constitutive. I then describe how they *are* related, before turning to an explanation of how this came to be so and the implications for altering this relationship in the future. The empirical chapters that follow will demonstrate why such an alteration in the inter-subjective understandings that underpin civilian protection discourse is of urgent importance for policy-makers interested in saving lives and promoting humanitarian law in international society.

According to Wendt (1999, 88), "ideas have constitutive effects when they create phenomena – properties, power, dispositions, meanings, etc. – that are conceptually or logically dependent on those ideas or structures, that exist only 'in virtue of' them." Unlike causal effects, which postulate independence and temporal asymmetry between independent and dependent variables, in a constitutive relationship, "X presupposes Y" (Wendt 1999, 25). For Kinsella's claim to be persuasive, at least according to this understanding of constitutive effects, the empirical record must show that the concept of civilian immunity cannot exist independently of the gender dichotomies that she has identified.

Instead, the immunity norm, while deeply gendered, is not contingent upon these gender binaries. Indeed, the gender sub-norm (specifying that gender/age groups in particular are to be spared death) and the immunity norm as such (specifying that *civilians* are to be spared) emerged independently from somewhat distinct, although overlapping, historical trajectories. They converged in the modern era due to specific normative and institutional processes.

The modern immunity principle emerged prior to its association with gender categories. It can be traced not to the sparing of women and children from the genocidal slaughter of ancient wars, but to the attempts of early just war theorists to secure immunity for clerics. Scholars of the immunity principle have identified inklings of this in Augustine, and more decisively in Aquinas (McKeogh 2002, 72). The culmination of this trend was the Peace of God movement in Europe, which between 975 and 1148 AD sought to render all clergy immune from attack during war (Johnson 1997, 105). While this trend was established purely out of institutional self-interest rather

42   *'Innocent Women and Children'*

than any spirit of humanitarianism (Gardam 1993, 12), it set the precedent of delineating protected groups on the basis of occupational status: the emergence of the distinction principle (Hartigan 1983, 69).

As cases such as Melos and Carthage suggest, women and younger children were sometimes spared massacre as such in ancient times as well, suggesting an early version of the gender sub-norm (Rahe 2002; Chalk and Jonassohn 1990). Norms prohibiting the slaughter of children and women were well-developed in the Islamic laws of war after the 7th century, as Johnson (1997) and Kelsay (1993) both discuss. However, this practice was distinct from the concept of civilian immunity in the "Peace of God" sense described above, or in the modern sense analyzed here. Instead, women and children were spared death due to their status as men's property. Whereas enemy men must be killed, women and younger males could be enslaved, thus enriching the victorious community rather than incurring the time and labor costs associated with massacring additional individuals (Ehrenreich 1997; Niarchos 1995). For example, early Islamic legal theories prohibit the killing of women and children, but make clear provisions for their capture, not merely as a right but a duty (Johnson 1997; Kelsay 1993). The moral basis for the prohibition on killing women (but not men) in this case is neither the perception that they pose less of a threat than enemy men nor that they are less responsible for the war, but that they, unlike the men, represent a potential resource of which belligerents have no right to deprive their own constituencies.

This is different from the broader immunity norm, for sparing people so they might be enslaved does not derive from the system of meanings by which we understand civilian immunity today. The gender norm (requiring fighters to appropriate women and children as property) originated distinct from the immunity norm (requiring fighters to avoid killing men in particular occupational categories). As I describe below, the "spare the women and children" gender norm then became reformulated in the context of immunity discourse and embedded as a sub-norm within the broader immunity norm during the Enlightenment. The normative understandings that constitute the current gender sub-norm have lost their basis in property relations and have rather been grafted onto Enlightenment notions of immunity as tied to material innocence: "women and children" are specified as immune today because they are perceived as unlikely to have been fighting (they are "distinct" from combatants), and therefore do not deserve to be mistreated (they are "immune" from death).

As these two sets of moral understandings emerged from different historical contexts, however, we can see that they are not logically necessary to one another. One need not presume a discourse of "immunity" to prescribe that women and children not be killed: this logic could be based simply on the desire to treat them as resources. Nor need one incorporate gender dichotomies into a discourse of "immunity" for it to have moral power:

occupational categories to whom this privilege extends might or might not include "women and children." That these ideas became interrelated during the Enlightenment does not mean that they necessarily need be related or that this relation cannot be strategically undone.

Indeed, far from being integral to the constitution of the "innocent civilian," the empirical case studies presented in the follow chapters suggest that such gender discourses undermine the very moral logic of the contemporary immunity norm. Since some women fight and many men do not, sex is not an adequate proxy for "civilian/combatant." That actors behave as though it is – and that this is generally seen by norm enforcers as unproblematic – demonstrates that the gender sub-norm *affects* the socio-linguistic practices through which the immunity norm is implemented in practice. As subsequent chapters outline, these effects on actor practice are both causal and constitutive. However, gender's effects on the norm itself are neither. Importantly, and contra to Kinsella's argument, this allows for the possibility that the immunity norm could be decoupled from its gender sub-norm without unraveling entirely, a point to which I will return in the final chapter.

Norm Evolution and Gendered Innocence

If the gender sub-norm – a prohibition on killing women – and the immunity norm – a prohibition on killing civilians – emerged from conceptually distinct normative trajectories, how did these two sets of normative understandings come to be associated in the modern laws of war? Although above I have emphasized their distinctiveness, both the immunity norm and the gender sub-norm exhibited points of convergence and overlap that set the stage for their later synthesis in the laws of war.

As anthropologists of war and a number of feminist historians recognize, organized warfare itself has historically been constitutive of masculinity and male social privilege (Keagan 1993; Lerner 1986). War took the place of hunting in early agrarian societies as the one occupation by which men could distinguish themselves as a social category (Dyer 1985; Ehrenreich 1997). If war was related to men's sense of honor and prowess vis-à-vis other men, little could be achieved by killing those who were excluded from the ritual of organized violence. Thus, the Romans prohibited the killing of women or children in terms of "honor" (McKeogh 2002, 36) and the "pre-Islamic tribal belief that it was not a sign of honor for a man to demonstrate his power to someone who is weaker" was incorporated into early Islamic jurisprudence (Tibi 1996, 133). As Lindner writes (2002, 152) the targeting of men for slaughter by men may have been as much about the perception that only other men are "worthy of death" as that they are threatening. This doctrine persisted throughout the Middle Ages in the chivalric codes

44 *'Innocent Women and Children'*

of European knights, "in which those having military prowess agree not to exercise their power against others weaker than themselves" (Kelsay 1993, 59) and is evident today in the norm that boys may not hit girls.[13]

It was in this discourse, in which women are not defined as property but are incorporated into the broader categories *civilians* ("materially innocent") and *weak* ("vulnerable"), that the older gender norms overlapped conceptually with the emerging concept of civilian immunity. This formed the basis for the later convergence of these two sets of discourses in the formal articulation of the immunity principle. This was not to occur until the early modern period when, in the wake of the brutal religious wars of Europe, calls for restraint were answered by scholars such as Hugo Grotius and later by Enlightenment thinkers (Best 1983). The immunity of "women and children" as a single ascriptive group was at that time linked to the general theory of occupational immunity by legal scholars, and to "protection" discourses of the modern nation-building era equating "women and children" with the national home-front.

As the next two sections demonstrate, the gender sub-norm was grafted onto the immunity principle because both the normative and the institutional environment were favorable to a convergence of these two pre-existing, but distinct, discourses. This explanation follows from Florini's evolutionary theory of international norms, which lists three factors accounting for a norm's success and survival: "whether a norm becomes prominent enough in the... norm pool to gain a foothold; how well it interacts with other prevailing norms... that is the 'normative environment'; and what external environmental conditions confront the pool" (Florini 1996, 374).

Norm Entrepreneurship

The first of these conditions is typically brought about through the efforts of a "norm entrepreneur," an individual or organization that aims to affect the behavior or beliefs of others (Finnemore and Sikkink 1998; Nadelmann 1990). In the 17th and 18th centuries, the intellectuals responsible for articulating the principle of civilian immunity chose to incorporate both the Christian just war theorists' arguments regarding the exemption of certain groups on the basis of occupation, and also the older prohibitions on killing women, children, the elderly and disabled, under the rubric that these groups posed no threat and thus deserved no maltreatment. This was in marked contrast to the earlier Augustinian "just war" tradition, in which the immunity of particular populations hinged on the right practice of their leaders (Johnson

---

13 Although, particularly with respect to growing children, it is as likely to be the case that the girl is bigger and stronger than the boy: with respect to the norm, sex serves as a proxy for "weaker," often trumping objective indicators of relative weakness.

Gendered Innocence 45

1999); and to gender norms requiring every woman and child to be enslaved by victorious troops.

According to McKeogh, the work of Francisco do Vitoria (1486-1546) brought the key break with earlier traditions on civilian immunity. "Vitoria's model brings a fundamental change in the basis on which people are classified as targets. The division of people into two categories, legitimate and illegitimate targets, is no longer on the basis of the just or unjust cause of the ruler; rather it is on the basis of combatancy and noncombatancy" (McKeogh 2002, 85). This shift required a clear articulation of the *distinction* principle as a basis for immunity: how to tell who was who in situations of armed conflict in order to determine how they should be treated. Vitoria resolved this in part through a logic of gender: into the ranks of the civilians, he included "women, children, clerics, foreign travelers, guests of the country, harmless agricultural folk and also the rest of the peaceable population" (quoted in Johnson 1975, 196).

Subsequent scholars of the early modern period followed suit. Hugo Grotius' (1583-1645) categories include "not only women and children but also all men whose way of life is opposed to war-making" (quoted in McKeogh 2002, 115). Decades before Grotius, Gentili had devoted an entire chapter of his work to the immunity of women and children from attack (Hartigan 1983, 44). For Emerich Vattel, the innocent included "women, children, feeble old men and the sick" (Vattel 1758, 251). Although the innocence of civilian men was a matter of argument, hinging on age and occupational status, women's innocence was treated, both by Enlightenment writers and later commentators, as "self-evident," or, in the words of Francisco Suarez (1548-1617), an "objective material fact": "It is implicit in natural law that the innocent include children, women and all unable to bear arms" (quoted in Hartigan 1983, 94-95).

If adult women were presumed "civilian" even when they were not, immunity theorists constructed adult men as "presumptive combatants,"[14] regardless of their actual societal roles. Of the Enlightenment theorists, Vitoria made this argument most forcefully: "Everyone able to bear arms should be considered dangerous and must be assumed to be defending the enemy king: they may therefore be killed unless the opposite is clearly true" (quoted in Hamilton 1963, 142). With regard to civilians, defined according to "objective criteria," (first and foremost age and sex) the presumption was innocent until proven guilty; but with regard to presumptive combatants, the early jurists sought proof of "innocence" in order to spare life rather than proof of guilt to take it. Suarez wrote, "Human judgment looks upon those able to take up arms as having actually done so" (quoted in Hartigan 1983, 94). The assumption that those "able to take up arms" are adult men can

---

14 This term was coined by former UNPROFOR negotiator David Harland (Respondent #8, Personal Interview, Geneva, August 2002).

46 *'Innocent Women and Children'*

be seen more recently in Walzer, whose discussion of guerilla war suggests that when there is doubt, any adult male should be considered a legitimate target: "A soldier who, once he is engaged, simply fires at every male villager between the age of 15 and 50... is probably justified in doing so" (Walzer 1977, 192).

To summarize, the philosophers, legal scholars and activists who were responsible for articulating the modern theory of civilian immunity drew on their own gendered understandings in constructing the social kind "civilian" as a gendered space.[15] These authors inscribed gendered notions of innocence and vulnerability into the civilian/combatant distinction. These gendered ideas did not constitute the category "civilian" itself, but rather the concept of distinction provided a site for inscribing the gender essentialisms. These then interacted and evolved with the particular gender hierarchies characteristic of the emerging state-system. Indeed, as I argue next, this interrelationship partly explains the emergence and persistence of the gender sub-norm in the modern period, despite developments that marked its increasing obsolescence.

Institutional Conditions

If the conflation of biological characteristics with social categories of non-combatant became prominent as a result of initiation and imitation by successive legal scholars, the association of women and children with non-combatant status became widespread because it both fit the broader normative environment and reinforced structural developments, namely the emergence of the Westphalian states-system. With respect to the normative environment, we have seen that the perception of women as weak, vulnerable and separate from war served both the mythology of war-making and the discourses legitimizing androcractic social hierarchies (Remy 1990). In this sense the extension of immunity on the basis of these same characteristics resonated with prevailing norms.

The argument about structural factors concerns the mutually constitutive relationship between institutional demands and normative processes. Configurations of normative belief may emerge and persist because they map conveniently onto and legitimate particular institutions. For instance, the concept of sovereignty has been analyzed as emerging in tandem with the consolidation of state power in the Westphalian system (Buzan 1993;

---

15 Kinsella's analysis also examines the ways in which these discourses reproduced particular hierarchies between states and cultures, postulating a "civilized" form of warfare appropriate and applicable to Western states only. This aspect of her analysis is borne out by research comparing levels of restraints between Anglo-European belligerents to that evident in colonial warfare (for example Andreopoulos 1994; Grimsley, 2002).

Gendered Innocence 47

Ruggie 1993; Spruyt 1994). It persists not because it corresponds to political reality (it does not) but because it legitimizes and constitutes the fiction of the Westphalian system itself (Walker 1993; Wendt 1992). In the modern period, norms seemingly based on ethical imperatives often emerged because they supported this institutional framework. For example, Thomas demonstrates that the need of actors in the emerging state-system to promote sovereign immunity, rather than an ethics-based logic, accounts for the emergence and persistence of the non-assassination norm (Thomas 2001).

Similarly, several authors have argued that the development of a norm of civilian immunity is partly explained by instrumental needs of political authorities and developments in military culture (Palmer-Fernandez 1998). As noted, the earliest immunity norms stemmed from the attempts of the Catholic Church to consolidate its power by protecting its clergy, and before that the desire to appropriate civilians as booty. In the early modern period, standing armies depended on local populations for provisions, and found cooperation readier if they restrained themselves from indiscriminate violence (Grimsley and Rogers 2002). Reciprocity operated to limit the wastage of resources involved in large-scale destruction of enemy civilians, which would invite reprisals (Mavrodes 1985).[16]

Like the assassination norm and the immunity norm more broadly, the association of women with children and with the civilian population was developed most systematically in the political thought of international legal scholars in the early modern state-building period (Best 1983). What united the discourses of these jurists were their beliefs that civilians deserved immunity because they did not pose a threat, and that the materially innocent were those who did not bear arms. Women were positioned as civilians partly because of the assumption that they *could* not fight, although as noted above, women could and at least some always did. But secondly the European laws of war provided an incentive for women to avoid participating in hostilities, by linking their protection as civilians to the provision that they avoid "taking the place of men," that is taking up arms (Hartigan 1983, 99).

Thus we can understand the gender dimension of the immunity principle both as a reflection of prevailing gender discourse and a factor in constructing the militarized sex-gender structure that came to be associated with the modern state. Two aspects of the European state-building context were particularly hospitable to the emergence of the immunity norm as a gendered construct: the legitimation of professional (masculinized) armies along with

---

16 The instrumentalist argument also explains the gradual breakdown of compliance with such norms where military developments, such as industrial mobilization of whole nations for war (Crane 2002), or resistance on the part of occupied populations (Blanning 2002), made the targeting of civilians strategically useful.

48   *'Innocent Women and Children'*

the emergence of mass adult male conscription; and the development of modern nationalism as a gendered discourse.

Modern Militaries and Gendered "Immunity" Discourse The modern laws of war emerged in this period partly as a means of delegitimizing the use of armed force by groups not affiliated with professional armies (Gardam 1993; Nabulsi 2001). Because the immunity of civilians per se is based on the reciprocal obligation to refrain from combat activities (Dongen 1991), these norms reinforced the political exclusion of women from combat (Kinsella 2001). This policy was strategically irrational in the age of mass armies, as the willingness of certain great powers to utilize female combatants during the World Wars attests (Braybon and Summerfield 1987; Goldstein 2001), but it was institutionally rational insofar as it corresponded to other developments in the European gender regime that accompanied the consolidation of the Westphalian state. The gendered division of labor inherent in modern militaries both reinforced the separation of women from war and legitimized domestic gender hierarchies (Enloe 2000; Hagemann 2000; Peterson 1992b).

The emergence of universal conscription in the Napoleonic era did much to bring the assumption of all men's combatant status into conformity with the facts (Forrest 2002; Nickerson 1940). Not every European country organized its levy on the draconian scale of revolutionary France; nor did conscription as such begin in the 18th century (Moller 2002). However, the transformation of combatancy from a professional occupation that excluded the majority of the population to an activity in which nearly all able-bodied young men could be expected to participate was pivotal in sedimenting the gender assumptions underpinning the concept of the "combatant." At the ideological level, mass conscription superimposed the "able-bodied adult male" onto the concept of the militarized state (Steans 1998, 89-90). At the institutional level, the bureaucratization of conscription ensured the impressment of young men and the exclusion of women from service, reifying age-old assumptions about gender and battle roles. "The hierarchical order of gender relations was ideologically underpinned by the designation of arms-bearing man as the protector of weak and defenseless woman" (Hagemann 2000, 189).

It is ironic that the gender sub-norm embedded in the immunity principle was reinforced by the emergence of mass armies even as the immunity principle itself was undermined by the concept of the "nation-at-arms." Able-bodied adult men were situated as citizen-soldiers, a strategy which held in check revolution from the lower classes while providing the manpower required to engage in extensive land campaigns characteristic of early 19th century warfare (Kestnbaum 2002). By contrast, women were positioned in support roles that simultaneously reinforced their de facto civilian status and undermined the protection that the immunity norm had previously afforded them. The French National Convention in 1793 stated: "The young men shall fight; the married men shall forge weapons and transport supplies;

the women will make tents and clothes and will serve in the hospitals; the children will make up old linen into lint; the old men will have themselves carried into the public squares to rouse the courage of the fighting men, to preach hatred against the kings and the unity of the Republic" (quoted in Nickerson 1940, 64).

Genealogies of total war make reference to the French National Convention in tracing the perception that wars were now total, that nations rather than professionals fought them, and that no longer could anyone be said to be morally or materially innocent (Carr 2002; Hartigan 1983; Nickerson 1940). Formerly presumptive civilians lost their immunity, not because they were now assumed to be fighting, but because their everyday tasks had been recast as vital to "war efforts" that now occupied entire societies.

This reinforced gendered assumptions regarding who fights and who is ostensibly protected (the distinction principle), even as the principle that "fighting" determines the right to be killed (the immunity principle) was weakened. This is evident in Stanley Baldwin's remarks to the British House of Commons in 1932, justifying the obliteration bombing of civilians: "The only defence is offence which means that you have to kill more women and children more quickly than the enemy can if you want to save yourselves" (quoted in Ford 1970, 34). This quote, while justifying the killing of civilians in the name of military necessity, still reinforces the gendered construction of the civilian by the substitution of the term "women and children." Presumably, killing able-bodied adult men was not questioned at all in calculations of whether strategic bombing was immoral: they were assumed to be away at the front. Correspondingly, those authors that sought to argue against this tendency to dissolve the civilian/combatant distinction also reproduced the belief that it was women and children, not men, whose immunity was at stake in the discussion:

> We must distinguish combatants from noncombatants on the basis of their immediate threat of harmfulness. Children are not combatants even though they may join the armed forces if they are allowed to grow up. Women are not combatants, just because they bear children or offer comfort to the soldiers. (Nagel 1985, 69)

In the 20th century, mass conscription has waned, due partly to advances in military technology, partly to the incongruity of forced conscription with democratic institutions (Mjoset and Van Holde 2002, 92). However, the discourse of citizen-warrior masculinity nonetheless remains influential within the institutional cultures of Western European states (Cohn 1998; Enloe 2000; Murphy 1998, 101; Whitworth 2004) and by diffusion, that of developing countries as well (Smythe and Prasad 1968, ix). The linkage between citizenship and arms, between the nation at war and the uniform mobilization of able-bodied men in the service of vulnerable women and children, has remained a cogent part of the way in which international actors

50 'Innocent Women and Children'

construct the civilian/combatant divide (Higate 2002; Mische 1989; Steihm 1982).

Feminists have pointed out that this construction of citizenship as a masculine realm linked to military service has been pivotal in excluding women from democratic participation (Elshtain 1987; Mische 1989). Others add that women who have served in the military have failed to benefit from the citizen-soldier contract in the same way as have men (Kerber 1990; Ritter 2002). The important point for my argument is that the linkage between masculinity, military service and citizenship meant that adult men in the modern European states-system, unlike either children or women, have been conceptualized as both agents of politics and as fighters in time of war. Both constructions run counter to the moral logic by which "innocents" (either in the moral or material sense) are said to be immune to attack.

The combination of hyper-aggressiveness and hyper-rationality that characterizes modern hegemonic masculinity (Connell 1987) and its connection to the Westphalian state, have been well documented (di Stefano 1991; Enloe 1993; Tickner 1992). Hegemonic masculinity constantly evolves and changes (Hooper 2001; Niva 1998); it is class and race-related (Pleck 1981, 40-41), often contradictory (Segal 1990); and it always masks and contests other forms of masculinity (Hearn and Morgan 1990). But regardless of context and time-specific variation in the attributes associated with dominant masculinity, the fundamental assumptions of men's autonomous subject status and relative societal power remain central to the imagery and language used in conceptualizing warfare (Goldstein 2001, 266). The responsibility to give one's life in protection of the nation is understood as the price by which men secure their privileged status within peacetime (Elshtain 1987; Enloe 1993; Mische 1989). Insofar as this contract is seen as uncontested, the assumption that the majority of men will rise to this responsibility, thereby making themselves legitimate targets during armed conflict, is naturalized.[17]

Modern Nationalism and Gendered "Protection" Discourse During this period, gender discourse influenced the development of the civilian/combatant distinction through a second conceptual trajectory: it became embedded in the idea of the "nation." With the territorialization of political community, the "civilian front" emerged as synonymous with the national homeland.[18]

---

17 The operation of militarized masculinity is far more complex and paradoxical than is sketched here. See for example Murphy (1998) and Hooper (2001). My key point relates not to men's gender identities as such, but to the societal perception that in time of war, men will adopt these identities unproblematically and assume culturally imposed gender roles.

18 According to Kinsella (2005), it was not until the 19th century that the word "civilian" entered into broad use.

Gendered Innocence 51

Civilians were juxtaposed to the military forces responsible for their protection. As various feminist scholars have pointed out, the nation-state, along with the international social order of which it is constitutive, emerged as a gendered concept (Blom, Hall and Hagemann 2000; True 1993; Yuval-Davis 1997). Mass armies, universal adult male conscription and the marginalization of women's previous wartime involvement embodied earlier ideas about the gendered character of war, articulated by Elshtain as the myth of the "just warrior" fighting for the "beautiful soul" (Elshtain 1987). Such policies aimed at reifying the myth that all men fought for the country, and that the "home-front" was composed of the women, children and elderly left behind (Steans 1998, 89-90).

According to Blom, "this process seemed to change the military from a joint masculine-feminine undertaking, as had been the case as long as women followed the armies to cook, clean and take care of the wounded, to a men-only project..."; concurrently, the rise of Darwinism, with the belief that gender was biologically inherent, supported the essentialist supposition that "*all* women were weak and needed protection, whereas to be strong and bellicose was a characteristic shared by *all men*" (Blom 2000, 15). Cooke argues that the "professionalization" of European wars in this period "codified the binary structure of the world by designating gender-specific tasks and gender-specific areas where these tasks might be executed" (Cooke 1993, 182).

These gendered representations of the front/home-front (along with accompanying dichotomies: "war/peace, good/evil, combatant/noncombatant, friend/foe, victory/defeat, patriotism/pacifism") came to underpin the idea of the nation-state as a sovereign political space (Cooke 1993, 182). IR feminists have demonstrated that the historical construction of the state reflects a masculine model: the state is represented as a hyper-rational sphere in which emotion and ideals matter little, one which both rules over and protects the nation (Tickner 2001, 52; Pettman 1996). By contrast, the nation is represented through a language of home, hearth, blood, family; the "domestic" space of the nation is juxtaposed to the "public" character of statesmanship in foreign affairs. "In [national] narratives, the nation is virtually always feminized and characterized as in need of protection... women are represented as the nation's social and biological womb and the men as its protectors" (Mayar 1999, 10).

The formulations associated with the gendered protection principle (women, like children, as dependent, vulnerable and in need of defense) reinforce the legitimacy of the modern state and guides its self-presentation as an actor in international affairs. We see examples of this in international social discourse, in which the gendered script of the masculine state protecting the feminine nation reproduces assumptions about the location of actual men, children and women. Enloe, writing about media coverage of the Gulf War, explains: "womenandchildren rolls easily off network tongues because in network minds women are family members rather than independent actors, presumed to be almost childlike in their innocence about international *realpolitik*... states exist, this media story implies, to protect womenandchildren... it follows that the Gulf Crisis story must also ignore the female attaché at the U.S. embassy in Kuwait, negotiating... for the release of these very same womenandchildren... her existence is not allowed to disturb the womenandchildren-protected-by-statesmen script" (Enloe 1993, 166).

The consolidation of modern sex-gender structures (in particular mass militaries) and modern gender narratives (in particular the gendered civilian "front") coincided and interacted with the articulation of the immunity principle as an Enlightenment discourse. This is different from claiming that it was gender dualisms that made the entire concept of the civilian/combatant distinction possible in the first place. To make such a claim suggests that in rethinking the way the law is gendered, the entire conception of distinction might collapse. Rather, I argue that gender essentialisms were grafted onto this principle in the course of a specific historical process. From the viewpoint of my analysis, the gender sub-norm can be best understood not as a constitutive aspect of the distinction principle, but as the combined result of gender assumptions made by norm entrepreneurs and the receptive normative/institutional environment of the emerging state-system. This leaves open the possibility of norm change. If the gender sub-norm were detached from immunity discourse, it might strengthen rather than eradicate the immunity norm. I return to this point in the final chapter.

Conclusion

In this chapter, I have provided an explanation for the way in which gender assumptions became embedded in the principles on which the civilian protection regime rests. The descriptive principle of the *civilian/combatant distinction* was constructed in part according to beliefs about the gendered division of wartime labor. The normative principle of *civilian immunity* emerged in the modern laws of war as a gendered construct because the modern state-system from which the contemporary international legal order stems also rests on the gender hierarchies, legitimated by the assumption of a corresponding sex-gender structure. Gender discourses associating men/manhood with soldiering and women/womanhood with the care of children legitimize the universal conscription of adult men and the exclusion of women from military service. The resulting sex-gender structure of national militaries reinforces the perception that women are separate from war. Thus, as I emphasize in the following chapters, those who now advance the principled idea of *civilian protection* frame their moral concern in terms of gender essentialisms as well.

Gendered Innocence 53

These gender discourses work best when war is conceptualized as a Hobbesian struggle between standing armies of male soldiers on territorial borders between states. Over the course of the 20th century they have been strained by technological innovation, both spotlighting women's participation in war-making from the home-front and undermining any biological rationale for women's exclusion from combat. More importantly, they have been belied by trends in warfare over the post-war period and particularly since the end of the Cold War. Political violence in the contemporary world seldom takes place between masculinized institutions of state. Cooke argues that guerilla war in particular, now endemic worldwide, subverts the gendered war paradigm, disrupting binaries on which the discourse of the state protecting the defenseless nation, men protecting innocent women and children, is based: "Front (male space) and home front (female space) are indistinguishable in a situation where war can break out at any instant in any place. Combatant (male) and (noncombatant) female are indistinguishable in a situation where civilians are drawn into skirmishes, or where they are specifically targeted" (Cooke 1993, 183).

All of this begs the question of why the innocent civilian persists as a *gendered* construct in the face of changes in women's societal roles and in the character of armed conflict. For although gender has been historically embedded in the concept of civilian immunity, it does not *constitute* the norm of immunity in an absolute sense (Wendt 1999): it is not a *necessary* component of the immunity norm. An un-gendered immunity norm could coincide with a society in which gender roles were less stratified. Indeed, in such a society, only an un-gendered norm would conceptually make sense.

Why then does the association of "women and children," but not men, with civilian status *persist* despite other sea changes in the global gender regime? The following several chapters suggest that it persists because it both affects and is reproduced by the practices of international actors – states and belligerents groups, transnational advocacy networks, and civilian protection agencies operating in zones of conflict.

Chapter 3

Implementing the Civilian Immunity Norm: Three "Gender Sub-Norm" Effects

The women and children will be left alone.
– Bosnian Serb Army commander to troops, quoted in Honig and Both 1997, 7

In the language of international relations theory, "principles" are broad descriptive beliefs about the nature of a particular problem, and broad normative understandings regarding how to address it. "Norms" set down specific obligations incumbent on particular actors in order to address the problem in accordance with collectively agreed upon principles. The previous chapter examined the key principles of the civilian protection regime. I argued that the concepts of innocence and vulnerability underpinning the immunity principle are gendered, so that the distinction principle, which defines what constitutes "civilians," has emerged as a gendered concept as well. This has happened despite the fact that in legal terms, the civilian/combatant distinction is to be determined based on what actors do – their agency rather than their ascriptive characteristics.

This chapter investigates what effect the gendering of regime principles has on the implementation of the norms that stem from the regime principles. I look in particular at the most basic regime norm: the prohibition on killing civilians. If gender beliefs exert no effect on the norm, we would expect efforts at compliance, denunciation and enforcement to be enacted on the basis of *who is actually a civilian* rather than according to sex and age proxies. If gender beliefs completely trump the logic of the norm, we would expect to see *all battle-age men* consistently identified as combatants and killed, and for *all women, children and old men* to be consistently identified as worthy of immunity.

I explore the relative merit of these two possibilities by examining three kinds of norm effects: the ways in which actors comply with the norm, that is, who gets targeted in war; the ways in which actors account for violations of the norm and the extent to which their accounts are accepted by bystanders; and the atrocity threshold beyond which outside actors feel compelled to enforce the immunity norm through "humanitarian intervention." I find that gender beliefs exert a probabilistic effect: along a continuum of norm effects from strong (unthinking compliance) to weak (justified violations), the immunity norm is relatively less robust – measured in compliance rates, accounts for violations, and reactions by bystanders – when the victims in question are adult men than when they include adult women. Women and younger children are less likely to be targeted for outright execution than are "battle-age" civilian males; belligerents are more likely to deny or apologize for such killings when they do happen; and third parties are more likely to point to the protection of civilian women and children than of civilian men as justifications for intervention in humanitarian emergencies. In short, the gender sub-norm "warps" or distorts the application of the regime norms themselves.

I make this case in the following manner. The first section below outlines my terminology and the approach to norm effects deployed here. The second section examines belligerent compliance with the immunity norm. Drawing on historical and contemporary examples, I demonstrate that civilian men are more likely than civilian women to be targeted for massacre in time of war. A case study of sex-selective massacre in the former Yugoslavia demonstrates that the logic behind these disparities has to do in particular with the gendered construction of the "civilian/combatant" divide. While additional ethnographic research on belligerent populations is required to determine the extent to which these sex-selective patterns of killing are norm-driven, this data suggests that the gender sub-norm exerts some effect on belligerents' interpretations of who is or is not a legitimate target in armed conflict.

In the third section, I examine the language through which atrocity, when it occurs, is interpreted both by the perpetrators and by bystanders. I demonstrate that what counts as an "attack" on civilians also varies somewhat according to the age and sex of the dead. Belligerents are less likely to claim that attacks on women are justifiable than those where adult men are the victims. Third parties are also more likely to condemn such attacks. I demonstrate the variation in the discourse used to define atrocity through an analysis of the My Lai massacre.

Fourth, I examine international efforts to enforce the civilian immunity norm. Here, I draw on literature regarding the "enabling" effects of norms and examine humanitarian intervention (arguably a violation of state sovereignty) as enabled by the civilian protection principle that enjoins bystanders to enforce or "defend" the civilian immunity norm when it is violated. This section explores the way that humanitarian intervention rhetoric is gendered. Because women and children signify civilians, their protection is more likely to be invoked as a justification for intervention. This will be the case regardless of the actual sex-distributions of the "innocent" and "vulnerable" in a particular case. I draw on examples from the post-Cold War era to make this case, and then demonstrate how gender discourse correlates with claims that intervention is justified, rather than with

Implementing the Civilian Immunity Norm   57

descriptive realities on the ground, through a case analysis of the Rwandan non-intervention.

The final section draws together these empirical claims through an in-depth analysis of the 1998-1999 war over the Serbian province of Kosovo. Sex-selective execution of men took place in Kosovo (in particular due to the perception by the JNA that men and boys were legitimate targets), but the rhetoric framing the war as a humanitarian emergency and justifying NATO's air war in the Security Council referred to the protection of "women and children." The fact that civilian protection principles are gendered explains these patterns in the application, interpretation and enforcement of the civilian immunity norm.

Norms and Their Effects in World Politics

So far I have argued that the *principles* underpinning the civilian protection regime are gendered. Does this matter in terms of how specific regime *norms* are implemented in practice? Norms are "standards of behavior defined in terms of rights and obligations" (Krasner 1983, 2). According to Hasenclever, Mayer and Rittberger (1997, 9), "norms serve to guide the behavior of regime members in such a way as to produce collective outcomes which are in harmony with the goals and shared convictions that are specified in the regime principles."

Numerous specific norms are embedded within the civilian protection regime, including (but not limited to): 1) a right of civilians not to be the object of attack (Bouchet-Saulnier 2002, 44-45); 2) an obligation of belligerents to distinguish themselves from the civilian population (Kalshoven and Zegveld 2001, 40-41); 3) an obligation to avoid methods and means of combat that are incapable of distinguishing between combatants and civilians (Hartle 2002, 152); 4) an obligation of civilians to avoid taking direct part in hostilities (Nabulsi 2001, 16); 5) and a right/obligation of third parties to take steps to *prevent* or alleviate the suffering of war-affected civilians, and to punish those belligerents who violate the civilian immunity principle (Dongen 1991; Wheeler 2000). The key norm of interest in this chapter is the most familiar and most fundamental: the obligation of belligerents to refrain from targeting civilians directly and to minimize indirect damage to civilians, or the "civilian immunity norm."

Norms contain both a *directive* aspect, which defines either what is required or what is prohibited, and *parameters*, which define the conditions under which the norm's directives apply (Shannon 2000, 295). The parameters within which the civilian immunity injunctions apply are expressed in the concepts of intentionality, proportionality and reciprocity (McMahan 1996, 88). The civilian immunity norm does not require actors never to kill civilians, but never to target them *deliberately as such*; never to kill them *unless* the military necessity outweighs the scale and brutality of their deaths; and not to kill them *as long as* they fulfill their reciprocal obligation to refrain from participating in hostilities (Gardam 1993).

As Shannon argues, both the likelihood of actors violating a norm and the way in which they account for their violations reflect the extent to which the norm parameters are fixed or open to interpretation (Shannon 2000, 294). Below, I argue that the civilian immunity norm has two sets of parameters, encoded by gender: a rigid one applying to presumptive civilian groups (including children, women, the elderly and the disabled) and a flexible one applying to adult able-bodied men whose civilian status may be doubted. Thus gender beliefs can in part account for variation in norm robustness in practice.

Three approaches to the effects of norms on actors' behavior are examined below. The most conventional approach to norms is as a supplementary explanation for why actors behave as they do. Norms exert causal effects when actors behave as they would not in the norm's absence (Goldstein and Keohane 1993). They may regulate actors' behavior either through a logic of consequences, in which actors respond to external incentives to comply, or through a logic of appropriateness, in which actors' identities are tied up with norm compliance (March and Olsen 1989). Actors may respond to a logic of appropriateness for instrumental reasons, where policies are changed as a tactical move but interests remain the same, or internalize the norms, which then take on a "taken for granted" character.[1] The first section below examines the extent to which belligerent restraint varies according to the age and sex of civilian targets, even in cases where many women are mobilized or where many men remain in the civilian sector.

Another strand of literature emphasizes not rates of compliance but the social language required by actors to explain their deviations from the norm (Jackson 2000; Kratochwil and Ruggie 1986; Risse 2000; Wheeler 2000). The section below examines how gender affects the strategies by which norm violators justify their actions and by which third parties condemn them. I argue that the communicative strategies by which belligerents defend their violations of the civilian immunity norm, and the likelihood of observers accepting these claims, differ depending on the sex and age of the victims. This is explained by the gender sub-norm's warping effect on the parameters of the immunity norm.

Third, norms can function to enable as well as constrain action. Flynn and Farrell argue that European states' commitment to democracy exerted enabling effects over time as it prompted a redefinition of sovereignty, loosening the norm of non-intervention in the affairs of the Commission on Security and Cooperation in Europe (CSCE) member states (Flynn and

---

1 Checkel (1999) has called these two pathways "simple learning" and "complex learning" respectively.

Farrell 1999). Likewise, the civilian immunity norm *enables* third party states to make arguments regarding the legitimacy of armed intervention on behalf of besieged non-combatants. The emerging doctrine of humanitarian intervention is another flashpoint around which gendered civilian protection norms are articulated and reproduced. Where compliance with the immunity norm itself is not enough to ensure that civilians are not targeted, third parties may legitimately take action to ensure that they are not. I demonstrate that intervention is more likely to be justified as humanitarian through references to "innocent women and children" than to the protection of civilian men.

The key argument of this chapter is that the extent to which there is "wiggle room" for belligerent actors to interpret civilian immunity norm parameters favorably – that is, to bend the norm and to justify doing so when in their interests – depends in large part on the age and sex of the civilians in question. In other words, the gender sub-norm influences not only what counts as a civilian but therefore what counts as an attack against civilians.

This explains why deliberate killings of women and children, while they do occur, are less frequent and widespread than the deliberate killings of adult men. It also explains why the social processes of dehumanization are so much more pronounced when women and children are targeted, and why actors are more likely to deny or excuse, rather than justify, the targeting of presumed non-combatants. Lastly, it explains why claims to be protecting civilians through forcible intervention are often buttressed by imagery of women and children at risk, despite the actual sex and age demographics of those at risk of massacre in complex emergencies. I lay out these claims in the three sections below before demonstrating their interrelationship through an analysis of the 1998-1999 war in Kosovo.

Regulative Effects: Belligerent Compliance

A gender sub-norm associating women but not men with civilian status is hidden or "stowed away" inside the civilian immunity norm. What effect if any does this have on patterns of compliance with the immunity norm? Does this make a difference in terms of which civilians are targeted in situations of armed conflict?

One way of tackling this question is to examine the conditions under which actors violate norms. Shannon's (2000) analysis of the political psychology of norm violation identifies a range of situations in which norm violation is more or less likely. Violations are not as easy as rationalists expect, Shannon argues, because where norms are absolute rather than ambiguous they are often followed despite utilitarian imperatives. However, they may be weaker than sociologists predict as well because "to the extent that 1) norms are ambiguously defined, 2) a situation lends itself to a favorable interpretation of an ambiguous norm and 3) an actor is motivated, there is great breadth in the range of norm interpretations and behavior within a social structure" (Shannon 2000, 311).

The parameters of the civilian immunity norm provide belligerents considerable leeway to violate the prohibitions. For example, the so-called doctrine of "double effect" states that civilians may not be targeted *directly* but they may be killed if their deaths were only incidental to the destruction of a legitimate military target (McKeogh 2002, 116). In these cases the belligerent is required to use force proportionally, minimizing collateral damage in relation to the military gains achieved (Gasser 1995; Kalshoven and Zegveld 2001). Because the "civilian" is socially constructed so as to create a gendered distinction between presumptive civilians and presumptive combatants, the flexibility with which to interpret the parameters depends on the sex/age demographics of the potential victims.

The Targeting of Civilians

The empirical record suggests belligerents are somewhat less likely to kill women and children outright than they are to kill unarmed adult men.[2] The propensity of belligerents to single out adult men for execution has now been documented in dozens of ongoing conflicts worldwide.[3] This martial tradition has roots in antiquity, and it remains widely practiced by irregular forces, if not always by state militaries.[4] More often than women, young children or the elderly, military-age men and adolescent boys are constructed as "potential" combatants and are therefore treated by armed forces – whether engaged in formal battle, low-intensity conflict or in repression of one's own civilian population – as if they are legitimate targets of political violence (IASC 2002, 175; Lindsey 2001, 28).

As suggested in the previous chapter, sex-selective massacre predates the civilian immunity norm. According to Lerner, "There is overwhelming historical evidence for the preponderance of the practice of killing or mutilating male prisoners and for the large-scale enslavement and rape of female prisoners" (Lerner 1986, 81). Yet the targeting of male civilians remains a defining feature of modern armed conflict, as well as mass killing in peacetime. Jones (2000) has carried out the most comprehensive comparative-historical survey on the phenomena of sex-selective massacre, which he terms

---

2   I emphasize "belligerents" rather than states because participants in armed conflict include paramilitaries, rebel bands and guerillas as well as regular forces.

3   The most comprehensive source for such data is the human rights watchdog group Gendercide Watch, whose website contains extensive case literature and news reports. See Gendercide Watch 2003a.

4   The paradigmatic examples are the treatment of the Melians at the hands of the Athenians or the sacking of Carthage. See Chalk and Jonassohn 1990; Jones 2000; Rahe, 2002.

"gendercide."[5] Citing among his examples the Stalinist purges, the Armenian genocide, inter-communal violence in South Asia, and counter-insurgency tactics in Peru, Sri Lanka, Iraqi Kurdistan, and Kosovo, Jones concludes, "it is... remarkable how regularly one comes across references, in the literature on modern mass killing, to staggering demographic disproportions of adult males vs. adult females" (Jones 2000, 187).

Although primary data on the motivations of belligerents who massacre men has not been collected for this study, several interrelated explanations can be gleaned from secondary literature on the subject. Some authors have emphasized the property status of women relative to men (Ehrenriech 1997; Lerner 1986; Niarchos 1995), suggesting that the ancient gender norm is itself salient in contemporary conflicts, rather than simply embedded and recast within the immunity principle. If the point of killing is to eliminate a human community, only the humans must be killed. Their chattel (domesticated animals, belongings, women, children) can simply be appropriated as booty.

A related explanation revolves around the cultural belief that men, but not women, carry ethnicity (Wing and Merchan 1993). According to this logic, eliminating an ethnic group only requires the destruction of male members; women, who simply absorb the ethnicity of those who "own" them and father the children to whom they give birth, can be appropriated as reproductive vessels (Allen 1996). Although this explanation would only hold in cases where target groups were delineated according to ethnicity, it does appear salient in some recent cases, such as Rwanda. According to a report from African Rights, collaborators with the genocidaires persuaded them to spare women because they did not have an ethnicity: "the bad ones were men" (African Rights 1995a, 692), and female survivors reported being told they were safe because "sex has no ethnic group" (Human Rights Watch 1999, 296). In Rwanda, as well, some Tutsi women were transferred as "wives" to the Hutu genocidaires after their husbands and children were killed.[6]

In other cases, sex-selective mercy can be explained by systems of reciprocity. Lindner, discussing women's relative security and freedom of movement during warfare in what she terms "honor societies," describes a "kind of contract between the warring parties not to rape each other's women" during the warfare in Lebanon (Lindner 2002, 143).

---

5   Much of the recent literature on sex-selective massacre also uses this term, but in my view there are serious theoretical and semantic problems with the label "gendercide." See Carpenter 2002b.

6   However, as Baines (2003, 9) argues, even this de-ethnicized construction of sex broke down in the later stages of the genocide, when Tutsi women were also constructed as a "threat."

62   *'Innocent Women and Children'*

But the common denominator that ties these elements together and is evident in the majority of the scholarship available is that men are, relative to women, viewed as likely combatants and therefore a threat. Of the ancient practice of sex-selective massacre, Kuper writes: "In the ancient world, killing all the men was often a measure aimed at destroying the military potential of a rival" (Kuper 1981, 11). Lindner suggests that "the killing of battle-age males is a sign of respect for males... these men are treated as dangerous and therefore 'worthy' enemies" (Lindner 2002, 152). Whichever set of meanings are attached to the mass killing of men, the result and the logic is the same: men of a particular group are killed because they are viewed as militarily threatening by other men.

There is evidence of the same strategic rationale today, particularly in counter-insurgency operations. Rummel reports that the Pakistani army initially sought to crush the East Pakistani independence movement by conducting "sweeps... of young men who would never be seen again... bodies of youths would be found in fields, floating down rivers, or nearby army camps" (Rummel 1994, 329). In Rwanda, where genocidaires took diapers off infants to discover which were boys to be killed (African Rights 1995a, 815), the "opening blast of the genocide was accompanied by an injunction not to repeat the 'mistake' of the 1959 revolution, when male children had been spared only to return as guerilla fighters" (Jones 2002b, 73).

A counterpoint to the argument that this effect is norm-driven would be to say that interests can account for the sex-selective targeting of men, since men are indeed more likely than women to take up arms and belligerents simply have less interest in eliminating young women. While it is impossible to refute this argument conclusively on the basis of anecdotal data alone, evidence of sex-selective targeting, even in cases where young women are also taking part in hostilities, throws into doubt the hypothesis that this is purely interest-driven behavior. For example, in Columbia, where the Revolutionary Armed Forces of Columbia (FARC) consist of between 30 and 40 per cent women (Penhaul 2001), massacres of rebel suspects by the government and right-wing paramilitaries have continued to predominantly target men (Human Rights Watch 1998; see also Gendercide Watch 2003b). Similarly, facing the Israeli Defense Forces, which include a large number of female soldiers, Yassar Arafat has asked suicide bombers to target "soldiers of the occupation" but that it is "wrong to kill a child or a woman" (Anonymous 2003).

The case for sex-selective massacre should not be overstated, as what Kuper calls "root and branch" genocide targeting all members of a victim population stands in stark contrast to the more demographically limited killings particularly associated with low-intensity conflict and counter-insurgency operations (Kuper 1981). Moreover, countless women and children have died and continue to die in wars. Historically, the extent to which they were spared from death often depended on the character of the attack:

Implementing the Civilian Immunity Norm

for example, although women and children were generally spared during medieval warfare, this immunity did not apply to cities that were taken by sack (Parker 1994, 46). Likewise, there is some evidence that indiscriminate attacks (such as high-altitude bombing) disproportionately kill women and children, as they not only constitute the majority of any population, but are also most likely to be in buildings when bombs hit.[7] Guerilla warfare, in which entire populations are perceived to be involved, can ratchet up the level of violence demanded by military strategists (Harkavy and Neumann 2001). When troops are manipulated by fatigue, alcohol and drugs, they are less likely to be constrained by moral inhibitions, no matter how strong.[8] Massacres of women and children alongside men are also more likely when the victims are of a different race or religion than the attacking army (Bourke 1999; Duster 1972).

All these things being equal, however (as they are if we look at variation within specific cases rather than across cases), women and young children have been and are less likely than men and older boys to be targeted outright by enemy forces, particularly at short range where perpetrators are least able to psychologically distance themselves from the act of killing. The association of men with combatant status explains this tendency. Grossman, who has conducted an extensive study on the psychological processes by which soldiers rationalize killing, argues that one of the most important elements in this process is being able to identify one's victim as a combatant. "If a soldier kills a child, a woman, or anyone who *does not represent a potential threat*, then he has entered the realm of murder (as opposed to a legitimate, sanctioned combat kill) and the rationalization process becomes quite difficult" (Grossman 1995, 174, italics mine).[9]

This explains why, even in cases where women and children are massacred, troops often exhibit a higher degree of resistance to taking part in the killing than is evident when the victims are adult men. Jones' (2002b) analysis of sex-selective killing patterns in Rwanda suggests that after the order was

---

7   Indiscriminate attacks are also considered lesser crimes than attacks that specifically target a civilian population. The deaths of such women and children then are more likely to be treated as regrettable than atrocious.

8   The use of drugs has become a means of coercing troops into following orders to commit atrocity. It is particularly widespread in the indoctrination of child soldiers, accounting for much of the barbarity, for example, in Sierra Leone (Richards 2002). The same was true of US soldiers in Vietnam, which has been called the "first pharmacological war" (Grossman 1995, 270-271).

9   Grossman points out that the inhibition to kill women is often just as strong even when facing armed female soldiers. "Bruce, a Ranger team leader in Vietnam, had several personal kills, but the one time he could not bring himself to kill... was when the target was a Vietcong soldier who was also a woman... many other narratives and books from Vietnam cover in great detail the shock and horror associated with killing female Vietcong soldiers" (Grossman 1995, 175).

64   *'Innocent Women and Children'*

given, mid-genocide, to kill women and children in addition to the men, the organizers encountered "significant popular opposition...it was this element of the campaign that largely gave rise to increasing disorganization and disorientation among the forces of genocide" (see also Human Rights Watch 1999, 297 and 555).

Similarly, participants in the My Lai massacre, in which several hundred children, older men and adult women were tortured and killed, initially and repeatedly questioned the orders they were given (Grossman 1995, 270-271; Holmes 1986, 391); many of those present passively disengaged by shooting chickens instead of people; some of these passive resisters were also pivotal in bringing to light the massacre a year later (Anderson 1999, 39). In comparison to the levels of restraint against killing women and children that existed even in this case, the killing of unarmed draft-age men in Vietnam was considered much less problematic (Hersh 1972, 47). For example, scout helicopters were routinely used to identify and apprehend "military-age males": pilots were offered five-day passes for bringing military-age Vietnamese men in for questioning, an operation which led to pilots deliberately killing civilian males by running them down with their helicopter skids or lassoing them and dragging them behind their aircraft (Hersh 1972, 46). In general, even those soldiers most shocked at the killing of women and children were able to countenance such killing of adult male civilians who, being "draft-age," were perceived to scarcely have immunity from attack at all. Given both that many Vietnamese women were mobilized as fighters and that many Vietnamese men were not, interests alone do not seem to account for this variation in behavior.

Sex-Selective Massacre in Bosnia-Herzegovina

The systematic practice of sparing women and children from lethal attack while targeting adult civilian males is epitomized by the actions of the Bosnian Serb Army (BSA) and Yugoslav National Army (JNA) in the war in the former Yugoslavia. Ethnic cleansing of Bosniacs[10] and Croats by the BSA, JNA and paramilitary forces followed a characteristic pattern discernible from the earliest periods of the war. First, the BSA and JNA troops would surround and blockade whichever town was to be attacked. Supplies to the town would be cut off, and indiscriminate shelling would commence, lasting

---

10 The term "Bosniac" designates Bosnian Muslims and reflects both local terminology and the fact that affiliations after the onset of the war were ethnic rather than religious. I use the term "Bosnian" to refer to all the people living in the disputed territory of Bosnia-Herzegovina during the war, including Bosniacs, Bosnian Serbs and Bosnian Croats, as well as those who chose to self-identify as multi-ethnic "Yugoslavs," as well as to the secular Sarajevo-based government, which sought to prevent the partition of Bosnia-Herzegovina. See Bringa 1995.

Implementing the Civilian Immunity Norm 65

between hours and months, depending on the town's ability to resist. When resistance flagged, BSA paramilitaries would enter the town on foot (Burg and Shoup 1999; Cigar 1995; Rogel 1998).

Unlike the siege itself, the violence of the irregulars during the fall of a town was both discriminate and highly systematic. Militiamen would begin by publicly torturing and executing the settlement's political and cultural elite (Maas 1996, 39; Silber and Little 1996, 244). Of the remaining population, women, younger children and the very old were typically permitted to flee or forcibly deported, experiencing varying degrees of harassment along the way.[11] Wounded men were sometimes evacuated as well, usually as part of a prisoner exchange facilitated by the ICRC (Mercier 1994). Younger women were frequently singled out for rape, some transported to concentration camps and held for indefinite periods; some were killed after being raped (Stigalmeyer 1994).[12] Able-bodied males between the ages of 16 and 60 were sometimes also detained, usually to face torture, forced labor and possibly death. However, adult males were frequently killed on the spot (Ball 1999, 128; Honig and Both 1997, 4; Johnson 1999, 150). One witness reported "a paramilitary gunman announcing, 'the women and children will be left alone...' as for the Muslim men, he ran his finger across his throat" (quoted in Honig and Both 1997, 76).

What was the rationale for this sex-selective approach to killing? Patterns of mass rape during the conflict suggest that traditional assumptions of women's property status played a role (Askin 1997; Brownmiller 1994; MacKinnon 1994). The practice of forcibly impregnating Bosniac women with what came to be described as "little Chetniks," suggested that in the region, ethnicity was assumed to inhere in the father's lineage (Fisher 1996; Wing and Merchan 1993). However, unlike in Rwanda, BSA and JNA fighters did not capture Bosniac women as wives. They did not seek to convert Bosniac women to their own ethnicity through rape/marriage. Rather, the women's bodies were used as tools of ethnic cleansing against their own ethnic group (Allen 1996). Sparing their lives cannot be wholly understood in terms of their status as booty to be appropriated, nor in terms of their lack of association with the ethnic "other."[13]

---

11 Although this was the general pattern, there were numerous examples of indiscriminate killing as well.

12 Although women and girls of child-bearing age were at the greatest risk of sexual violence in Bosnia, women of all ages, as well as men and boys, were sexually abused during the war. See Askin 1997.

13 It should be noted that not all rape victims were spared. Rape itself can be directly fatal, depending on its brutality and the age of the victims, and some rape victims were then killed. As Askin reports (1997) women who were detained and forced to serve as sexual slaves for male soldiers were more likely to be killed than those who were detained in rape camps with the intent of forced impregnation. See also Wilmer 2002.

66 'Innocent Women and Children'

Instead, commentaries from humanitarian workers in the region consistently describe the perception of the BSA authorities that every battle-age male was an actual combatant (Harland 1999; Hollingworth 1996; Rhode 1998; Sudetic 1998). In short, the BSA fighters used sex and age as proxies for "combatant." Gendered assumptions provided a cognitive short-cut given the uncertainty as to who was involved in fighting, which enabled the BSA to at least appear to be complying with the obligation to distinguish civilians from combatants. This perception may have been grounded in the Yugoslav tradition of "people's war" or the fact that in Bosnia, as in other cases of such internal warfare of this type, many adult men were mobilized.[14]

But many other adult men were not combatants. Indeed, Wilmer's study of the war describes mass resistance to mobilization among draft-age men on all sides (Wilmer 2002, 147). Moreover, although the levels of women's participation in the Balkans did not rise to those in regions of Latin America and Asia, women did fight alongside men and many of those participating in the war effort, especially in besieged enclaves, were women and older children. "There were women in all of the militias and national armies throughout the former Yugoslavia" (Kesic 1999, 188). In short, age and sex categories did not overlap neatly with the civilian/combatant distinction. Only the presence of a gender sub-norm within the immunity norm can explain the sex-selective targeting of adult men in the Balkans.

This does not necessarily mean that the BSA military planners had internalized such a norm. In the Bosnian case (particularly given the BSA authorities' willingness to orchestrate mass rape campaigns), it is more likely that women and children were spared from outright massacre as a means of placating Western concerns with BSA atrocities (Cigar 1995, 144). In other words, belligerents responded to a perceived logic of appropriateness as a tactic for reducing Western propensity to intervene, or as a form of "strategic self-presentation" (Jones and Pittman 1982), rather than on the deeper level associated with complex learning. Some of the most dramatic examples of BSA generosity toward "civilians" were orchestrated so as to be captured by the media. During the fall of Srebrenica in 1995, General Ratko Mladic handed out bread and candy to Bosniac children in front of television cameras, emphasizing that the BSA was a "civilized" fighting unit (Silber and Little 1996, 272).

Violence against civilians in Bosnia and Croatia suggests that the immunity norm was implemented in a highly sex-specific way. Conclusive arguments about whether and how the gender sub-norm motivated this behavior (alongside assumptions of ethnicity, women's property status, constructions of hegemonic masculinity and interest-based considerations) require the more systematic collection of narratives from the fighters themselves, a task which has not been undertaken here. However, available evidence suggests

---

14 See, however, Mueller's (2000) analysis of ethnic mobilization.

that the association of adult men, but not women, with combatant status played an important part in bringing about the sex-disparities in lethal atrocity that we see in this case.

Discursive Effects: Violators' Accounts and Bystanders' Reactions

But some women and children were murdered in Bosnia. Sometimes, even those civilians most likely to be spared are instead brutalized and killed at the hands of enemy troops. Such events neither refute the relevance of the civilian immunity norm nor its gendered character. When Kratochwil and Ruggie (1986, 767) claim that norms are "counterfactually valid" they mean that the existence of a norm is not refuted by even repeated violations. What demonstrates a norm's *salience* is the extent to which it is invoked in reacting to violations. Indeed, the presence of a norm is constitutive of "violations" themselves. What demonstrates a norm's *gendered* character is the extent to which it is invoked differently with respect to men and to women.

If the innocent civilian is gendered, the sex as well as age demographics of the dead should exert some measurable effect on not only the propensity of actors to violate the norm (as shown above) but also the social mechanisms they employ to avoid censure for having done so. Shannon distinguishes between four such social mechanisms which actors use when violating norms: denial (it never happened), excuses (we had no choice), apology (forgive us) and justifications (it was legitimate in this case because...) (Shannon 2000, 304). Actors judging whether a violation has taken place can accept or refuse such explanations, and condemnations of norm violations will vary in intensity accordingly.

There is a qualitative continuum of moral difference between the denials, apologies, excuses and justifications. Denials, apologies and excuses all admit the wrongness of the act, in varying degrees, while attempting to exonerate the perpetrator. But justifications reaffirm the existence of the norm by denying that the particular case is a violation at all.

Gendered Constructions of Atrocity

Shannon argues that to the extent that a norm is ambiguous, perpetrators have greater leverage with which to build an interpretation of the violation that positions victims beyond the parameters of the norm. Because "women, children and the elderly" are *unambiguously* defined as civilians, killing them deliberately is likely to be denied by belligerents and condemned by onlookers; killing them accidentally evokes apology. But because adult men's civilian status is seen as ambiguous and contested, actors have greater leverage to exclude them from the norm parameters and to do so with legitimacy. Thus, it is easier for belligerents to justify and for onlookers to excuse the deliberate killing of adult men than even the accidental killing of "women and children." In short, the sex and age of the victims partly constitutes what it means to have "attacked civilians" and thus the moral framework of atrocity itself.

For example, the BSA repeatedly justified its treatment of civilian males in Bosnia and Kosovo as within the bounds of humanitarian law. Military-age Bosniac men were constructed as combatants and likely "war criminals." The BSA authorities' desire to be viewed as complicit with the laws of war is demonstrated by Mladic's insistence that UNPROFOR Major Franken sign a document confirming that the evacuation of Srebrenica had been carried out in accordance with the Geneva Conventions (Honig and Both 1997, 45). Later, on trial for the crimes committed at Srebrenica, Radovan Krstic attempted to defend himself by arguing that the freeing of women and children was enough to demonstrate BSA compliance with civilian immunity norms (Simons 2001). The men of Srebrenica, who had allegedly committed war crimes of their own in Bratunac two years earlier, presumably did not count as civilians and were therefore legitimate military targets.

Even in cases where actors arguably mean well, a double standard is often applied to civilian casualties in armed conflict. Although the US defense establishment had previously acted as if a certain level of collateral damage in Afghanistan was acceptable, it was unable to avoid apologizing for the accidental bombing of a Pashtun wedding party in Oruzgan early in July 2002. Until that point, the Bush Administration had brushed aside claims of indiscriminate bombing as an inevitable part of legitimate military operations.[15] For example, after allegedly killing dozens of tribal elders at Khost in December 2001, US General Tommy Franks said: "We believe it was a good target" (Beaumont 2001). The Oruzgan incident, which was widely publicized as having resulted in the deaths of "women and children," did not elicit such justifications from the Pentagon and in fact drew immediate expressions of regret (CNN 2002).

US officials initially attempted to excuse themselves by way of having mistaken celebratory weapons fire for a ground-to-air attack; later, in the face of outrage from Afghan authorities and international public opinion, combined with relatively extensive media coverage, this was replaced by an outright admission of error and an investigative inquiry.[16] The comparison of the incidents at Khost and Oruzgan is illustrative. The former could be

---

15 For example, the top spokesman for Central Command said: "There is no question that we have killed and injured people we did not intend to in the course of the war." Quoted in Cummins 2002.

16 Until July 2002 there was relatively little coverage of civilian casualties in the Western press (Fairness and Accuracy in Reporting 2001). Nor had human rights organizations convinced the US to investigate or produce any estimates of collateral damage (Cummins 2002).

considered semi-legitimate because the civilian status of the dead might be doubted (although elderly, they were male), whereas in the latter case, the age and sex of the dead automatically conferred them status as civilians, drawing far more extensive condemnation and ultimately an apology (Radio Free Europe 2002).

It is not the case that massacres of adult civilian men never provoke censure, denial, excuses or apology. To import the language of causation into constitutive analysis, the relationship is probabilistic rather than deterministic. It is *possible* to claim that killings of men are killings of civilians: Krstic was found guilty at the Hague, and Srebrenica has been defined as a genocidal massacre (Harland 1999; Rhode 1998). But in these cases it is usually the scale, context or brutality of the killings that support claims of atrocity. Holding such factors constant, it is far easier to make the claim that civilians are dead if the dead in question included at least a few children or women. This explains the frequent use of the term "including x women and x children" in describing massacres. The number of men killed frequently exceeds those of women and children put together, but it is the female and child dead who decisively signal the civilian status of the victims. For example, "In the first three weeks of the Nablus offensive… at least 80 Palestinians were killed, including seven women and nine children" (Anderson 2002). As I discuss at greater length momentarily, this logic also applied to the way in which attacks on the civilian population of Kosovo were framed in international society.

Interpreting the My Lai Massacre

The massacre of hundreds of unresisting villagers by US troops at the Vietnamese village of My Lai is a classic example of the failure of the civilian immunity norm to restrain belligerents from wanton slaughter. On March 18, 1968, soldiers of Charlie Company, 11th Brigade, Americal Division, entered the village presumably on a "search and destroy" mission aimed at rooting out enemy combatants. Although they received no fire from the village as they approached, Lieutenant William Calley ordered his men to shoot as they entered My Lai. Finding no armed fighters in the village, Calley's troops then rounded up between 300 and 500 children, old men and women, who were shot and stabbed to death. A number of girls were raped and sexually mutilated before being killed (Bourke 1999).

Although many of the perpetrators initially hesitated based on the age and sex of the victims, many of them ultimately did participate in the massacre. What is more interesting for the purposes of this argument is the way in which the massacre was later represented, both by perpetrators and onlookers. Efforts to define My Lai as a massacre, as well as interpretations of the events by those involved and by outside observers, were shaped by the gender beliefs within the protection regime principles.

70 'Innocent Women and Children'

Sex as well as age was used at the outset to *distinguish* whether the victims were civilians or combatants: that is, to determine whether a massacre, as opposed to combat, was taking place. The most direct attempt to protect the My Lai villagers was undertaken by the crew of a scout helicopter commanded by Warrant Officer Hugh Thompson. Thompson's helicopter passed over the village on the morning of the massacre and, realizing what US ground troops were doing, the crew touched down between the troops and Vietnamese civilians. while his gunners trained their sights on the US soldiers, Thompson assisted the terrified civilians onto the helicopter and used it to evacuate them from the killing zone (Peers 1979). Thompson also filed a report on the events of the day to his superior officers, few of whom believed him and several of whom later covered up the massacre (Hersh 1972).

In testimony at a conference on My Lai in 1999, Thompson described how he and his crew had realized that a massacre, rather than combat, was occurring below: "Everywhere we looked, we saw bodies. These were infants; women, very old men, but no draft-age people [sic: men] whatsoever. What you look for is draft-age people" (Anderson 1999, 28). It is reasonable to think that had Warrant Officer Thompson looked down at a village of dead adult men, he and his crew would not have been as quick to assume that something was amiss. Similarly, when attempting to piece together what had happened in the first hours after the massacre, Colonel Oran Henderson, commanding officer of the 11th Brigade, demanded that Charlie Company return to My Lai and produce a body count including the age *and sex* of victims and how they had died (Peers 1979, 55).

That the massacres could simply not be justified or excused as the destruction of legitimate targets is evident by the fact that the Army initially covered it up. Reporting on one of several parallel massacres in the vicinity of My Lai on the morning of March 16, in which between sixty and ninety women, children and elderly were later reported to have been killed, the official log made a point of reporting that "none of its victims were women or children" (Hersh 1972, 19). Both Captain Ernest Medina, Charlie Company's commander during the operation, and division commander Major General Koster who arrived shortly thereafter, apparently tried to impede Henderson's investigation of the age and sex ratios of the dead (Peers 1979, 81).

The very fact that My Lai received such attention underscores the extent to which it was considered exceptional, and exceptionally atrocious. My Lai was framed as unbelievably wrong both because of the number of victims in one place and because of their sex as well as age. It is for these reasons that this incident, unlike many others during Vietnam, received such notoriety and caused such controversy. William Eckhardt, who supervised the prosecutions in the courts-martial of those charged with the My Lai killings, said, "I saw lots of things as I moved around the country, but I never saw anything like

Implementing the Civilian Immunity Norm 71

this" (quoted in Anderson 1999, 41). The acknowledgement that such a massacre was beyond justification is reflected in the social mechanisms used for explaining it away. As might be expected, when the story broke in 1969 the charges were at first denied or the perpetrators excused as having acted under orders.

These mechanisms were as obvious among the US public as among the participants in the killings (Bourke 1999, 182). A survey of citizens' reactions to the accusations in 1969 suggests that the most common reaction was denial (Opton 1972, 62-63):

Our boys wouldn't do this. Something else is behind it.

I can't believe an American serviceman would purposely shoot any civilian... any atrocities in this war were committed by the Communists.

I can't believe that a massacre was committed by our boys. It's contrary to everything I learned about America.

I don't believe it actually happened. The story was planted by Viet Cong sympathizers and people inside this country who are trying to get us out of Vietnam.

As facts came to light, Americans gradually accepted the killings had occurred; then they turned to excusing the soldiers as having merely followed orders: "What would have happened to them if they hadn't? Would they have been shot?" "They were given an order to do something. They will shoot you if you don't. They had no choice" (Opton 1972, 63).[17] Most Americans opposed the conviction of Calley, whose life sentence was later reduced to a few months of house arrest (Bourke 1999, 183). By contrast, no one in the Opton survey said that the killings themselves were justifiable.

As for the soldiers of Charlie Company themselves, some also denied the massacres outright: "It is my opinion that what they say happened did not happen" (David Mitchell, quoted in Opton 1972, 63). Most, however, excused themselves: it was terrible, but they had no choice; they were acting under orders. Conveniently, those to whom the direct orders would likely have been traced had either been killed in action, left the military, or escaped court-martial through procedural luck. Others accused of giving such orders denied it and were not convicted. Captain Medina, who had been accused by some of directly ordering the massacre, told the Peers Commission, "I did not say anything that would indicate to an individual in a proper state of mind that he was to go in and slaughter women and children" (quoted in Peers 1979, 79).

---

17 Opton does not distinguish between "excuses" (they had no choice) and "justifications" (the civilians were really the enemy) – he calls these both justifications, but he categorizes them into two different types.

72   *'Innocent Women and Children'*

A few members of the military explicitly justified the massacre. In a letter to the *San Francisco Chronicle*, four army sergeants wrote in December 1969, "Our job is to destroy the enemy… I want to come home alive… if I must kill old men, women or children to make myself a little safer, I'll do it without hesitation" (quoted in Opton 1972, 65). But this discourse was the exception rather than the rule (Anderson 1999, 9). Lt. Calley, who supervised the massacre and was later tried for war crimes, did attempt to justify the killings as legitimate and the victims as "enemy." But this display of remorselessness itself was a deviation from social norms. Indeed it contributed to the popular perception that Calley had simply "gone crazy" and this accounted for the massacre (Anderson 1998, 41).

Moreover, even those who suggested that perhaps the immunity principle was inapplicable to *these* civilians still tended to define civilians per se in terms of gender categories, while denying their moral innocence. Lt. Calley testified that he was convinced that "the old men, the women, the children, were all VC or would be in about three years" (Bourke 1999, 162). One respondent interviewed by Opton (1972, 64) questioned whether the civilians were "innocent": "Now, had these civilians, had these women set booby traps for these people?" (Opton 1972, 64). While questioning whether the immunity principle should be applied, the respondent did not deny the distinction principle in general, and reinforced the gender sub-norm by using sex as an indicator of civilian.

The social construction of My Lai in its aftermath demonstrates that the gender sub-norm affects inter-subjective understandings of what constitutes an attack on civilians. Belligerents are quicker to realize they have done something unjustifiable when they choose to kill women than when they can claim to have killed "potential combatant" men. They adopt different methods of avoiding social censure for having done so (denial, excuses and apologies) whereas male civilian deaths are generally justified as being beyond the parameters of the immunity norm. Bystanders are also more likely to accept such justifications when the civilian dead are male. They are readier to insist that atrocity has occurred when it is clear that "presumed civilians" have died, and adult women as much as children or the elderly are included in this category.

Enabling Effects: Humanitarian Intervention in International Society

In addition to constraining state behavior or shaping representations of atrocity, norms can alter the context in which action is circumscribed, enabling actors to behave in ways that would otherwise be avoided (Flynn and Farrell 1999). For example, Tannenwald (1999, 437) has argued that in addition to regulating the use of nuclear weapons, the nuclear non-use taboo has exerted an enabling effect on the use and proliferation of non-

Implementing the Civilian Immunity Norm 73

nuclear weapons demarcated as more "civilized" by a discourse of nuclear atrocity. The civilian protection norm also exerts such an enabling effect. By delineating the limits of acceptable conduct in international society, it provides legitimation for third party military intervention in internal conflicts for ostensibly humanitarian reasons.[18]

Following Mertus and others, I define "humanitarian intervention" as "the use of force with the stated aim of preventing or ending widespread and grave violations of fundamental human rights of individuals other than their own citizens" (Mertus 2002, 134). This definition excludes interventions to which the receiving state has given its consent, as well as military action on behalf of the third party states' own nationals. It also excludes non-military forms of humanitarian action in complex emergencies. These forms of action do not require an enabling norm because they do not involve the breach of an otherwise robust norm: sovereignty.

Forcible third party intervention to save civilians from the predations of their own state involves precisely this. The emerging doctrine of "humanitarian intervention" is based on the belief that such breaches of territorial sovereignty are justified in cases where the protection of the civilian population is at stake: indeed, the plausible claim to be saving civilians from slaughter defines what a humanitarian intervention is (Finnemore 1996b; Wheeler 2000). Because the "innocent civilian" is gendered, part of what makes such claims plausible is the argument that "women and children" will be the beneficiaries of military action. This explains why attempts at such legitimations generally include references to "saving women and children," regardless of who is actually at risk in a particular humanitarian crisis. It also explains the avoidance of such rhetoric in cases where third parties wish to avoid the obligation to intervene.

Humanitarian Intervention in the 1990s

A consideration of the emergence of humanitarian intervention discourse in the post-Cold War period makes this clear. The first post-Cold War military campaign *legitimately* viewed as humanitarian was undertaken by the US in Northern Iraq, in the wake of the Gulf War (Weiss 1999; Wheeler 2000).[19] The soothingly labeled "Operation Provide Comfort" was

---

18 Flynn and Farrell (1999) have made a similar argument with respect to democratization within the European Community.

19 Humanitarian intervention was once considered a legitimate causus belli, but lost legitimacy as the non-aggression norm solidified in the post-war era (Coll 2001, 133). The US, like other states, claimed humanitarian motives for various other unilateral operations, but it required a multilateral effort backed by the authority of the Security Council to legitimate the doctrine in post-Cold War international society (Finnemore 1996b). It is ironic that Operation Provide Comfort, an aggressive intervention into a sovereign state, coincided with the Gulf War, which took place

74   *'Innocent Women and Children'*

motivated by press coverage of helpless Kurdish women and children. This struck a chord with a US population who had so recently learned to think of the Iraqi "regime" as the enemy against whom (Kuwaiti) civilians needed protection, and whose support for the Gulf War had peaked when Kuwaitis drummed up allegations of Iraqi atrocities against newborn infants (Stauber and Rampton 1995, 172-174).[20] Turkey's persuasive letter addressed to the Security Council, while mostly concerned with its border stability, cited humanitarian concern and drew attention to the fact that the refugees were mostly "women and children" (Murphy 1996, 169). Commentators characterized the intervention as a response to Iraq's repression of "women, children and rebels" (presumably all the males involved were rebels, but the women and children were innocent bystanders) (Weiss 1999, 50). Years later, when the US government drew fire for the continuing no-fly zones, it continued to invoke such threats as reasons for its presence in Iraq: "We are protecting civilians, who had suffered from Iraqi attacks, including the use of poison gas against women and children," Peter Burleigh told the General Assembly in September, 1999.[21]

Subsequent intervention efforts, as well as calls for intervention, threats to intervene, and condemnations of acts that could warrant intervention, have made stock use of this formula throughout the 1990s – whether or not they made any sense based on the sex-distribution of the victims of conflict and the goals of the intervention. In Somalia as elsewhere in the Horn of Africa, images of starving women and children provoked a quick response from US public opinion that something must be done (Christian Century 2000). But not all women and children were passive victims of Somali politics and receptors of aid. Some took up arms with their clansmen against the humanitarians (Shoumaff 1994). Although the resulting casualties were technically "combatants" rather than "unarmed civilians," the female/child deaths resulted in an outpouring of moral condemnation by the US Senate of American soldiers' lack of martial restraint (Pine 1993).

Nor did the relative invulnerability of women to slaughter in a particular context deter intervention-proponents from espousing the need to save them from slaughter. In Bosnia, where women were being displaced, starved and sexually assaulted but generally left alive, US Representative Ron Coleman argued for decisive action to stop the genocide by saying, "The US will have

---

in large part to punish aggression. Perhaps the fact that Iraq's status as a "civilized" nation had been disrupted through its actions in Kuwait facilitated Western sympathy for the Kurds.

20 Not surprisingly given this argument, it was the Kuwaiti ambassador's young daughter, posing as a traumatized witness, who was chosen to sob out these allegations on global television.

21 Notably, although women and children, along with men, died in the Halabja attacks, most of the victims of the Anfal campaign were military-age men. See Moeller 1999, 243.

to accept the moral responsibility to intervene where innocent women and children are being slaughtered in the name of ethnic cleansing" (Garnett News Service 1993). Save a few international relations scholars-cum-activists (for example, Jones 1999), no one argued for intervention on behalf of "innocent men."

These examples suggest that during the precedent-setting cases of intervention or, in the case of Rwanda, failure to intervene, appeals to be saving "innocent women and children" correlated neither with women's and children's actual roles in the conflict, nor with their actual relative vulnerability to slaughter, but with the desire of international actors to justify humanitarian action. Such discourse can be understood as what Risse (2000, 7) refers to as "argumentative rationality," a process in which actors "seek a consensus about their understanding of a situation as well as justifications for the principles and norms guiding their action." When actors are engaged in a process of trying to convince one another through the force of argument, they marshal the most effective tools they can in the service of their position.

Because "women and children" signify "innocent civilians" in a way that adult men do not, arguments that action is required to protect civilians will be more convincing if they are framed in terms of "women and children." As I describe below, in Kosovo this was accomplished by focusing on displacement rather than massacre, and by focusing on a few dead women and children, rather than many dead men, in the case of specific massacres such as that at Racak. For the same reason, when actors wish to *avoid* moral obligations to protect civilians, they likewise avoid drawing attention to "women and children." As the case on Rwanda illustrates below, such language resurfaces in condemnations of the *failure* to protect. Either way, references to "women and children" being killed, or lack thereof, have less to do with women's innocence in a particular case or with their relative vulnerability to slaughter, than with the fact that "women and children" denotes "civilians."

Rwanda: Framing Intervention Failure

The construction of the Rwandan genocide as a failure of civilian protection demonstrates the correlation of gendered discourse to evocations of the protection norm, and refutes the hypothesis that this gendered language simply reflects empirical realities on the ground. Many Rwandan women were not "innocent" of participation in the violence; nor were women and children the primary victims of the slaughter, although many died alongside civilian men and nearly all were sexually tortured. References to innocent Rwandan women and children, when they appeared, correlated not to the actual sex-age distributions of the atrocity being described, but to whether the references were being made to support or refute claims that intervention

76   *'Innocent Women and Children'*

was warranted. Such references were absent during the genocide when decisive action might have saved lives but when those making such references sought to avoid intervening, but appeared in the aftermath when actors in international society constructed non-intervention as a grave error that had cost civilian lives.

The origins of the Rwandan genocide are often traced to the legacies of first German and then Belgian colonial rule, during which ethnic differences between Tutsi, Hutu and Twa were re-constructed and pre-existing hierarchies exploited so as to facilitate and maintain colonial control (Prunier 1997, 38; Lemarchand 1997, 409). Since independence in 1962, the Hutu-led government had initiated a system of discrimination against the Tutsi, reversing the colonial system of ethnic hierarchy. In response, Tutsi leaders mobilized a guerilla insurgency from expatriate communities in southern Uganda (Campbell 2001). The Rwandan Patriotic Front (RPF) claimed to represent the ethnic Tutsi population in Rwanda and sought to overthrow the sitting Hutu government. Massacres occurred throughout the 1960s and early 1970s, and an economic recession worsened the ethnic tension in the late 1980s (Klinghoffer 1998, 24).

In the early 1990s the RPF launched an open invasion into northern Uganda, against the Forces Armee Rwandaises (FAR), trained by the French and aiming to prevent the Tutsi "filth" from coming to power (Campbell 2001, 73). The Organization for African Unity organized a peace agreement in August 1993, and in October the UN Security Council authorized a peace-keeping force, the United Nations Assistance Mission for Rwanda (UNAMIR), to oversee the cease-fire. Over the course of the winter, particularly after Juvenal Habyarimana was sworn in as president of the new coalition government, the UNAMIR leadership became increasingly concerned about the stockpiling of light arms and promulgation of incendiary propaganda by Hutu radio (Chalk 1999), but General Romeo Daillare could not convince the UN to send reinforcements or expand UNAMIR's mandate in order to protect civilians should violence break out (Wheeler 2000).

When Habyarimana's plane was mysteriously shot down on April 6, 1994, the presidential guard immediately began killing Hutu moderates and Tutsi political and civil leaders in Kigali. Incited through the use of hate radio, the violence soon spread to the countryside and was directed at the Tutsi civilian population in general, as well as any Hutus who refused to kill or attempted to protect their Tutsi neighbors. Hutu civilian men, children and women were forcibly conscripted to join in the task of killing. Most victims were killed with clubs or machetes, locked inside structures and burnt alive, or thrown into pit latrines (Gourevitch 1998; Lemarchand 1997). According to Human Rights Watch (1996), nearly every Tutsi female who survived the genocide had been raped or sexually tortured during the course of the violence (see also Baines 2003; Hamilton, 2002). Within two months, this grassroots genocide had claimed an estimated 800,000 lives.

Implementing the Civilian Immunity Norm 77

The international community was aware of the genocide as it unfolded (Barnett 2002). But reeling from the Somali disaster, the US in 1994 was no longer prepared to undertake military action for purely humanitarian purposes by the time violence erupted in Rwanda (Campbell 2001). References to "women and children", like the use of the term "genocide," are strikingly absent from US rhetoric on the unfolding violence in April of that year. For example, of all press briefing transcripts from the US State Department during that month in which the keyword "Rwanda" appeared at least once, not a single reference is made to "women and children" being under attack. According to data available from the US National Archives and Records Administration (1994), neither is the phrase used in presidential statements on Rwanda during that time period (US State Department 1994a).[22] Nor is it used in any of the statements made by the Security Council President in the first half of 1994 (UN, 1994a-e). Instead, the duty to protect *foreign* civilians and UN peacekeepers was stressed in US discourse. For example, a cable from the State Department to the US Mission to the UN in New York advised delegates to stress the responsibility to "ensure the safe withdrawal of... international personnel and civilians" in presenting the US position that UN troops should be withdrawn from the country (US State Department 1994b).

The "women and children" trope does appear later in both Security Council resolution 912 and 918 in which the UN attempted to appear to be doing something while minimizing its involvement in the genocide through the reduction in UNAMIR troops (Wheeler 2000). It also appeared in legal analyses at the US State Department that influenced Administration officials' gradual acceptance that the killings constituted "genocide." Government officials were originally careful to avoid labeling the killings "genocide."[23] This position gradually changed as public awareness of the killings grew and as the State Department became concerned that otherwise "our credibility will be undermined with human rights groups and the general public" (US State Department 1994e). When on May 21 Secretary of State Warren Christopher authorized State Department officials to use the phrase "acts of genocide have occurred" (Ferroggiaro 2001, 8), his decision was based partly on two legal analyses, both of which emphasized that women and children were among the civilian dead: "Massacres in Rwanda have claimed from 200,000 to 500,000 lives, according to international humanitarian organizations. Most of those killed have been Tutsi civilians, including women and children" (US State Department 1994c; see also US State Department 1994d). In short,

---

22 Full text of both sets of transcripts is on file with author.

23 For example, in a May Department of Defense discussion paper, which cautions Administration officials against authorizing a legal investigation into whether the killings constituted genocide: "Be careful... genocide finding could commit USG to actually 'do something'" (US Defense Department 1994).

78 'Innocent Women and Children'

evidence of female and child deaths was used, along with other factors, to build the case that not only was genocide occurring, but that the US would appear callous if it denied as much.

However, narratives of "innocent women and children being slaughtered" were most pronounced in post-genocide efforts to deal with international guilt over non-action: "Do we, the members of the international community, really require that more innocent women and children be slaughtered by the thousands to cause a change in our priorities and level of concern?" asks a 1998 report to the Carnegie Commission on the failure of early intervention in Rwanda (Feil 1998; see also Hranski 2000; Cornell and Smyth 1998). The language used to describe the genocide as an "intervention that should have been" frames "women and children" as both particularly vulnerable to the genocide and as innocent bystanders who deserved protection.

The *empirical realities* of the conflict demonstrate that Tutsi females were not the primary victims of the slaughter. While tens of thousands of women and girls did perish (and nearly all female survivors were targeted for non-lethal forms of violence, especially rape and sexual slavery), the majority of civilian deaths in the Rwandan genocide were Tutsi men and boys, including male infants (Baines 2003; El-Bushra 2000; Human Rights Watch 1996; Jones 2002b; Lentin 1997b). The genocide swept up Tutsi indiscriminately in its later stages, but initial targeting was intricately sex-specific (Baines 2003, 9), leading Tutsi men to attempt to disguise themselves as women in order to save their lives and Hutu genocidaires to take diapers off infants in order to determine which were boys to be massacred (African Rights 1995a, 815).

This is borne out by post-genocide Rwandan demographics: in the early years after the genocide, a considerable sex-disparity was apparent in the Rwandan Tutsi population (Hamilton 2000, 1). Jones (2002b) has conducted a detailed analysis of testimonies regarding the targets of the killing, extrapolating from major human rights documentation of the genocide, including reports from Human Rights Watch, Africa Rights and the Organization of African Unity, and identifying a number of stages with various patterns of sex-related targeting. He concludes that "the general thrust of human rights reportage suggests that, on balance, males were overwhelmingly targeted in the genocide's earliest and most virulent stages" (Jones 2002b, 71).

Yet most *portrayals* of the genocide emphasize its indiscriminate rather than sex-selective character, drawing on the smaller numbers of women who also died in the early stages and on evidence from the more systematically indiscriminate killings later in the genocide. "Innocent men, women and children [were] subjected to the abomination of genocide" (Pope 1999); "Tutsi women were killed during the 1994 genocide in numbers equal to, *if not exceeding*, those of men" (Taylor 1999, 154).[24] The need to emphasize

---

24 Italics added by author.

Implementing the Civilian Immunity Norm 79

women and children as *the* victims in depictions of the genocide extended to those who recognized that men had primarily died: since women and children are the ones left behind, they are the "real victims" as it is they who bear the toll of the aftermath (Human Rights Watch 1996, 2; for other examples, see Jones 2002b, note 58.)

In fact, two separate crises claimed lives in Rwanda: the initial series of massacres and the resulting epidemics. Women and small children were the primary victims of the latter, largely because they were the primary demographic categories left alive after the earlier violence abated. The media coverage of Rwanda did not distinguish between these patterns of death, and humanitarian aid was primarily mobilized to combat the cholera epidemic among the refugees, where women and children were the victims, rather than to stop the massacres of men (Moeller 1999).

Nor were all women innocent bystanders to the genocide. African Rights (1995b) has documented the participation of Hutu women in the massacres and their aftermath, as policy-makers, as individual genocidaires, and as catalysts inciting Hutu men to kill. Nonetheless women were constructed as bystanders in international discourse on the genocide (Hamilton 2002). Sadako Ogata, condemning the humanitarian side-effect of perpetrators in the midst of refugee camps, said, "My staff had to continue feeding criminals as the price for feeding hundreds of thousands of innocent women and children" (quoted in Weiss 1999, 147). The UN, condemning RPF retaliation on the camps sheltering the perpetrators, urged restraint: "We realize there are genocidal killers among these refugees. But a majority of these refugees in eastern Zaire are innocent women and children" (United Nations, 1997).

These statements reproduce the assumption that female and child refugees had not participated in the violence. As Lentin writes, "the involvement of women in the genocide and murder of Hutu political opponents failed to attract national and international attention, precisely because of the construction of women as the universal victims of that particular catastrophe" (Lentin 1997b, 12).[25]

What makes the use of military force "humanitarian" and thus defensible in international society is the claim that innocent people are at risk from their own states and require protection from third parties. In cases of internal conflict, such a claim is constituted by the existence of "innocent civilians" in need of rescue. Above I argued that international actors claiming to act for humanitarian purposes are more likely to claim they are protecting "women and children" than men. Correspondingly, as the Rwandan case study illustrates, when actors wish to avoid the obligation to intervene, they will avoid such language. Such language may resurface later if attempts

---

25 Heather Hamilton has traced the way in which the perception of Hutu "women and children" as "innocent" paralyzed UNHCR's response to the militarization of the refugee camps, possibly leading to the Kibeho massacre (Hamilton 2002).

80   *'Innocent Women and Children'*

are made to argue that such intervention should have occurred. This use of rhetoric to legitimate action often has little to do with the actual age/sex distributions of the besieged.

The Protection of Civilians in Kosovo

In this chapter, I have argued that the civilian immunity norm is more robust in application when the civilians in question are women and children than when they are adult men. Through short thematic case studies, I have illustrated first that belligerents are less likely to attack women and children than adult civilian males. Second, the reaction of third parties and perpetrators' strategies for explaining their actions are qualitatively stronger when the victims are women and children. Third, to the extent that the immunity norm is invoked by third parties to justify forcible "protection" measures, they are likely to frame such justifications in terms of protecting "women and children," regardless of the sex-distributions of atrocity in a particular case. Correspondingly, actors seeking to avoid responsibility to protect civilians are likely to avoid references to "women and children." To explain this, I have pointed to the existence of a "gender sub-norm" associating women and children, and men on only a more contingent basis, with the category "civilian." In this final section, the interrelationship between these sub-norm effects will be illustrated with respect to NATO's intervention on behalf of the Kosovar Albanians in Spring 1999.

Historical Background

Kosovo was an autonomous province of Serbia until Slobodan Milosevic revoked its autonomy in 1989 (Calic 2000; Vickers 2000). The ethnic majority Kosovar Albanians had always faced discrimination at the hands of the minority Serbs, in what many commentators refer to as an apartheid system (for example, Mertus 1999). After 1989 this situation became intolerable. Initially Albanians responded by mobilizing a peaceful resistance movement under Ibrahim Rugova (Clark 2000; Kostovicova 2000). But the lack of any provisions regarding Kosovo in the Dayton accords, which ended the 1991-1995 war in the former Yugoslavia, delegitimized Rugova's strategy of non-violence and facilitated the growth of the Kosovo Liberation Army (KLA). The KLA had existed since 1991 but only after the failure at Dayton and the collapse of the neighboring Albanian economy in 1997 could the KLA consolidate legitimacy in the eyes of the Albanian people and gain access to the light arms necessary to engage federal forces (Campbell 2001; Judah 2000).

Throughout early 1998 the KLA conducted armed attacks against Yugoslav police forces and, occasionally, both ethnic Serb and ethnic Albanian civilians

Implementing the Civilian Immunity Norm 81

(Independent Commission 2000). In response, the JNA engaged in increasing levels of counter-insurgency violence, which resulted in 2000 deaths and 400,000 displaced by Fall 1998 (Demjaha 2000, 34). NATO countries, fearing a repeat of Bosnia, orchestrated talks, issued condemnations of violence on both sides, and dispatched human rights observers to monitor the situation. But violence flared up in January 1999, and when talks in France failed in early March, NATO initiated air strikes against Serbia, ostensibly to avert a "humanitarian catastrophe."[26] In response to the NATO attacks, Milosevic cracked down further on Albanian civilians, resulting in thousands of additional deaths and the additional forced displacement of nearly two million people (Buckley 2000, 4). Averse to the possibility of casualties, NATO eschewed ground troops and concentrated on strategic bombing, eventually expanding its target list to include civilian infrastructure (Arkin 2001). The war to protect civilians ended up costing, by conservative estimates, up to 500 Yugoslav civilian lives directly and many more as a result of destroyed infrastructure and depleted uranium poisoning (Human Rights Watch 2000a; Kashnikov 2002, 240). Milosevic capitulated on June 3. By July the refugees were returning home, only to terrorize the Serb and Roma populations in Kosovo, who then began a reverse exodus into Serbia with, as Mertus notes (2001), little outcry from the West.

Most commentators believe NATO's air war over Kosovo was an important historical turning point in the history of the civilian protection principle. As such, it has much to tell us about the interconnection between gender discourse and the protection of civilians. The parameters of ethical debate are clearest at points in history when normative disputes occur between members of a moral community.

NATO's actions in Kosovo were highly contested. Russia and China, permanent members of the Security Council, believed the very concept of "humanitarian intervention" undermined the entire basis of international society. Nay-sayers within NATO countries, on both sides of the political spectrum, argued the war was wrong for various reasons: because it served no national interests, because NATO's motivations and means were inconsistent with humanitarianism, or because insufficient grounds existed to justify a war (Mertus, 2001). Even non-NATO states who tacitly supported the intervention did so with ambivalence. Predominantly Muslim countries, for example, both cheered the rescue of their Balkan brethren and expressed

---

26 Opinions on whether NATO's motives were purely or even primarily humanitarian are mixed. Chomsky (2001) and Ali (2000) suggest that oil interests, or even the desire to use up weapons that could be rendered useless by the Y2K bug, trumped humanitarian concerns, especially considering the lack of attention to analogous atrocities elsewhere and the "counter-humanitarian" means employed to supposedly protect people. Roberts (1999a) and Daalder and Ottenlon (2000) argue that the diplomatic record shows that the key concerns were shame over the failure to intervene in Bosnia, as well as a desire to retain credibility.

concern about the precedent of large countries forcibly violating the sovereignty of small ones in order to enforce Western standards regarding the treatment of minorities (Karawan 2000). Thus, the scope and shape of the debate over the air war, both at the time and post-hoc, is an indicator of the normative landscape regarding the active protection of civilians as a right or duty incumbent upon all members of international society.

Kosovo is also a hard case for testing the hypothesis that the gender sub-norm enabled or guided humanitarian action. Women and children were not at the greatest risk of massacre in Kosovo, and the international community was aware of this. Moreover, with the memory of Srebrenica guiding Western expectations of JNA behavior, one might even guess that the *need* to refer to women and children in order to justify action would be mitigated by the growing recognition that adult men, too, could and were likely to be victims of atrocity (Roberts 1999a). Thus, the extent to which this language is still apparent in condemnations of attacks on civilians or in justifications for humanitarian action indicates the gender sub-norm's salience even in unlikely cases.

Sex-Selective Massacre in Kosovo

As in Bosnia, human rights abuses in Kosovo were highly sex-selective (Danner 2000). A Human Rights Watch study after the conflict gathered evidence on 3,453 execution victims during the conflict. Of those whose gender was known to the analysts, 92 per cent were male (Human Rights Watch 2001, 5). A report on the conflict published in 1999 by the Organization for Security and Cooperation in Europe (OSCE) devotes an entire chapter to "Young Men of Fighting Age." The report states:

> Young men were the group that was by far the most targeted in the conflict in Kosovo... every young Kosovo Albanian man was suspected of being a terrorist. If apprehended by Serbian forces, the young men were at risk, more than any other group of Kosovo society, of grave human rights violations. (OSCE 1999)

These violations included horrendous torture, detention and summary execution, a pattern that is corroborated by several other key human rights reports on the conflict (American Association for the Advancement of Science 2000; Human Rights Watch 1999; Physicians for Human Rights 1999). Kosovar males were first systematically separated from women, children and the elderly (Human Rights Watch 2001), and then subjected to massacre, detention, torture and forced labor. The separation of men from women and children occurred either in villages or in refugee convoys: an aid worker across the border described a "planet without men, only women and children. It was unbelievable. The old men were there, but I'm talking about young men, between 17 and 45" (quoted in Buchanan 2002, 99).

Implementing the Civilian Immunity Norm

It would be misleading to conclude that no children and women died in the cleansing. Wilmer's account of the Balkans wars includes an interview with a former JNA fighter, who described how his commanding officer demanded 20,000 German marks from an elderly Albanian in exchange for his grandchild's life. When the old man produced only 5,000, the soldier beheaded the toddler with a knife, saying, "Five thousand is only enough for the body" (Wilmer 2002, 208). In other cases, children and women died alongside men of all ages in indiscriminate attacks (Demjaha 2000, 34). Nearly the entire extended family of a prominent KLA official was killed in September 1998 at Gornje Obrinje village. However, after the adult men along with their wives and several of their children had been killed as they fled into the forest, JNA soldiers captured the remaining children and turned them over safely to a female relative in another village, before killing her husband with an axe (Human Rights Watch 1999).

Thus despite sporadic killings of children and women, or indiscriminate attacks where they died alongside their male kin, they were not systematically targeted for execution as were draft-age males (Human Rights Watch 2001, 7). As in Bosnia, some young women were targeted for rape (Human Rights Watch 2000b), but most survived this ordeal.[27] Although some children died with their families during sieges or were picked out sporadically by particularly sadistic soldiers, most of the time JNA fighters chose to terrorize, rather than to kill, young children and their mothers. That women and children generally were immune from direct lethal attack is evident in the massive gender disproportions in refugee flows during the crisis.

Framing Atrocity

Since the international community was cognizant of the specific risks faced by young men in the crisis, we might expect to see less emphasis on "women and children" in rhetoric condemning the attacks. However, although the international community understood that military-age men were being killed en masse, it was precisely those cases where women and children also were victims that drew the greatest condemnation from international actors. For example, according to one NATO official, the killing of one seven-months-pregnant woman "represented a breach in the 'atrocities threshold'" (quoted in Daalder and Ottenlon 2000, 43).

In January of 1999, 45 Kosovar Albanian civilians were tied up and shot near the village of Racak. At least 37 of the victims were military-age men,

---

27 However, although most female Kosovar rape victims were not killed by their attackers, it is important to note the indirect consequences of war rape for women's life chances, particularly in a conservative society such as rural Kosovo. Some victims faced rejection by or even death at the hands of family members in the aftermath of the conflict. Many committed suicide. See Igric 1999.

many of whom had been singled out for torture and interrogation before being taken to a hillside and executed. According to Human Rights Watch, "four boys were taken out of this group, including the twelve year old who later spoke with Human Rights Watch, and were locked up together with the women and other children... the conscious decision to return him, while later executing the others, suggests that the police had a clear order to kill the adult males of the village" (Human Rights Watch 1999b, 4). The Serbian authorities released a report denying that a massacre had occurred and claiming that although many men had died, they had been armed KLA personnel engaged in combat (UN 1999j). The President of the Security Council condemned the massacre, saying "civilians were killed, including seven women and at least one child" (UN 1999d, 1).

The Racak massacre is generally viewed as the pivotal turning point in the resolve of NATO leaders to take military action to avert "a humanitarian catastrophe" (Campbell 2001, 88; Wheeler 2000, 264). This took the form of massive air strikes against targets in Serbia, beginning on March 24. In addition to emphasizing a few dead females rather than many dead males, the international media also focused on displacement as atrocity (in which the majority of the victims were women with families in tow) rather than the issue of mass killing (in which the majority of the victims were "battle-age" men). According to Livington (2000), CNN carried 30 per cent more stories on refugees during the crisis than on both fighting and atrocities combined. Livington's analysis itself collapses "fighting" stories and "atrocities" stories into the same category "owing to the impossible task of distinguishing 'normal' battle from atrocities" (Livington 2000, 372). Presumably, the same difficulty accrued to journalists covering the war and statespersons relying on media imagery to generate public support. Because the dead were in both cases adult men, it was difficult to distinguish between battle and atrocity.

The suffering of women, children and the elderly in camps, however, was crystal clear to NATO publics. Now, rather than isolated stories of dead men filtering out of Kosovo, the media and statespersons could rely on actual footage of hungry and weary mothers and families. Whether or not the refugee explosion was factored into NATO's calculations, it is certain that attention to victimized "women and children" played a decisive role in legitimizing the Kosovo war among Western publics, policy-makers, analysts and governments. Letters to the editor of *Newsweek*, after a story detailing the indiscriminate shelling of one village, read: "it embarrasses me to think that not too long ago I was doubting the wisdom of NATO's involvement" and "thank you for helping me feel as though I, too, were there, wailing with the mothers of innocent babies who were murdered in the name of a political struggle" (*Newsweek* 1999).

Legitimizing Intervention

NATO did not bother to seek UN approval for its "humanitarian war," guessing that both China and Russia would veto such a resolution. Instead, the Russian Federation forced the Security Council to debate the legitimacy of the intervention by sponsoring a draft resolution condemning the airstrikes (Roberts 1999a). On March 26, the members of the Security Council vigorously debated the legal and moral right of NATO countries to use military force in the absence of UN authorization. Those sponsoring the draft resolution cited international law and non-aggression norms; those opposing it emphasized the duty to protect the civilian population of Kosovo (Shinoda 2000; Wheeler 2000).

To what extent does gender discourse appear in these debates? Although the civilians most at risk were adult men, no delegate referred specifically to the protection of men and boys. Instead, several of those countries opposing the draft resolution on the basis that the war was morally just couched their justifications in terms of the protection of "women and children":

> Every day, the situation worsens and it is the civilian population - principally women and children – that suffers. (UN 1999e, 5)

> ... systematic repression by the Yugoslav authorities to drive innocent civilians, especially women and children, out of Kosovo... (UN 1999e, 9)

> Civilians, especially women and children, have been forcibly displaced from their homes and villages. (UN 1999f, 8)

In these passages, the suffering of women and children is couched in terms of the forced displacement issue. Indeed the intervention was framed as a response to refugee flows rather than to internal massacres.[28] Thus, the suffering of women and children (who had been primarily displaced rather than killed) could be pointed to as the justification for a military campaign that was in other respects illegal.

Whereas the main tendency of Security Council delegates, as well as the mainstream media, was to focus primarily on displacement rather than killings, one delegation specifically referred to women and children, rather than men, as victims of *massacre*: the Namibian delegate, Ambassador Andjaba, said:

---

28 In some cases, refugee flows can be framed as a breach of sovereignty (as India claimed in 1973) or a "threat to international peace and security" (as the Security Council claimed of the Kurdish emergency in 1991). In the case of Kosovo, however, the emphasis was on the humanitarian dimensions of the problem. The term "international peace and security" appears once in the debates; reference to regional stability appears twice; reference to the "civilian population" appears 18 times and the term "humanitarian catastrophe/situation/disaster" appears 46 times.

86   *'Innocent Women and Children'*

> The degree of brutality perpetrated on the civilian population, the massacre of women, children and the elderly, the displacement of people from their homes, kidnapping and the wanton destruction of property continue to take place in Kosovo. (UN 1999e, 10)

This is an especially intriguing passage because Namibia went on to vote *for* the resolution condemning the air strikes. It thus appears to throw off the hypothesis that actors opposing humanitarian intervention will always avoid drawing attention to "women and children," a hypothesis that is borne out by the rest of the content analysis. A closer examination of the Namibian position in the earlier debates on the protection of civilians provides some insight into this discursive anomaly. Russia and the other anti-interventionist countries criticized the intervention on the grounds that no humanitarian catastrophe was occurring and if it were, it was an internal matter. Their claim was that norms of sovereignty and non-aggression trumped the importance of protecting civilians in this case. This argument was raised repeatedly in the conversations on civilian protection just prior to the initiation of air strikes. Namibia, by contrast, had been extremely concerned to protect civilians against violence. But the Namibian position was that this should not take place through the use of armed force, particularly high-altitude bombing campaigns, which put additional civilian lives at risk.[29] In the case of Kosovo, the Namibian explanation for their position was thus:

> What we have been yearning for in the Federal Republic of Yugoslavia, as in any crisis situation, is peace. More violence and destruction cannot salvage peace. In numerous cases of conflict it has been the view of the Security Council – and rightly so – that military action is not the solution, but rather that peaceful means should be resorted to… My delegation wishes to underscore that military action against the Federal Republic of Yugoslavia may not be the solution. Furthermore, the implications of this action may go beyond the Federal Republic of Yugoslavia, thereby posing a serious threat to peace and security in the region. Therefore, my delegation appeals for the immediate cessation of the ongoing military action and for the exhausting of all possible avenues for a peaceful resolution of the conflict. (UN 1999e, 10)

This rhetoric is markedly different from the Russian position, which avoids the question of protecting civilians, stating that "attempts to justify the NATO strikes with arguments about preventing a humanitarian catastrophe in Kosovo are completely untenable." Instead, Russia (along with Ukraine, Belarus and China) emphasized the illegality of the intervention and the threat to international order:

---

29 Mertus (2001) distinguishes between categories of "nay-sayers" who opposed the intervention for sovereignty reasons and those who opposed it because it was an inadequate means to protect civilians in practice.

The Russian Federation vehemently demands the immediate cessation of this illegal military action against the Federal Republic of Yugoslavia... Russia is profoundly outraged by NATO's military action against sovereign Yugoslavia, which is nothing less than an act of open aggression... A dangerous precedent has been created regarding the policy of diktat and force, and the whole of the international rule of law has been threatened... For its part, the leadership of the Russian Federation will review its relationship with NATO as an organization, which has shown disrespect for the fundamental basis of the system of international relations. (UN 1999e, 3)

The contrast between these passages supports the conclusion that rhetoric of saving "women and children" correlates to a concern for the "protection of civilians." However, it also demonstrates that there is no current consensus in international society that armed humanitarian intervention is the best means to this end. Indeed the tide shifted when NATO's errant missiles began to produce their own civilian casualties (Human Rights Watch 2000a). Because missiles do not distinguish by age or sex, many of the victims were indeed women and children, a fact seized upon by those who sought to question the legitimacy of the air war (World Socialist Website 1999; Fisk 1999).

Case Summary

The Kosovo case demonstrates that the implementation of the civilian protection regime principles is affected by the gender beliefs embedded therein. Because sex and age are used as indicators of the civilian/combatant distinction, belligerent actors implementing the distinction principle often assume that military-age men may be classified as combatants. They are thus more likely to kill adult men and more likely to justify doing so. In Kosovo, young men were singled out for attack and the Serbian government argued that this was a legitimate response to terrorism. Bystanders, including other states, the international media and academics, consider the killing of women and children as a higher order atrocity than the killing of civilian males. Thus, in attempts to frame political violence as atrocity, references to female and child victims signify massacre in a way that adult male victims may not. In Kosovo, international actors condemning the violence capitalized on the relatively fewer female and child deaths, as well as non-lethal violence and deprivation to which women and children were exposed, rather than on sex-selective killing of males. Finally, the protection principle requires the international community to take active steps to enforce the civilian immunity norm where it is being violated. When enacted, this principle involves forcible military intervention, which in non-humanitarian cases itself constitutes a violation of the sovereignty norm. Only evidence of massive human rights violations can be used to claim that an intervention is "humanitarian," and in times of civil war, it is women and children who stand in as the innocent victims whose protection can justify such a claim.

88 'Innocent Women and Children'

Thus, during the Security Council debates over the legitimacy of NATO's response to ethnic cleansing in Kosovo, those arguing that the intervention was legitimate spoke of women and children, rather than civilian men, as the beneficiaries of NATO's action.

Conclusion

Because the "innocent civilian" is gendered, the protection of civilians – whether through state compliance with norms, persuasion or condemnation by third parties, or military intervention – reflects the perception that "women and children" are more clearly entitled to the protection that the civilian immunity norm affords. Although civilians of all categories die in indiscriminate warfare, and although cases of women and children being massacred exist, warring parties are less likely to *specifically* select women and children for execution, and are less likely to attempt to justify or rationalize such killings. The targeting of civilian men and boys en masse is more frequent, is more frequently justified as within the bounds of humanitarian law, and is less explicitly condemned within international society. Third parties are more likely to condemn atrocity when victims include women and children and to exaggerate claims to be protecting women and children in service of arguments that armed intervention is legitimately humanitarian.

The moral language of humanitarian intervention draws on the "home-front" idea whereby state forces actively serve to protect the innocent at home from attack, but expands the community of moral obligation to civilians per se rather than nationals. By 1999, even the Security Council, which had previously legitimized "humanitarian interventions" only on the basis that spillover effects were threatening international peace and security, was actively redefining its mandate to include civilian protection as such (Roberts 2001). In short, states are now actively debating not merely their responsibility to uphold humanitarian law, but their obligation to respond when others breach it. References to "innocent women and children" have played an important part in framing this agenda. It seems to matter very little that women and children themselves are increasingly mobilized, or that adult civilian men continue to be most at risk of lethal attack in internal conflicts.

What of the "protection" afforded by compliance with immunity norms itself? The fact that belligerents exercise restraint at any level is heartening to those accustomed to grisly anecdotes from war-affected regions worldwide. Yet the disparity in the reaction of observers to civilian deaths based on sex and age poses an enabling as well as a constraining effect. Indeed, this dual effect is at the root of the civilian immunity norm more generally: "the morally relevant distinction between non-combatant and combatant prohibits the intentional killing of the former at the same time as it justifies the killing of the latter" (Fullenwider 1985, 91; see also Norman 1995, 161). To the extent that it is considered legitimate to use sex and age as proxy variables in applying the distinction principle, this legitimizes the sex-selective killing of adult men and older boys. That the killing of "women and children" is seen as both morally different and worse than killing "men and boys" explains both patterns of sex-selective massacre and the disparate response of the international community to atrocity.

But it also begs important questions about the relative value of human life that one might expect to have received more attention from scholars and human rights practitioners. In the next two chapters, I demonstrate that this has not so far been the case. Indeed, both the language used by human rights advocates to set the agenda on "protection of civilians" and the strategies adopted by humanitarians in the field *coincide perversely with the very gendered logic that legitimates belligerents' sex-selective targeting of men and boys*. From a human rights perspective, this seems extraordinarily puzzling. I argue that it is the gender sub-norm (and its appeal to transnational constituencies, belligerents and even humanitarian workers themselves) that accounts for this paradoxical approach to civilian protection in international society.

Chapter 4

Advocating for Civilians: Gender Discourse in Transnational Human Rights Networks

The message is more important than the so-called
facts being used to deliver that message.
– Respondent #24, Personal Interview, Geneva, September 2002

As noted in Chapter 2, the UN Security Council, once the farthest removed from "soft" issues such as human rights and humanitarian affairs, has recently incorporated the protection of civilians into its mandate, at least in principle. This unprecedented interest and flurry of activity resulted directly from the concerted efforts of a transnational network of advocates mobilized around the issue of war-affected populations, who succeeded in setting the international agenda on civilian protection in the 1990s (Keck and Sikkink 1998). In this chapter, I analyze the impact of the gender sub-norm on the socio-linguistic strategies used by these network actors in the 1990s. I argue that the civilian protection network, including key humanitarian organizations, drew strategically on older gendered imagery to promote its agenda, and that this in part accounts for the deeply entrenched gender essentialisms now so pervasive at the UN Security Council.

From an empirical perspective, this outcome presents a puzzle for two reasons. First, in the early 1990s, the time was ripe for an understanding of conflict-affected populations that relied less on gender essentialisms than previously. Development and humanitarian assistance organizations were already beginning to adopt a "gender-mainstreaming" approach in vulnerability analysis, that sought to disaggregate target populations according to specific demographics including but not limited to age and gender, and replace essentialist assumptions with contextual analysis (March, Smyth and Mukhpadhyay 1999; Baines 2004). In 1989 the General Assembly of European NGOs adopted a Code of Conduct on Images and Messages Relating to the Third World that aimed in particular at reducing stereotypical gender imagery (Benthall 1993, 182). By the late 1990s, gender-mainstreaming policies had proliferated throughout the humanitarian

92   *'Innocent Women and Children'*

assistance community,[1] defined as "ensuring a gender perspective is fully integrated into all humanitarian activities and policies" (ECOSOC 1998). This approach was to include "equal protection of human rights of women *and men* in carrying out humanitarian and peace-building activities" (IASC 1999, 2).[2]

Moreover, several of the key conflicts in the early 1990s that put the protection of civilians on the international agenda were particularly notable for atrocities against civilian men and boys. Indeed it was images of emaciated male prisoners at Trnopolje, invoking Holocaust imagery, that initially signaled to the West the moral responsibility to intervene in Bosnia (Moeller 1999); Srebrenica, a massacre which took the lives primarily of men and boys, haunts the international community (Zarkov 2002); the failure to intervene in the Rwandan genocide, in which the majority of those killed were males (El-Bushra 2000, 73), has become emblematic of the need for decisive action to protect endangered civilians (Barnett 2002).

Yet as this chapter demonstrates, the language used to frame the protection of civilians as an international issue appealed in the 1990s primarily to the protection of women and children. Indeed this continued to be the case during the period when I conducted field research as part of this book project. One humanitarian field worker told me in 2002, after describing what s/he referred to as the sexual slavery of young boys under the Taliban, "Especially in conflict situations in certain countries, one simply does not talk about the abuse of young men" (Respondent #2, Personal Interview, May 2002, Geneva).

Why has the network, whose aim is to protect all civilians, reproduced rather than challenged these gender essentialisms that undermine the protection of civilian men and older boys? Below, I argue that network actors have attempted to establish a "frame" that "resonates" with the moral language familiar to international donors, belligerents and the global media, and that is acceptable to political allies in the women's network. Simply put, the pre-existing gender essentialisms embedded within the immunity norm – "all the women are victims, all the men are in the militias" (Enloe 1999) – have been seen as a useful normative resource for mobilizing attention to the broader problem of civilians. Often cognizant of the political tradeoffs inherent in these representations, many protection advocates are nonetheless convinced that the overall goal of civilian protection is served rather than undermined by this frame distortion; and those who question whether that is the case have so far been unable, given strategic and discursive constraints, to establish a salient counter-frame.

---

1   A summary of documents on gender-mainstreaming in humanitarian assistance can be found online through the OCHA Protection of Civilians website. See IASC Sub-Working Group 2001.

2   Italics added by author.

The analysis in this chapter contributes to recent theoretical work in international relations on the role of transnational advocacy networks in contributing to inter-subjective understandings. A number of recent studies have imported research from comparative politics on the strategic use of ideas in mobilizing collective action (McAdam, McCarthy and Zald 1996; Snow et al. 1986; Swidler 1986; Tarrow 1994), to explain why certain collective meanings and not others emerge at the international level (Finnemore and Sikkink 1998; Florini 2000; Joachim 2003; Khagram, Riker and Sikkink 2002; Smith, Chatfield and Pagnucco 1997). This line of inquiry advances scholarship on international norms, which has been criticized by several authors for failing to capture the extent to which actors manipulate norms in their own strategic interests (Barnett 1999, 7; Joachim 2003, 249); for inadequately specifying the conditions under which actors are successful (Checkel 1998, 325); and for focusing primarily on "good" dogs that barked (Legro 1997). Even this emergent literature, however, has tended to treat norms as static and as inherently functional. Here, I want to argue that even seemingly good norms may emerge as dysfunctional, and therefore their robustness may be diminished, if they are framed in a way that undermines their moral logic (Payne 2001).

Civilian protection discourse exemplifies this phenomenon. Activists have succeeded in galvanizing attention to "innocent civilians": by 1999, even the Security Council, which had previously legitimized "humanitarian interventions" only on the basis that spillover effects were threatening international peace and security, was actively redefining its mandate to include civilian protection as such (Roberts 2001). For some norms scholars, this would in itself be considered a success. But network actors have simultaneously replicated a gender stereotype in their agenda-setting efforts that some within the network argue undermines the entire agenda itself. Moreover, they have missed opportunities to correct this "misframing" (Snow et al. 1986) in such a way as to provide a more normatively and empirically consistent frame. This can be explained through understanding the role played by pre-existing cultural norms, interacting with ongoing environmental factors, in providing incentives for actors to privilege certain network frames – even those they understand to be distortions – over others.

The analysis in this chapter is drawn from a review of international documents put forth by major international and non-governmental organizations in their appeals for funding, in press releases describing complex emergencies, in the content of their Internet sites, and speeches and statements given in international fora. Semi-structured in-depth interviews, primarily with officials at UNHCR, ICRC and OCHA, were then used to gather data on network actors' rationale for using such essentialisms. Those interviewed include officials from the Protection and Donor Relations divisions in the organizations, as well as Gender Units, whose staff are

94   *'Innocent Women and Children'*

typically embedded in both the civilian protection network and the women's network. In addition, I attended the ICRC's Seminar on the Protection of Special Categories of Civilian in May 2002 as a participant-observer. This experience enabled me to examine the use of gender essentialisms in a training setting as well as to assess ways in which humanitarian practitioners may be challenging them as part of an ongoing "reframing" process.

In the sections below, I situate the civilian protection network in the context of the emerging literature on transnational advocacy networks. I then demonstrate that civilian protection network frames reproduce the three prominent gender essentialisms characteristic of the older discourse on civilians: women as civilians, women as mothers and women as vulnerable. Third, I explain the emergence of this gendered rhetoric as part of a strategic framing process in which network actors sought to promote an image of their work that both resonated with traditional humanitarian ethics and drew strength from the emerging activity around the issue area of war-affected women. Finally, I consider the possibilities of incipient norm change within the network.

The Civilian Protection Network

As already detailed, the targeting of civilian populations has been a feature of international politics throughout history (Carr 2002; Chalk and Jonassohn 1990; Rummel 1994), but in the late 1990s, this phenomenon became an *issue:* powerful countries began explicitly addressing it as both a pragmatic and a moral problem for the first time in history (Roberts 2001). This international shift toward a global concern with war-affected populations was generated by the advocacy of numerous committed groups, organizations and individuals, who succeeded in mobilizing international attention to the needs of civilians through the skillful use of persuasive rhetoric (Habermas 1986; Risse 2000).

Keck and Sikkink refer to such principled communities as transnational advocacy networks (Keck and Sikkink 1998): "sets of actors linked across country boundaries, bound together by shared values, dense exchanges of information and services, and common discourses" (Khagram, Riker and Sikkink 2002, 7). In contrast to the *civilian protection regime*, which I defined previously in terms of shared norms and rules pertaining to civilians, the *civilian protection network* is the transnational community of citizens, journalists, protection organizations and statespersons who, believing that civilian immunity norms should be respected, aim at the more widespread implementation of those norms, through persuasion or purposeful action.

The concept of transnational advocacy networks explicitly goes beyond inter-state interactions to emphasize the transnational public sphere (Guidry, Kennedy and Zald 2000; Khagram, Riker and Sikkink 2002; Smith, Chatfield and Pagnucco 1997). Governments do play a role in such networks, in this case as the creators of the Hague and Geneva conventions and more recent instruments demarcating humanitarian law and established to enforce it. In venues such as the Security Council and in the manner that they justify armed intervention for humanitarian purposes, states also play an important role in reproducing and clarifying civilian protection norms (Sandvik-Nylund 1998, 89). However, those actors on the ground most often engaged in the protection of civilians are international or non-governmental organizations, and those most vocal about condemning violations of the immunity principle are often embedded in transnational advocacy networks existing alongside the state-system, rather than members of government bureaucracies per se.

Non-state entities in the network include the global media, international organizations established by states, such as UNICEF, and non-governmental organizations such as Medicins sans Frontieres (MSF) (Shiras 1996). Organizations may also occupy a quasi-international status. The ICRC is an international organization in the sense of being the repository of the Geneva Conventions (a treaty between states), in being charged with its implementation, and in being funded primarily by signatory governments. However, it is a non-governmental actor in the sense that it is independent of any particular government's control, is composed of a committee of private individuals, and is responsible to the victims of conflict rather than to governments per se (Berry 1997). Coalitions of many actors around particular issues also constitute discrete focal points in the broader network. The International Campaign to Ban Landmines and the Coalition to Stop the Use of Child Soldiers are two such examples: landmines and child soldiering became salient issues as part of a broader social concern with the effects of armed conflict on the innocent (Hughes 2000; Mekata 2000; Price 1998).

Of the formal agencies in the civilian protection network, none has an explicit mandate to protect civilians in particular (Cohen and Deng 1998, 197). Some organizations are mandated to protect war-affected populations more generally, such as UNHCR and the ICRC; others address the needs of civilians in the context of their broader work in development and assistance (Save the Children Alliance) or human rights (Human Rights Watch). For some entities, such as the UN Office for the Coordination of Humanitarian Affairs (OCHA), the "protection of civilians" figures prominently as a subset of its broader agenda, exemplified by a link from its homepage to a specific website on the issue (Protection of Civilians 2003).

As in most transnational advocacy networks, these actors are diverse, informally connected, and embedded in broader issue networks concerning human rights, humanitarian affairs and development. Their modes of operation also vary, spanning the range of network political tactics specified by Keck and Sikkink (1998, 16). Amnesty International and Human Rights Watch expose and condemn violations of international human rights and humanitarian law, "quickly and credibly generating politically usable

96 *'Innocent Women and Children'*

information and moving it to where it will have the most impact"; journalists and external relations departments of major protection agencies frame atrocity by calling upon "symbols, actions or stories that make sense of a situation for an audience that is frequently far away"; concerned citizens engage in "leverage politics" vis-à-vis their own governments; other actors, such as the ICRC, avoid shaming belligerents externally in favor of direct persuasion, or what Keck and Sikkink call "accountability politics" (1998, 16). In many cases, addressing violations themselves takes a back seat to negotiating access to needy populations in order to deliver aid or alleviate suffering. As Sikkink (2002, 309) points out, actors within networks often disagree strenuously on how to negotiate such tradeoffs, and organizations engaged in humanitarian operations are no exception (Cohen and Deng 1996; DeMars 1997; Minear 2002).

Despite vast differences in outlook, strategy, mode of operation and organizational culture, groups within an advocacy network are members of the same community by virtue of their shared values and common discourses (Smith, Chatfield and Pagnucco 1997, 65). One of the most important roles in which advocacy networks are engaged is the construction or transformation of norms and discourses at the international level, in an effort to "teach" (or in this case "remind") political actors how they should behave (Finnemore 1996a; Thomas 2001) and incite others to join their cause (Cohen 2001). It is on this aspect of network activism, which Keck and Sikkink call "symbolic politics," that this chapter focuses. I am less interested in the diversity of approaches or procedural disagreements within the network than on the set of values that they hold in common and the way these are represented in appeals to their targets of influence (belligerents) and the international community. Here, I explore how these principled and causal beliefs about civilian protection have been articulated and politicized in the post-Cold War era, and the way in which pre-existing gender discourses influenced this process of strategic social construction.

Gender in Civilian Protection Network Discourse

Despite opportunities to reformulate or challenge the language used by states and legal scholars to define and delimit the moral parameters of the civilian immunity norm, activists in the transnational network instead tend to mirror several of these gender essentialisms to press their cause. These are evident in a broad array of empirical sources: documents submitted to international fora, statements by network officials, appeals to citizens and donor states for resources or involvement, condemnations and depictions of specific atrocities. Each gender essentialism situates women alongside children as innocent, dependent and vulnerable, therefore civilians and therefore worthy of protection. These generalizations, even when rooted in

Advocating for Civilians 97

empirical realities, draw attention away from the fact that able-bodied adult men may also be civilians worthy of the protection network's concern.

Civilians as "Women and Children"

As described in Chapter 2, the term "innocent women and children" abounds in international discourse, but protection agencies often make this association explicit. Their appeals for donations or international concern tend to picture women as both the primary civilian victims of slaughter and the living in need of relief; their brochures picture hungry mothers or desolate refugees (Cohen 2001; Moeller 1998). The same year that 8,000 men and boys disappeared from Srebrenica, the ICRC published a slick brief entitled "Civilians in War," which contained no images of un-uniformed adult men, and included sections on "women" and "children" alongside "mines," "water" and "humanitarian law," without discussing patterns of attack against civilian males. Web sites of major humanitarian organizations, such as the ICRC and the OCHA, contain "protection of civilians" web pages with links to "women," "children" and sometimes "elderly" and "displaced" but not to "men."[3] Civilian protection advocates invoke the language of "innocent women and children" to call on belligerents to restrain themselves; on powerful states to intervene; and on potential donors to send aid:

> Rebel groups should demonstrate the quality of their leadership, by halting the slaughter of innocents such as women, children and the disabled. (Nelson Mandela, quoted in Ardery 2000)

> I call on all sides to give up violence in Kosovo, which is forcing tens of thousands of people to flee their homes, bringing suffering upon many women and children. (UNHCR 1998)

The ICRC's report on "Women and War" specifically calls into question the use of such gendered language. "The juxtaposition of men as fighters and women as civilians, both in text and photos, fails to recognize the danger to which male members of the civilian population are exposed and the role that women play in the military" (Lindsey 2001, 64). However the bulk of the study itself is likewise concerned only with the wartime experience of women as civilians (Lindsey 2001, 33).

The equation of women and children with civilians, concurrent with efforts to mobilize attention to the issue, can operate more subtly. For example, although there are no reliable global statistics on the proportion of civilians killed in wars (Goldstein 2001, 399-402; Smith 1997, 100; Liu Institute, 2005), it has become commonplace for scholars and network advocates to assert that

---

3   See Protection of Civilians 2003; ICRC 2003.

"90 per cent of casualties in recent wars are civilians," frequently followed by the expression, "the vast majority being women and children":

> Today, 90 percent of war casualties are innocent bystanders, and the majority of them are women and children. That's a dramatic reversal from a century ago, when civilians made up fewer than 5 percent of war's victims. (Reliefweb 2003)

> Civilians now account for 90% of war casualties, the majority of whom are women and children. (Tickner 2001, 2)

> In conflicts throughout the 1990s, civilians constituted up to 90 percent or more of those killed with a high proportion being women and children. (Chesterman 2001, 2)

Although this statistic is sometimes attributed to the UN, no one at the Department of Statistics could tell me where it came from. During interviews at different protection agencies, humanitarian practitioners readily rattled it off, yet none were certain how it had been calculated or by whom. Although an analysis of the data provided in the few primary sources identifiable by tracing citations does not unequivocally support the view that civilian targeting is on the rise (Beer 1981, 34; Sivard 1991, 20-25; Small and Singer 1982; Smith 1994, 2), no one seemed to think the validity of the statistic was an issue. "Where the numbers come from isn't important," a facilitator at a Training Seminar on Humanitarian Law for University Teachers sponsored by the ICRC replied when asked. "What's important is what they show about the situation of war-affected civilians." Invoking the "90 per cent casualty" trope has become a ritual within humanitarian discourse, even among those who admit that the data on which it is based are not reliable: "While there is little data on how many of war's recent casualties have been women, it is known that women and children compose the majority of civilian deaths and the majority of all refugees" (Save the Children 2002, 9).

When injuries, brutalization through typically non-lethal means (such as sexual violence),[4] and indirect deaths and displacement are factored in, women and children indeed become the majority of "casualties" *not* because they are targeted specifically for massacre as some advocates claim,[5]

---

4 Wartime sexual violence can be fatal, however, either because of the injuries sustained or because it is followed by murder (Aafjes and Goldstein 1998; Askin 1997; Wilmer 2002). Moreover, war rape can be indirectly fatal depending on its social context. Suicide rates among war rape survivors, due to the secondary stigmatization they often experience from their societies, are sometimes high (Ghobarah, Huth and Russett 2003, 199), as is the risk in some societies that they will be killed by their families for having been "dishonored" (Aafjes and Goldstein 1998).

5 For example: "Recruitment and use of child soldiers... the indiscriminate use of land mines, large scale forced displacement and ethnic cleansing, the targeting of women and children... are all too familiar features of war." UN Doc S/2001/331:1.

but because they demographically represent the majority of any random population.

Thus where it is implied in these statements that women and children are being specifically targeted for death in vast numbers, the statement is misleading. Although male and female children as well as adult women are sometimes killed (Rehn and Sirleaf 2002), often targeted for rape (Kelly 2000), and nearly always affected indirectly by the long-term effects of armed violence (Ghobarah et al. 2003), there is little convincing evidence that women and children are *specifically* targeted as victims of the *majority* of *deaths* in current armed conflicts (Goldstein 2001, 400; see also Murray and Lopez 1996). Moreover, this discourse obscures the endemic sex-selective targeting of male civilians in these contexts.

Parents as Mothers/Mothers as Peacemakers

As detailed in Chapter 2, women have traditionally been associated with child-rearing, and the special protections that have accrued to women under international humanitarian law have historically addressed only their specific needs as mothers rather than the vulnerabilities they face as a result of gender hierarchies prevalent in society before and during armed conflict (Gardam and Jervis 2001). This conceptualization values and protects women primarily in their role as caretakers of children. Equally, it assumes that women alone are responsible for or vital to the survival and developmental needs of children, marginalizing the importance of fathering. As mentioned in Chapter 2, the Additional Protocols to the Geneva Conventions specify that pregnant women or mothers of children under five may not be executed even if convicted of a capital offense, whereas the father of the same child has no such immunity. The relative devaluation of fathers is also reflected in the priority given to mothers accompanying children during humanitarian evacuation, as demonstrated in Chapter 5.

Similar maternal imagery has often been used by humanitarian and development organizations. UNICEF has begun to define child well-being as synonymous with women's well-being through the slogan "child rights are women's rights" (OCHA 2000a; see also Beigbeder 2002; Goonsekere 1992; UNICEF 1999). While this frame is rooted in a valid empirical understanding of the link between maternal health and child protection (rather than war-affected civilians' issues per se), it equates women with mothering and does not consider the relevance of fathers' health for the protection of children.

This construction has mapped easily onto the specific issue of war-affected populations, and has been mirrored in the narrower issue of war-affected civilians. Save the Children, for example, has begun a parallel campaign to call attention to mothering at a global level. The "Every Mother Every Child" campaign cuts across issue areas and is development-oriented, but its 2002

State of the World's Mothers report specifically emphasizes armed conflict. Here, women are positioned as both mothers and civilians:

> It has become increasingly clear that the lives of children are jeopardized when the lives of women are not protected... the global community can and must do more to make the protection of women, of mothers, of children in armed conflict a priority. (Save the Children 2002, 2)

> When houses, schools and hospitals are bombed, food supplies are cut off, agricultural fields are strewn with land mines and wells are poisoned, mothers struggle mightily to preserve their way of life and keep children safe and healthy. (Save the Children 2002, 4)

> Belligerent parties deliberately inflict violence on civilian populations, and women and children are killed... (Save the Children 2002, 8)

This language is also reflected in the web content of the OCHA page on "Women and War," situating women (but not men) as civilian care-givers: "in spite of all they endure in camps, towns, villages, and fields across war zones, women persevere and work to preserve the integrity of their families and communities." Here, women's role as mothers is linked to an assumption that they are inherently peaceful, which has led some actors to frame women as peace-building resources, in efforts to get major UN organs to see women's rights as part of their broader agenda with security and peace (Cohn et al, 2004). This discourse also draws on traditional imagery, deployed by some UN agencies, situating women in the private sphere. As Erin Baines has noted, UNHCR's discourse on refugee women emphasized domestic labor and reproductive roles: "UNHCR narratives repeatedly defin[e] women as apolitical, private sphere actors who [are] particularly vulnerable and in need of help" (Baines 2004, 27).

Within the dataset analyzed here, there are 29 references to women as peacemakers. The frame obscures the caring and supportive roles of civilian men, but also the role that women play in supporting, promoting and engaging in armed conflicts (UNSC 2002, 13). There are only two references to fathers in the dataset, and none to men as peacemakers. Similarly, the "women and children" of civilian protection network discourse are often women *with* children: mothers whose men have "gone off to fight" (Save the Children 2002, 12) and who now struggle to provide for and protect their children, often without access to resources that were once channeled through male heads of households and community leaders:

> In many cases, women and teenage girls in conflict zones are the sole providers and protectors for their families, as wives, mothers and sisters, since their husbands, brothers, sons and fathers have either been exiled or killed or are away on combat duty. (IASC 1999, 2)

Advocating for Civilians 101

Women's usual position as primary caretakers of infants and young children makes them vulnerable to forms of psychological torture if their children are also victimized. (Bunch and Reilly 1994, 41)

It may be harder for women to flee the fighting if they have babies and small children. (Lindsey 2001, 65)

In these passages, the disappearance of men is both assumed and treated as a factor affecting their families' plight rather than a protection issue in its own right. The burden of parenting and care-giving is presented as entailing risks only for women. Civilian fathers, before and after separation from their families, are invisible in a frame that assumes their absence and associates childrearing with women.[6] As Save the Children emphasizes: "the care and protection of women and children must be *the humanitarian priority* in ethnic and political conflicts" (Save the Children 2002, 6).

Vulnerable Groups "Including Women, Children and the Elderly"

Attention by the protection network to "especially vulnerable populations" still tends to include every possible category except able-bodied adult civilian males. This discursive usage, which is to be distinguished from the sorts of vulnerabilities and capabilities assessment instruments popularized in the development community (March, Smyth and Mukhpadhyay 1999), equates "women and children" with vulnerability and is used to draw international attention to specific demographic groups (Caversazio 2001; Baines, 2004). Describing the concept of "vulnerability," and considering whether adult men could be vulnerable, a representative of the UN Office for the Coordination of Humanitarian Affairs told me: "Commonly when you speak of vulnerability you have the image of women, children and the elderly. The idea of a 20-year-old man who can't defend himself [laughter] he can just run away and join the army or join the rebel force" (Respondent #29, Phone Interview, October 2002).

This framing of vulnerability is most evident in the attempt to place the protection of civilians on the agenda of international institutions. The Secretary-General's 1999 Reports to the UN Security Council on the Protection of Civilians refer to the "special needs" of women as well as children (UN 2001 and UN 1999g). By contrast, no reference is made to the vulnerabilities of adult men, other than one statement in the September report that they are most likely to be killed. (This is buried in the section

---

6 Also hidden from this frame is the fact that many women are facing difficulties (such as reintegration for female ex-combatants) quite distinct from issues of providing for children; and the fact that in some cases, such as forced pregnancy, emphasizing biological motherhood may not result in the protection of children or women (Allen 1996; Carpenter 2000).

on page 3 regarding women's special needs.) In 2001, the UN Office for the Coordination of Humanitarian Affairs disseminated a pamphlet entitled *Reaching the Vulnerable* which emphasized deprivation rather than lethal attack and whose images included no civilian males (OCHA 2001). The opening statement of the Report on the Civilian Protection Workshop in South Africa states: "Civilians are no longer just victims of war today. They are regarded as instruments of war. Sex is no defence, nor is age: indeed women, children and the elderly are often at the greatest risk" (OCHA 2002, 1).

When mention of the risks to men does appear in policy documents or speeches, it is seldom followed by analysis or policy recommendations. A recent report on gender-based violence in conflict settings acknowledges that "GBV programming targeting men and boy survivors is virtually non-existent among conflict-affected populations" (Ward 2002, 4) but the report goes on to focus almost entirely on women and girls, and includes no recommendations regarding men other than the need to incorporate them into initiatives to eradicate violence against women. OCHA's Emergency Relief Coordinator pointed out in a 2000 public statement that "While research has been undertaken on types of violence and traumatic stress disorders experienced by women during war, less is known about the psychosocial consequences of violence, including sexual violence, suffered by men during conflict" (McAskie 2000, 3). But none of the policy recommendations at the end of her talk included gathering data on such issues.

Actors within the civilian protection network have never agreed on how to define "vulnerability." Protection workers I spoke to made reference to two partially conflicting definitions. To some, "vulnerability" accrues from *physical* characteristics, such as age or disability, which make certain individuals inherently less able to withstand attack or escape from harm. For example, very young children are physically more susceptible to disease and malnutrition; the elderly or the disabled are less mobile and self-sufficient than able-bodied adults. It is persons with these types of physical vulnerabilities for which the Geneva Conventions set down specific guidelines for treatment, and this definition was offered at the ICRC's Seminar on the Protection of Specific Categories of Civilian, Geneva, May 2002.

Women are often included as such in this group. Some respondents seemed to see women as inherently vulnerable "due to physical reasons and these kinds of factors" (Respondent #25, Personal Interview, September 2002, Geneva). Others, when probed, made it clear that it was only certain aspects of biology that rendered some women vulnerable some of the time, but these aspects were being generalized to women as a group. In particular, pregnant or lactating women possess inherent vulnerabilities stemming from

Advocating for Civilians 103

their biological sex (IASC 1999).[7] Overall, however, it makes objectively less sense to define able-bodied adult women without nursing infants as innately vulnerable. Although social vulnerability can vary greatly across societies, in strictly biological terms, a healthy adult woman is far more similar to a healthy adult man than to an elderly invalid or a child under five (Goldstein 2001, 132-134).

Others emphasize *socially induced* vulnerability. Regardless of physical characteristics, some groups in some contexts are more vulnerable than others to particular forms of threat based upon societal inequities in access to resources, role expectations or geographic location. It is perhaps less empirically problematic to include women as women in this construction of vulnerability. For much of the time under any given social system, women are indeed *made* vulnerable by social factors, and this is particularly true during times of armed conflict (Lorentzen and Turpin 1998; Moser and Clark 2001). Displaced women are vulnerable as heads of households in situations where resources are customarily distributed through male heads of households who may not be accompanying their families (Mertus 2000). In addition to the risk of attack from enemy forces (particularly sexual assault), women's vulnerability to violence and deprivation from their "own" side increases in times of war (Enloe 2000). In other words, "the vulnerability of women during armed conflict is a direct consequence of the discrimination that women face throughout their lives" (Gardam and Jervis 2001).

Thus, there is a case to be made for conceptualizing all women as always socially vulnerable because of the gendered structure of power within war-affected communities. If empirically undistorted, however, such a frame would account as well for *men's* socially induced vulnerabilities. While able-bodied men, as adults, are among the least vulnerable group *physically*, they become far more vulnerable than women, children and the elderly to certain forms of attack in certain situations because of socially constructed assumptions about male gender roles (IASC 2002).

The Gendered Civilian as Strategic Social Construction

Before a problem becomes an issue, norm advocates must place it on the agenda of those actors – in this case the Security Council – with the ostensible power to address it. This requires a carefully crafted interpretive frame that connects the problem to pre-existing principled and causal schemas of those whom advocates wish to influence, and proposes a solution (Snow and Benford 1992). "Frames are the specific metaphors, symbolic representations,

---

7 The Geneva Conventions provide for special protection on this basis, including evacuation priority for pregnant women and mothers of young children. See de Preux 1985.

104 *'Innocent Women and Children'*

and cognitive cues used to render or cast behavior and events in an evaluative mode and to suggest alternative modes of action" (Zald 1996, 262).

Framing efforts by norm advocates draw upon pre-existing symbolic technologies: "inter-subjective systems of representations and representation-producing practices" (Laffey and Weldes 1997). Encoded in language and imagery, frames are ideational constructs; however, they do not exist within human minds, but are rather encapsulated or "envehicled" within symbols, "a symbol being anything that denotes, describes, represents, exemplifies, labels, indicates, evokes, depicts, expresses... anything that somehow or other signifies" (Geertz 1980, 135). These symbols and signifiers – such as the category of "women and children" as a signifier for "civilians" – form the "cultural tool-kit" (Swidler 1986) with which norm advocates build the frames that then succeed or fail at mobilizing collective action.

Network actors' efforts to transform pre-existing cultural symbols into calls for action that resonate with their target publics are mediated by the strategic environment in which they operate (Joachim 2003; Payne 2001). Social movement literature, on which the emerging work on transnational networks builds, typically discusses the strategic environment into terms of two aspects: political opportunity structures and mobilizing structures.[8]

Political opportunity structures are "those consistent dimensions of the political environment that provide incentives for or constraints on people undertaking collective action" (Khagram, Riker and Sikkink 2002, 17; see also McAdam, McCarthy and Zald 1996 and Tarrow 1998). This typically refers to how much *access* network actors have to key institutions or targets of influence such as states, international organizations and, in this case, belligerents. At the international level, the acceptance of the involvement of NGOs in international decision-making as an international norm has altered the political opportunity structure for advocacy networks (Gordenker and Weiss 1996). But proximate events can also provide opportunities: shifts in political alignment, such as the ending of the Cold War, or events of seemingly world-changing significance, like the Holocaust and bombings of Hiroshima, or the terrorist attacks on the World Trade Towers in 2001, can affect the social and discursive space in which network actors can press their demands (Joachim 1998; Minear 2002).

Mobilizing structures are "those collective vehicles, informal as well as formal, through which people mobilize and engage in collective action" (McAdam, McCarthy and Zald 1996, 3). In domestic social movements, these structures include churches, families, neighborhoods, friendship networks and professional associations. In the transnational public sphere, advocates mobilize by building alliances with networks of like-minded actors who can generate support for their cause by leveraging different points in the global

---

8   In reality, it is often difficult to analytically disaggregate these interrelated concepts, so I refer to both as aspects of the "strategic environment."

system. Powerful *allies* can include states, international organizations and the global media (Risse, Ropp and Sikkink 1999). In addition, networks seek to build a heterogeneous transnational *constituency*, enhancing both their mobilizing base and the legitimacy of their cause (Joachim 2003, 252). Finally, advocacy networks attempt to "extend" their frames so as to coincide with and thus draw on the energy of other networks working on issues seen as similar or analogous (Snow et al. 1986). Networks working on overlapping issues can become important as *partners,* by increasing the pool of "experts" on which activists can draw: both "directly affected individuals who can provide testimonies based on their experiences" (Joachim 2003, 252) and "epistemic communities" consisting of professionals able to share scientific, technical or legal expertise (Haas 1992).

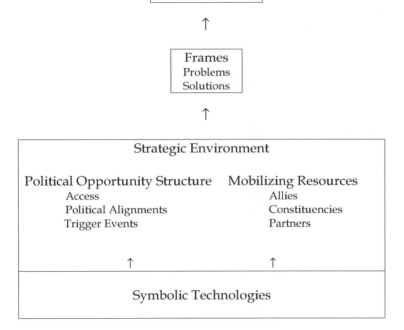

Figure 4.1 Agenda-setting in world politics

As illustrated in Figure 4.1, all these aspects of what I call the strategic environment are shaped, however, by pre-existing norms (Smith, Chatfield and Pagnucco 1997, 70). In some cases, the emergence of a political opportunity itself can be caused, or its meaning constituted by, changes in international or transnational understandings. For example, the end of the Cold War is

106 *'Innocent Women and Children'*

said to have opened "agenda-space" for transnational social actors (Joachim 1998). But it was also the presence of such post-World War II narratives of democracy, human rights, and self-determination that provided a context in which this particular "new world order" was conceived, by powerful states redefining their foreign mission, by international agencies redefining their mandates, by democratization movements, and by transnational networks seizing the opportunities provided by the sudden issue-vacuum to fit their old agendas into new and suddenly successful frames (Risse 2000).

Similarly, the relationship of advocates to the structures through which they mobilize is not self-evident but hinges on the distribution of underlying norms and the ways in which norm advocates deploy them. For example, the development of coalitions among like-minded groups depends on the ability to construct a narrative of "like-mindedness" that is highly contingent on the cultural tool-kits available (Swidler 1986) as well as the inventiveness with which actors deploy them (Barnett 1999).

Framing is about politicizing the "envehicled meanings" evident in these cultural symbols. A key insight of the social movement literature is that successful agenda-setting requires establishing a frame that "resonates" with pre-existing norms (Barnett 1999, 9; Klotz 1996, 31; Meyer 1995, 175; Payne 2001 , 43; Smith, Chatfield, and Pagnucco 1997, 70) as well as with the symbolic technologies used by other actors with overlapping interests and identities (Snow and Benford 1992). For example, the chemical weapons norm was successfully developed in part because norm entrepreneurs successfully linked chemical weapons to poisons, which were already outlawed (Price 1997). Therefore, smart norm advocates will adopt language that coincides with pre-existing cultural discourses in order to press their claims. Snow et al. (1986, 468-469) identify several ways in which activists seek to align their frames both with "structurally unconnected but frame-compatible sentiment pools" and with "values presumed basic to prospective constituents."

When symbolic technologies are invoked not in their own right, but rather as signifiers of something not conceptually contiguous, frames are vulnerable to what Payne (2001) calls "frame distortion." For instance, the term "international relations" as a signifier for the study of relations between states uses the term "nation" to signify "state" – a frame that misleads because nations almost never coincide entirely with territorial political entities (Lapid 1994). This language reifies the notion that states represent nations and suggests that this type of political arrangement is both empirically evident and normative, neither of which is necessarily true. A number of scholars of nationalism and political geography have blamed dysfunctional processes (including ethnic cleansing campaigns) on this distorted idea (Horowitz 1985; McNeill 1986; Williams 1997).

In our case, it is not the protection of women and children per se that is being promoted by the network, but the protection of *civilians*. Images of women and children, however, represent the innocence and vulnerability according to which the civilian population is to be conceptually constituted and understood: they *denote* "civilians." But the use of ascriptive characteristics to identify "civilians" undermines the moral logic of the norm, which is based instead on who is doing what. Gender imagery proves a potent cultural resource in terms of agenda-setting, precisely because it resonates with pre-existing gender discourses, but since this gender essentialism is fundamentally misleading, it *distorts* the civilian protection frame it is intended to promote.

According to Payne, frame distortion occurs when "normative debates fail to meet basic standards of communicative rationality," which "imagines actors' reciprocally challenging one another's validity claims in order to find shared truth" (2001, 46-47). Payne asserts that only through such "genuine" persuasive practices can "true" norm-building take place. If the resonance of a norm is based on misleading or distorted claims, the process of norm-strengthening itself can be undermined by norm advocates' internal contradictions (Smith 2001, 45). Target populations may respond to the frame rather than the norm: "We are civilized troops, so we will kill only the adult men." Moreover, intentionally distorting a moral claim by appealing to only partially compatible symbolism can undermine the broader moral claim itself when the gap between the norm and its frame becomes evident to constituencies: "Women and children are under arms, so there is no longer any such thing as a civilian." Particularly in the human rights field, "information that turns out to be exaggerated or biased harms the organization's credibility and ultimately the interests of the people it seeks to help" (Caversazio 2001, 102).

Why do advocates sometimes engage in seemingly counter-productive frame distortion in order to promote their agenda? Part of the answer lies in the existence of such distortions prior to the process of framing. Pre-existing cultural tropes are the stock of ideational resources from which the frames themselves are built. If these symbolic technologies already contain distortions, challenging them can reduce the potential for a resonant frame. But the extent to which this is the case will be contingent on strategic factors, through which these cultural tools are filtered, and which therefore provide the incentive structure that drives framing choices. This combination of factors determines the way in which issues will be framed once they reach the agenda of elite organizations in international society, such as the UN Security Council.

Understanding this process renders explicable the persistent use by civilian protection actors of gender stereotypes they know to be outdated and which some claim to be destructive to their cause. The network's relationship with its most important allies, its ability to appeal to its international constituency, and its success in relating to partners in overlapping issue areas, are perceived to have been enhanced by the use of gendered rhetoric. Moreover, powerful

108   'Innocent Women and Children'

network actors see the advantages of these gains as outweighing the gaps created by relying on such frame distortions.

Ensuring Access to Targets of Influence

A key aspect of network actors' political opportunity structure is their ability to maintain access to belligerents, and through them to the civilian populations they wish to serve. In order to advocate with belligerents on behalf of war-affected civilians, humanitarian organizations must create an environment in which the belligerents are willing to listen and negotiate (Cutts 1999). Moreover, to carry out humanitarian operations themselves – the delivery of relief, the removal of civilians from besieged areas, the provision of medical care – protection organizations require access to civilian populations, which also typically involves negotiations with the belligerents who control the territory in which the civilians find themselves. These negotiations take place in a context in which warring parties may at best be very suspicious of humanitarian organizations, and at worst may wish to exploit them in their own interests (Cohen and Deng 1998; Darst 2003; DeMars 1997).

In order to maintain this access, most humanitarian organizations rely upon a discourse of neutrality: "each organization asserts that it is concerned only with the human needs and rights of the victims of conflict – not with influencing the political and military contest between adversaries" (DeMars 1997, 104). While different organizations have conflicting conceptions of neutrality (DeMars 1997; Minear 2002), and while it has become clear in the post-Cold War era that the very concept of neutrality may be dysfunctional in some contexts (Jones and Cater 2001), it remains a powerful principle governing humanitarian discourse and practice in war-affected regions.

Because the discourse of neutrality is contingent upon avoiding actions that could be interpreted as assisting participants to one side of a conflict, it is typically easier to argue for the right to assist those individuals least perceived as participants. Given the gendered parameters of the immunity norm, and the fact that warring parties generally see adult men as agents during time of war, providing explicit assistance to men can undermine the perception that humanitarian actors are in fact neutral. Take the example of British relief shipments to German-occupied Greece during World War II. Junod (1951, 185) describes British concern that humanitarian aid would be channeled to Greek collaborators and thus sustain the German war effort: "Mr. Jordan, the commercial attaché of the British Embassy, was all in favour of relieving the sufferings of women and children, but he insisted that men should not benefit… 'you really must see that Her Majesty's Government can never agree to feed factory workers in Greece who are working for the enemy'."

As Frohardt, Paul and Minear write (1999, 45), gender assumptions often become grafted into humanitarian efforts to maintain neutrality in contemporary contexts as well: "Because provision of social services to the elderly, women or children often are less threatening to the authorities, relief programs can sometimes be used as points of entry to areas where populations are at risk." In his extensive analysis of negotiating access to civilians in Bosnia, Mark Cutts (1999) details the ways in which UNPROFOR's policy of smuggling draft-age males out of war zones had the effect of undermining the credibility of all the aid organizations in the region (Cutts 1999). Or as a UNHCR protection officer formerly based in Sarajevo described, "One of the accusations was that we were fueling the war, feeding the men of Sarajevo, who may wear civilian clothes when they came to pick up the bread but would later fight... we worked very hard to avoid saying we were feeding the army" (Respondent #31, Phone Interview, October 2002).

By claiming to be protecting only the "objectively" innocent, a UNICEF official explained, agencies attempt to "depoliticize" their role in complex humanitarian emergencies where indeed de facto neutrality is increasingly recognized as untenable: "We simplify the issue, simplify the scenario, 'we are just here to help innocent civilians, innocent women and children, we're not here to interfere with the conflict...' so bringing it down to a very fundamental level – in that sense, the simplistic nature of the analysis is meant to reduce controversy and make it easier to work" (Respondent #30, Phone Interview, October 2002).

Unfortunately, an approach to neutrality that validates false assumptions about who falls into the populations under an organization's mandate undermines a second humanitarian principle, *impartiality*, which requires "human rights and humanitarian organizations [to] conduct protection activities not on the basis of race, national or ethnic origin, language, or gender" (Caversazio 2001, 19). Impartial humanitarian action demands equal protection of all victims on the basis of need. But the exigencies of maintaining access to civilian populations often require a language that ensures belligerents' ease, and this can necessitate a *partial* approach. When aid organizations adopt gendered language to maintain access, they legitimize the neglect of civilian men and boys as deserving of protection or aid.

Maintaining Media Alliances

The most important political ally for the humanitarian relief community in general, and civilian protection advocates in particular, is the global media. Humanitarian and human rights organizations "need the material and moral support of the public if they are to act freely and effectively... the reactions of governments and the UN to major crises are inextricably bound up with public opinion" (Braumann 1993, 149). Particularly in the case of acute crises such as famine, epidemic or massive refugee flows resulting from armed conflict, the influx of resources to provide for afflicted populations depends on media attention (Moeller 1999).

Advocates for the protection of civilians in times of war – both humanitarian workers and those journalists who might themselves be considered "inside" the network[9] – therefore have an interest in attracting media coverage of the areas in which crises are most severe. Well aware that news coverage will drive donations to agencies as well as, possibly, a resolution to crises, achieving both their moral and organizational goals depends on it. Many humanitarian agencies have established extensive public relations departments whose primary role is to serve as liaison with the press. "Relief agencies depend on us for pictures and we need them to tell us where the stories are," a BBC correspondent covering Somalia once said (quoted in Moeller 1999, 108). Thus, while relief agencies are often frustrated by journalists, who ignore certain crises and sensationalize others, they are also dependent on the media and exert a powerful influence over it (Rosenblatt 1996, 130).

Media narratives of humanitarian emergencies aim to parse complex events into a simplistic frame that will capture the attention of an audience (typically that of Western donor states) that is generally ignorant of and apathetic to world affairs. Braumann (1993, 150) argues that a persuasive emergency story must involve "scene-setting" appropriate to the capacity of Western viewers to respond: "pictures, not words… an isolated upheaval… a personality or volunteer from a humanitarian organization to 'authenticate' the victim."

The roles ascribed to women and children in these media dramas are invariably the starving widow, the disheveled rape victim, and the refugee columns of elderly women in kerchiefs (Ignatieff 1998, 294). The recent Hollywood film *Wag the Dog* articulates this theme vividly, as film producers conspiring with the government to provide media representations of a fake "humanitarian war" work to generate just the right image of a blond, blue-eyed female victim, holding a cat, to symbolize the entire besieged foreign population. "Images of victim girls function as political symbols," writes

---

9 I am thinking of those war correspondents who have tirelessly risked or given their lives to keep the situation of war-affected civilians in the news or to draw international attention to specific hotspots. These are the authors who, frustrated by the inefficacy of their work in Bosnia, then wrote and published extensive memoirs on the politics of humanitarian action (for example, Neuffer 2002); those like Roy Gutman and David Reiff whose well-timed exposes actually protected civilians and whose efforts have included public information campaigns (Gutman and Reiff 1999); and individuals who have consistently placed the protection of actual war victims above their own professional interests (for example, Ricchiardi 2001). These are to be contrasted to self-serving journalists interested primarily in selling stories, such as the journalist who took a Pulitzer-winning photograph of a starving Sudanese toddler being stalked by a vulture, but who did not pick up the child.

Advocating for Civilians 111

Nordstrom, "as policy justification, as military propaganda to engender nationalist loyalties, and to call people to arms" (1999, 65). According to Moeller (1999, 234), television coverage of Rwanda, "showed the dead, preferably in large piles, and the hollow-eyed survivors, *preferably women and children*, although men and children or just gaunt men alone were also shown."[10] More often, men are pictured as the perpetrators of violence, the roving bands of warlords ransacking relief convoys or those with the machetes and light arms (Jones 2002a). Describing the Western response to Rwanda, a *Washington Post* reporter wrote: "Women and children were hacked to pieces by machete-wielding gangsters who reveled in the gore…" (quoted in Moeller 1999, 222).

Such gender archetypes are not surprising: as Braumann argues in his list of criteria for engineering "international events," an important requirement for eliciting sympathy is the construction of a victim who is "spontaneously acceptable to Western viewers in his or her own right" (Braumann 1993, 150). Acceptability is dictated foremost by "100 per cent victim status" – the symbolic victim must be seen as entirely lacking agency; s/he must be both unable to help her/himself and an unequivocal non-participant in the political events from which his/her misery results (Braumann 1993, 154). In short, the victim must be unambiguously "innocent." As former *Boston Globe* correspondent Tom Palmer said, "People being killed is definitely a good, objective criteria for whether a story is important. And innocent people being killed is better" (quoted in Moeller 1999, 34). Because adult men and boys may be viewed as "potential participants" in any society, journalists assume evidence of male victimization will elicit less sympathy and therefore sell fewer stories; women make better symbolic victims, especially in wartime, precisely because they – either as dependents or as mothers of helpless children – can be seen as innocent.[11]

Given its interdependence with the global media, how have actors in the civilian protection network responded to this tendency to simplify and distort? Generally, they have also elected to craft these simplistic frames or "synecdoches" (Ignatieff 1998, 194). With respect to Western publics, the aim is not to educate about complex realities, but to generate public sympathy, donations and (perhaps) political will for multilateral intervention (Shiras 1996, 97). According to Hammock and Charny (1996, 130), "just as the media continue to rely on stereotypical images, so the relief agencies continue to perpetuate the images of helplessness and despondence among the beneficiaries of the work." Foreign aid bureaucracies in major donor states

---

10 Italics added by author.

11 Occasionally men stand in for women in images such as the man holding an infant that became emblematic of Hussein's attacks on the Kurds of Halabja (Moeller 1999, 287); or signify a narrative, such as that of the Holocaust (represented by male prisoners in Bosnia) which invokes reaction in its own right.

112 'Innocent Women and Children'

even hand out guidelines to disaster workers on how to relate stories to the media: "Keep it simple. Simplify and summarize your major points... remember that the audience is the general public" (OFDA 1994, I-4).

Not surprisingly, these simplified frames often include gender essentialisms designed to resonate both with journalists' repertoire of narratives and with the mass public. A UNICEF official put it this way: "It's in many people's best interests to maintain [the association of women and children with civilians]. Think of the media, who create many of our visions and images of such situations. They want a story and the story is about the relationship between good and evil, it's about bad men with guns and good, innocent, women and children who suffer and they are starving and raped. It's a hell of a story. You don't want to complicate it" (Respondent #30, Phone Interview, October 2002).

Thus, both in framing particular crises and in representing war-affected civilians as a general population, protection network actors often represent them as a mass of women and children in particular trouble (Enloe, 1993). During the breakup of the former Yugoslavia, UNHCR skillfully deployed its newly formed public relations wing to court the media, both in drawing attention to the crisis and carving out a space for itself as the lead agency in the region (Loescher 2001, 290). Documents released by the UNHCR External Relations Unit to the public highlighted the agency's efforts to assist women and children, and officials enjoined the international community to protect the "innocent women and children" of Bosnia in statements to the press, governments, and international assemblies (for example, UNHCR 1994a; UNHCR 1994b; UNHCR 1998; UNHCR/UNICEF/WHO, 1992). One read: "As in all conflicts, those most affected are the innocent: women, children, the disabled and the elderly" (UNHCR 1992a), 10). In a letter to the Secretary-General encouraging the 1993 evacuation of civilians from Srebrenica, Ogata wrote: "Civilians, women, children and old people, are being killed, usually by having their throats cut" (quoted in Sudetic 1998, 175). Special Envoy Jose Mendiluce also stated, "The whole point of this war is to direct as much of the violence as possible against women and kids" (quoted in Reiff 1995, 201).

These statements, while perhaps helpful in attracting international attention to the crisis, obscured the complexity and nature of the political violence. In fact, women and younger children were the least likely in general to be killed at close range, and were more often raped and subjected to deprivation and displacement, or indiscriminate attacks such as shelling. The civilians most likely to be taken aside for slaughter were adult men and older boys (Honig and Both, 1997). When international bodies moved to condemn the atrocities, however, they responded not to the empirical realities but to the frame provided by the protection network: "The conflict in the former Yugoslavia is marked by ethnic cleansing and barbarous

Advocating for Civilians

violence against civilians, in particular women and children" (Council of Europe 1993).

Appealing to Donors and Transnational Publics

Besides utilizing the media as an indirect agenda-setting mechanism, the civilian protection network engages directly with donor governments and with transnational civil society, as a site for both fundraising and norm-building. Donor governments are encouraged to provide financial resources for humanitarian actors and, having identified themselves as members of the network through their donations, to play an economic and military role in protecting civilians when necessary. Individual citizens are called upon to send money for blankets, food and other relief programs, and to pressure their governments to take a stronger stand with respect to an issue. Transnational appeals of this sort work by appealing to moral sensibilities (both principled and causal) to invoke action.

As Joachim notes, one way that transnational networks appeal to moral ideas is to establish a frame that resonates with the widest and most diverse set of actors possible. The mobilization of a heterogeneous international constituency can increase the legitimacy of a frame by "making it more difficult for opponents to discredit it as representing the interests of only certain groups [and] enabling NGOs to exert pressure at different levels and with different tactics" (Joachim 2003, 252). The ICRC engaged in such cross-sectoral mobilization when it conducted its *People on War* survey in 1999. The survey, which "allows [the] voices [of] people who have experienced war... to be amplified and heard in the councils of nations" involved interviewing tens of thousands of people from all backgrounds, both combatants and civilians, in twelve war-torn countries and several "Security Council" countries, and disseminating the results at various levels within international society (ICRC 1999a). The data was useful to the ICRC in fashioning its own advocacy efforts with respect to communities in war-torn societies themselves (Harroff-Tavel 1998), but also in enhancing its transnational claim that humanitarian law, in particular the civilian immunity principle, is widely – or as the ICRC puts it, "universally" – recognized as legitimate.

Such efforts are often shaped by the perception within the network that the protection of women and children is even more indisputable than the protection of civilians in general, both because gender norms governing protection of "women and children" seem universal, and because of widely held assumptions that women and children are "objective" non-combatants (Respondent #33, Personal Interview, August 2002, Geneva). Whereas intervening in civil wars (or promoting women's empowerment) can be seen as the deeply politicized processes they are, "protecting women and children, well nobody can argue with that" (Respondent #4, Personal Interview, July 2002, Washington, DC). The gendered aspects of the immunity norm are "amplified" so as to resonate with individuals' sense of familial obligation, and draw attention away from possibly divisive moral arguments about agency and neutrality, which are nonetheless an intricate part of the protection network's activities on the ground (Snow et al. 1986).

Frame amplification is used to encourage action as well as to broaden the legitimacy of a frame. Activists frame an issue in such a way as to provoke a response: a check in the mail, a letter to an elected official, an interventionist force. They are faced with distinguishing their cause among the litany of appeals that potential "conscience constituents" will receive, and with overcoming the pervasive denial that afflicts donor populations (Cohen 2001; Moeller 1999). Frames are amplified when they are "clarified or invigorated to bear on a particular issue" (paraphrasing Snow et al. 1986). According to these authors, both principled and causal beliefs can be amplified in order to enhance the resonance of a particular frame.

Rhetoric on civilian casualties within the network is calculated to affect constituents' sense of moral urgency (principled beliefs) as well as their empirical understanding of the current situation (descriptive beliefs). By claiming that most of the affected are women and children, the appeal is designed to invoke unconditional sympathy and response. By claiming that the severity of the situation is new, unprecedented, a break from the normality of the past, a sense of urgency is conveyed, along with a sense that things can again be "put right."

The appeal distorts the frame because it is empirically specious. It reifies the association of women but not men with civilian status. More misleadingly, it suggests that of all adult civilians, women are *most* likely to be singled out for attack: "Civilian women are the primary victims of modern-day warfare," reads the Midterm Review of the 2000 Consolidated Inter-Agency Appeals, publicized by the UN Office of the High Commissioner on Human Rights (OHCHR 2000, 2). This is the view that has been internalized and reproduced at the Security Council:

> The most vulnerable in society – women, children and the elderly – are often targeted and deprived of the most basic human right, the right to life. (UN 1999a, 14)

> Among the civilians who bear the brunt of such conflicts are women and children, the most vulnerable groups. They are targeted for physical elimination and abuse. (UN 1999a, 18)

> Civilians have thus become the first and main target in armed conflict. Women, children, the elderly, the sick refugees and internally displaced persons have been attacked in large numbers. (UN 1999b, 3)

But as previously described, available data show that civilian men and older boys are more likely to be *directly* killed in war or civil strife (Goldstein

2001; Jones 2000); women and younger children are particularly affected by conflict's long-term, *indirect* effects, in part because they tend to be disadvantaged socially during reconstruction (Cockburn and Zarkov 2002; Gardam and Jervis 2001; Meintjes, Pillay and Turshen 2001), in part because they are more likely to survive the immediate conflict period (Ghobarah, Huth and Russett 2003) to suffer in the aftermath. By conflating these factors, "women and children" are framed as the primary "targets" of armed violence, obscuring sex-selective targeting of men and boys.

The use of numbers to suggest a drastic rise in proportions of civilian deaths is also questionable, as the Indian delegate to the Security Council pointed out in the 1999 debates, citing centuries of atrocities against colonized populations (UN 1999b, 16-19).[12] The current statistics include deaths from indirect and long-term causes, which have usually been excluded from casualty counts of earlier periods to which they are being compared. It also suggests civilian *fatalities* have increased rather than *casualties* in the broad sense of dead, injured or displaced, but many of the still living seem to actually be factored into the current estimate, exaggerating the novelty of the current situation compared to the past (Small and Singer 1982; Smith 1994, 2; Wood 1968, 24, cited in Beer 1981, 37).[13] This frame produces the appearance of drastically rising civilian casualty rates. But as Frohardt, Paul and Minear write (1999, 17): "Data does not substantiate the view that civilians are increasingly being targeted by belligerents."

So why does this view persist? While distorting, it presumably appeals to constituents' immediate sense of urgency and agency: if wars were once "civilized," perhaps they can be so again. It is reiterated strategically to the public by figureheads of protection agencies, even as those same agencies' statistical divisions produce empirical data contradicting the public

---

12 Notably, his references to scholarly data on the issue and his reminder that "women are also under arms" did not substantively alter the discourse at the debates, which continued to reiterate the standard tropes.

13 Sadowski, citing only secondary source (Ahlstrom 1991, 57) claims: "During World War I, civilian casualties constituted 14 percent of all deaths. During World War II, the percentage of civilian deaths skyrocketed to 67 percent of the total... Since World War II, the share of civilian deaths has been rising for all types of warfare." He then interprets the long-term effect of UN sanctions on Iraqi children over the ten years after the end of the first Gulf War as "a civilian death share of 95%" for the Gulf War itself. But the death rates from epidemics, famine, disease and pogrom are excluded from much of the early-20th century data: if factored in, the World War I civilian death rate would have been much higher and the gap in civilian/military ratios over time much smaller. For example, Wood's 1968 appraisal of World War I military v. civilian casualties, cited in Beer (1981, 37) included only civilians "killed or died from injuries" but does not factor in deaths from epidemic or deprivation. By these criteria, the post-Cold War civilian to military death ratio would be much lower.

116 *'Innocent Women and Children'*

statements. For example, in the same year that the ICRC published a report stating that only 35 per cent of weapons injuries it had treated since 1991 were women, children under 16 and men over 60 (ICRC 1999b), the President of the ICRC told the Security Council:

> The ICRC is faced today with 20 open conflicts the world over, in many of which civilians are the first and principal target. Women, children, the elderly, the sick, refugees and internally displaced persons have been attacked in large numbers and methodically driven from their homes. (UN 1999h, 2-3)

Alleged refugee numbers have similarly been disseminated by public relations divisions of humanitarian agencies and by the media, so as to appeal to moral sensibilities. In September 1992, UNHCR's Assessment Mission Report on the situation in the former Yugoslavia claimed that "the overwhelming majority of displaced persons are children (50 percent), women (30 percent), and the elderly and disabled (10 percent)" (UNHCR Update 1992b). Such data is useful in calls for appeals but of little use in programming or understanding the gender balance in the context. Is an elderly woman counted as a woman or as an elder? Exactly where are the men? Although more systematic data is now available from UNHCR's Population Data Unit (see UNHCR 2001a), as Crisp (1999) notes, few journalists, public relations officials, women's rights advocates or scholars seem to be asking these questions.

The political association of refugee numbers with "women and children" generally abstracts away from the issue of missing men where it exists, as in Bosnia (UNHCR 2000b). According to official UNHCR statistics, however, the oft-repeated statistic "80% of the world's refugees are women and children" is more often simply wrong or, at best, meaningless. Women may be over-represented in some camp populations, but are under-represented among asylum-seekers in Western and Central Europe (UNHCR 2000a).[14] An official from the Population Data Unit at UNHCR pointed out that all females plus males under 18 would make up a majority of *any* population: "There wouldn't be a population person in the whole world, a demographer or a head of statistics office or a head of census who would issue a statement saying that 75% of the population in the US was women and children – not that it wouldn't be accurate, but that they don't see the point" (Respondent #24, Personal Interview, September 2002, Geneva).

To bureaucrats in the Population Data Unit and Evaluation and Policy Unit of UNHCR, the misuse of data is an irritant; to officials in the Donor

---

14 This under-representation is due to well-documented gender-based barriers to women seeking asylum, such as a hesitancy to consider gender-based violence a form of persecution, and some women's difficulties in producing identity documents distinct from those of male family members. See Goldberg 1995; Baines, 1999; Mertus 2000.

Advocating for Civilians   117

Mobilization and External Relations Unit, it is a moral resource (Respondent #33, Personal Interview, August 2002, Geneva). One respondent told me s/he receives frequent calls from journalists and activists wanting to cite the percentage of female/child refugees globally. "I ask what kind of children do you want, what do you mean by women, women of all ages, women above a certain age, for example, and then there's a silence…The facts are often not paid attention to because the message is more important" (Respondent #24 2002).

UNHCR's 2000 Report directly refuted the statement that there exist more female than male refugees. "From a statistical and demographic viewpoint, there appears little reason to combine the two groups [women and children] into one statistic"; and suggested furthermore that "combining the two is unsuitable for programmatic reasons" (USCR 2002). But the availability of this data has not affected the use of the "women and children" rhetoric in describing refugee populations. "The message" *is* "the point." The candor with which public relations officials at UNHCR spoke with me about their use of these distortions indicates both their cognizance that the facts are misleading and the inter-subjective acceptability of distorting evidence to generate political action.

It is not entirely clear whether such frame distortions are actually required to generate donor sympathy. There is little systematic research on whether states and citizens actually *do* respond better to gendered imagery of civilians than to gender-neutral appeals (Cohen 2001, 169; Harff 1987).[15] However, it does seem that the protection community assumes such a connection. The ICRC's *People on War* study explicitly compared responses to a scenario in which "civilians" were said to be targeted with the same question where the wording was changed to "women and children." They noted a near-identical response to the two questions. The survey analysts had clearly expected that the term "women and children" would generate different results, and interpreted the lack of a gap as demonstrating that "specific protections for women and children have dissolved" (ICRC 1999, 8).

This example tells us very little about how gender affects the thinking of transnational constituencies,[16] but a great deal about the expectations thereof by the protection advocates conducting the survey, and the impact these

---

15 Harff's (1987) study on how students ranked human rights violations in terms of severity and obligation to intervene suggests that the age and gender of victims may be less important than the brutality and cruelty of killings and the graphic manner in which they are portrayed. Cohen (2001) and Moeller (1999) also describe various factors in addition to gender that bear on whether humanitarian appeals issue a response.

16 It is possible that the near-identical response reflected the respondents' failure to draw any distinction between the category "civilian" and the category "women and children," which would be consistent with the operation of the gender sub-norm.

118 *'Innocent Women and Children'*

expectations have on network framing strategies. "If we look at civilians in general, people are more willing to cross the line than when you say women and children," an ICRC staff-person associated with the *People on War* project told me (Respondent #3, Personal Interview, May 2002, Geneva). Whether or not it is empirically founded, network activists believe that successful advocacy hinges on emphasizing that "women and children" are the beneficiaries of civilian protection (Cohen 2001, 183). When asked about whether to highlight civilian men and boys as a "vulnerable group," participants at the ICRC's Seminar on the Protection of Special Categories of Civilian responded: "I don't think it's a good strategy. I wouldn't do that" and "If you suggest a program for 'vulnerable men' no one will fund it."

Cultivating Network Partnerships

A final important institutional pressure on the civilian protection network's mobilizing strategies has been the need to align its discourse with "partners" – activists working on overlapping issues, whose frames might either clash with and undermine, or coalesce with and mutually support, those of the protection network. Beginning in the early 1990s, when women's advocates linked women's rights to the human rights frame, one of the most important such strategic "partners" in the transnational human rights network has been women's advocates (Respondent #5, 2002). Humanitarian organizations are now under both activist and donor pressure to demonstrate what they are doing for women, and this pressure provides an additional incentive to de-emphasize civilian men in their discourse or as programmatic targets (Respondent #15, Personal Interview, August 2002, Geneva).

Like the protection of civilians, women's issues have been on the international agenda for some time (Penn and Nardos 2003; Steinstra 1994), but in the early 1990s both issues were redefined in a way that catapulted them to prominence at the level of international institutions. This process of reformulation coincided with a general shift in the "global security" agenda to encompass concerns such as the environment, refugees and humanitarian affairs (Joachim 1998, 147). Civilian protection advocates joined with other human rights groups to argue that massive violations of human rights constituted a threat to global stability and security (Roberts 2001; McRae 2001). Women's advocates, concerned with the marginalization of women's issues by mainstream human rights groups, reframed women's rights *as* human rights (Bunch 1990) by focusing on the issue of violence against women (Keck and Sikkink 1998). Departing from an earlier and more controversial emphasis on political and economic rights, this campaign emphasized the ways in which "peacetime" often renders women insecure and sought to link the personal security of all individuals, including women, with international peace.

Advocating for Civilians 119

Although civilian protection and women's human rights are quite distinct as issue areas, they overlap both empirically and conceptually. While not all war-affected women experience armed conflict as civilians, the majority do, and they face specific issues both as civilians and as women (Gardam and Jervis 2001; Lindsey 2001). From the perspective of civilian protection advocacy, while not all civilians are women, a large percentage of them – as in any population – are, a percentage that rises if they are conflated with the category "children." Violence that is specific to civilian women in time of war constituted a focal point around which both networks mobilized conjointly in the early 1990s.

As noted above, the civilian protection network strategically framed civilian women as the primary victims of war as part of a general strategy to draw greater attention and resources to civilians in general. For women's advocates, the emphasis on war-affected women was part of a strategy to promote women's human rights in general, rather than those of civilians (Joachim 1998; Penn and Nardos, 2003; Thompson, 2002). As Keck and Sikkink describe (1998, 195), of all issues affecting women's human rights, women's advocates successfully seized upon "violence against women" because it was an issue that could unite a broad constituency.

While not all women who experience gender-based violence are war-affected, the problem of violence against women in armed conflict became a potent symbol for the broader problem of violence against women (Barstow 2000c, 238-239), which then epitomized the claim that the international community must take seriously the human rights of women (Respondent #5, August 2002). Widespread outrage over reports of mass rape in Bosnia provided a proximate political opportunity (Joachim 1998, 156): the Bosnian Muslim rape victim came to symbolize the plight of civilian women in war, at the hands of male (Serbian) soldiers (Slapsak 2001; Zarkov 1997).[17] Thus, while violence against women is only one problem on the women's network's agenda, and while war-affected women is only one small subset of that problem,[18] it coincided with the emerging emphasis on war-affected populations to become emblematic of the need for greater international attention to both sets of issues.

The emergence of the violence against women frame coincided with the opportunities and mobilization strategies seized upon by civilian protection advocates. Civilian protection advocates correctly recognized that, at an empirical level, addressing the needs of civilians meant taking

---

17 Many protection officials I spoke to cited the mass rapes in Bosnia as a catalyst in humanitarian practitioners' awareness of the plight of war-affected women.

18 Violence against women is defined very broadly and is understood to encompass family violence, honor crimes, harmful cultural practices such as bride burning and female genital mutilation, sexual violence and exploitation, and sex-selective abortion, among other practices. See Penn and Nardos, 2003, chapter 1.

120   *'Innocent Women and Children'*

women's concerns into account, in particular by (selectively) listening to and validating the concerns raised within the women's network (Respondent #29, 2002; see also Rehn and Sirleaf 2002). But moreover, at an ideational level, the increasingly successful women's movement represented a mobilizing resource for attention to "civilians," particularly to the extent that the civilian population continues to be conceptualized primarily as a women's sphere. Likewise, as Thompson relates, the international women's network actively sought to cultivate relationships with mainstream human rights groups and to influence and transform their discourses. "Human rights NGOs became part of the transnational network around women's human rights, contributing significantly to information development and exchange in the area of state practices" (Thompson 2002, 106). Drawing greater attention to "women and children in armed conflict" rather than civilians per se was the programmatic aim of women's advocates, and they worked actively with organizations in the civilian protection community to achieve this goal. In a 2000 briefing to the UN Department of Public Information, the Special Advisor on Gender Issues and the Advancement of Women praised a "linked awareness" between the women's movement and multilateral advocacy for the "protection of women and children in armed conflict" (UN DPI 2000). Organizations such as WCRWC also actively supported sex-specific protection initiatives such as the "United States Women and Children in Armed Conflict Protection Act of 2003" (WCRWC 2003).

The connectivity between women's network frames and those of the civilian protection network is evident throughout the post-Cold War era. In the early 1990s the discourse of women's activism on war-affected women dovetailed in key respects with the civilian protection network's focus on "women and children" as innocent victims of violence perpetrated by men. Both the Vienna Tribunal and the 1995 Beijing Conference, occurring in the aftermath of the Rwandan genocide, focused almost exclusively on women as *civilian* victims of war, despite some women's participation in both the Bosnian conflict and the Rwandan genocide: "Those making the war are not women, however those being raped, yes, we are women," lamented the judge appointed to hear the cases at the tribunal (quoted in Barstow 2000b, 236). Scholarship on war-affected women during this period also tended to emphasize women as civilian victims, and as particularly vulnerable to political violence (presumably in comparison to men).

> Women and children, in particular, are victims of widespread and apparently random terror campaigns by both governmental and guerilla groups in times of civil unrest or armed conflict. (Charlesworth, Chinkin and Wright 1996, 267)

> Civilians – women, children and elderly men – are often the targets in [ethnic] conflicts. (Mertus 2001, 21)

Advocating for Civilians 121

Women's advocates have often been reluctant to highlight women's roles as agents of political violence or war crimes against men, children or other women.[19] Part of this stems from a fear that acknowledging women's agency will reduce international leverage on their behalf as victims; and that acknowledging men as victims will draw hard-won resources away from women.[20] Moreover, because women's advocates have understandably focused on the human rights of women, they have tended to avoid addressing the victimization of civilian men in armed conflict, except insofar as it affects women. Therefore:

> Women are often forced to witness the brutal torture or murder of loved ones… Minka watched out of the bushes as her father was murdered. They killed him and then cut him in pieces with a yard axe… (Bunch and Reilly 1994, 40)

> As a result of the genocide, many women lost male relatives on whom they previously relied for economic support and are now destitute. (Human Rights Watch 1996, 2)

> Women have always been the primary victims of war. Women lose their husbands, their fathers, their sons in combat. (Hilary Clinton, 1998, quoted in Jones 2000, 91-92)

The use of such frames among women's advocates has both reinforced and provided a disincentive for the protection network to challenge gender essentialisms associating women and children with civilian victim-hood and men with armies. Officials in the protection units of major protection organizations often cited the activity of the women's network as crucial in their understanding of how to protect war-affected women; others felt constrained by the need to legitimize their work on behalf of "women and children" by appealing to the concerns of women's advocates.

> In the media women and children are often mentioned, especially if there are casualties, children who have died in the conflict. In UNHCR we often do use it as well. And I think it is linked to the way in which within the organization we are struggling to mainstream gender in our operations, and it's also linked to the fact that a lot of HCR staff members, and a lot of donors are really pushing women

---

19 Butalia (2001) and Mukta (2000) discuss the leverage the feminist activists have sometimes gained from defining women as a uniform victimized group, an assumption that their analyses of women's participation in communal violence demonstrate cannot be sustained.

20 Domestic feminist movements and literature have sometimes grappled with the same dilemma, as Gordon acknowledges in her study of family violence: "Defending women against male violence is so urgent that we fear women's loss of status as deserving, political 'victims' if we acknowledge women's own aggressions" (1997, 317).

122 *'Innocent Women and Children'*

and children all the time, and NGOs say we are still not doing enough for women and children. (Respondent #15, Personal Interview, August 2002, Geneva)

Some individuals in the gender units of these organizations, most of whom are drawn from the women's movement and are aligned with both networks, often justified the use of such essentialisms and specifically advocated against a focus on men as victims:

> I recognize our discourse is a bit outdated. But it's very difficult because as soon as you stop talking about women, women are forgotten. Men want to see what will they gain out of this gender business, so you have to be strategic. (Respondent #18, Personal Interview, August 2002, Geneva)

> If you have a situation in which women are already reasonably empowered and men are already reasonably prepared to cooperate, yes in that case you can get them together; in other places where there is complete oppression of women I think if you involve men there would be a danger that they hijack the process again and you've lost what level of achievement you've reached. (Respondent #21, Personal Interview, September 2002, Geneva)

In short, the protection network is institutionally and ideationally reliant on the international women's network in a way that constrains its ability or desire to challenge their discourses on civilian women. Protection agencies draw on women's organizations to provide professional expertise on women's issues, relieving them of the necessity of fully mainstreaming gender in their own programs. Data-gathering on women's issues is often delegated to partners, such as the Women's Commission for Refugee Women and Children (WCRWC), and gender experts to fill the few "gender focal point" positions in major protection organizations are gleaned from within the women's network, in lieu of a systematic mainstreaming process.[21] Moreover, protection agencies, who have often been accused of failing to adopt a gender-aware approach, look to the women's network to legitimize their attempts to improve their policies. Often this is assumed to be better served by emphasizing what they are doing for "women and children" than to work systematically at a "gender-aware approach," understood by most analysts as involving an awareness of gender as it affects both men and women (Anderson, Howarth and Overholt 1992; Benjamin and Fancy 1998, 10; Morris 1998, 3).[22]

---

21 Most of those whom I interviewed in the "gender unit" or "women's units" had a previous background specifically in broader women's issues, rather than broader protection issues.

22 Barbara Harrell-Bond told Doreen Indra in a 1998 interview: "No one believes that those outside feminist circles who talk about gender studies are actually including men or considering the dynamics of relationships between men and women" (Indra 1999, 56).

Advocating for Civilians 123

This results in both networks failing to address civilian men as victims in armed conflict. For the women's movement, men's victimization of one another is seen as simply beyond their mandate, except as this affects women. On the other hand, the mandate of the civilian protection network, which owes its attention to civilians per se, very much includes civilian men. Yet these advocates avoid the issue because they are invested in a discourse that associates civilians, innocence and vulnerability with everyone but the able-bodied adult male. Thus, while many interviewees readily – and often without prompting – rattled off a list of ways in which men and boys could be particularly vulnerable in armed conflict, few saw a politically realistic way to broach this problem at the level of official discourse.

Transnational networks' need for their frames to resonate with partners in overlapping issue areas would also explain why both sets of actors are moving in tandem beyond certain other gender essentialisms that both can agree are problematic. For example, in recent years, the tendency to cast women as vulnerable and helpless has been increasingly reframed among women's advocates (Rehn and Sirleaf 2002; Cockburn and Zarkov 2002, 17), with cascade effects on protection network discourse. A site for this reframing was Security Council Resolution 1325 on Women, Peace and Security, which emphasized the need to draw on women's capacities in peace-building efforts. Since then, protection network imagery of women has moved toward an emphasis on their strengths rather than simply their victimization. Consistent with calls from women's advocates, OHCHR's "Checklist for Integrating Gender and Human Rights" specifically asks practitioners and researchers to make sure that women are not simply being described as a "vulnerable group" or discussed only in connection with children (OCHCR 2000). A 2000 bulletin produced for OCHA by WCRWC reads: "Women are often seen only as victims of war. The reality is far more complex... women have an essential role to play in the resolution of conflict." The OCHA webpage on "Women and War" specifically refers to the agenda-setting role of the women's movement: "Recent trends by leading scholars and activists tend to emphasize women's strengths not their vulnerability. Women play a prominent role in rebuilding war-torn societies... women community leaders facilitate mediation and reconciliation." Between 1999 and 2003, references to women as a vulnerable group declined, and references to women as constructive actors in peace-building and post-conflict decision-making increased (see Table 4.1).[23]

---

23 These trends peaked in the year 2001, in which the Security Council passed Resolution 1325 on Women, Peace and Security and when women's groups arguably had a greater influence than before or since in shaping Security Council discourse.

Table 4.1 Change in number of references to vulnerability, peace, and decision-making, as a percentage of total number of references to women, PoC documents 1999-2003

	1999	2000	2001	2002	2003
W/Vulnerable	24.0	21.0	23.0	4.5	13.0
W/Peace	1.6	0	23.0	18.0	15.0
W/Decisions	0.8	0	2.0	4.5	3.0

This frame change was facilitated by the fact that it resonated in some respects with both networks' previous frames. The women's movement, while securing attention to violations of women's rights, also sought to empower rather than simply to "help" women. The notion of strong, maternal women as peacemakers resonated with conventional protection network gender discourses. Indeed, as several scholars have noted (Helms 2003; Lentin 1997b; Skjelsbaek and Smith 2001), women's putative peace-making skills are juxtaposed in this discourse to men's presumed belligerence, replicating the women-as-peacemakers/men-as-warriors discourse that underwrites the gender sub-norm.

The "women in peacemaking" frame has also continued to position women as civilians (Kinsella 2002). Some women's advocates have recognized that this frame too is problematic, in particular since it obscures the existence of female ex-combatants, who remain one of the most underserved populations in humanitarian assistance. Recent documents contributing to international discourse on women and armed conflict have begun to incorporate a recognition of women's belligerent roles alongside their capacities as peacemakers (Rehn and Sirleaf 2002; UNSC 2002; Lindsey 2001). However, these efforts are far from constituting an *emphasis* on women's roles as participants in armed conflict. The Secretary-General's study entitled *Women, Peace and Security* does specifically state in a number of places that "women and girls are also active agents and participants in conflict" and "it is important... not to generalize about 'women' as not all women work for peace" (UNSC 2002, 3 and 54). However, the study, commissioned by the Security Council, includes an entire chapter on women's peace-making activities without a corresponding chapter on women as agents of armed conflict. Similarly, the ICRC's "Women and War" study, while careful to mention that women may also be combatants (Lindsey 2001, 23-25), focuses almost exclusively on women's experience of war as civilians (Lindsey 2001, 33). Nonetheless, that women's advocates are adopting more nuanced language and carefully qualifying their generalizations may be having a gradual impact on broader protection discourse as well. While civilian protection tropes do continue to identify women as members of the civilian population, and while there are only six explicit references to women as combatants or ex-combatants in the entire dataset analyzed here, it is notable that OCHA's PoC webpage entitled "Armed Groups" (as actors involved in civilian protection) contains an image of female rather than male soldiers.

While representations of women in both networks are gradually shifting to include women's agency and their roles as perpetrators and facilitators of violence, men as victims of armed violence continue to lie largely outside of these frames. For example, the Secretary-General's study on *Women, Peace and Security* specifically critiques the tendency to cast women as a "vulnerable group," calling attention to two problems: the need to disaggregate essentialized vulnerable groups into different sectors, and the risk of overlooking women's capacities. A third problem, the obfuscation of civilian men's vulnerabilities, is not mentioned in this section of the study.[24]

I am not arguing that it is the responsibility of women's advocates to explicitly address wartime violence against men, or that a study on the issue of "women, peace and security" is the appropriate place to do so. The point made here is that while civilian men as victims tend to be justifiably absent from women's network frames, by extension (and much more problematically) they are also absent from the protection network's frames about vulnerable groups. To the extent that the protection network is institutionally and ideationally reliant on the international women's network in a way that constrains its willingness to depart from their frames about gendered wartime violence, this creates additional disincentives for norm advocates within the protection network to highlight civilian men as an underserved population.

Reframing "Vulnerability"?

The imagery through which the protection of civilians has manifested on the UN agenda remains profoundly gendered, despite the fact that most civilian protection advocates recognize the misleading and potentially destructive aspects of this imagery. Because the pre-existing civilian immunity discourse is gendered, and because of the particular strategic environment in which the civilian protection network finds itself, gender essentialisms have been reproduced within the framing processes of the network.

Given pre-existing cultural assumptions about the innocence and vulnerability of women and/with children, and the importance of resonating with such ideas in order to frame an issue in international society, the use of this language and imagery should come as no surprise. But it can also come at a cost. According to Michael Ignatieff (1998, 292), "Nothing is intrinsically

---

24 The study does, however, take note that men, as well as women, may be subject to sexual violence (UNSC 2002, 16); and while it is not explicit about the effects of armed violence on men, it does mention men and boys as members of the civilian population (p. 14).

126   *'Innocent Women and Children'*

wrong about this resort to fictions and simplifications. Dramatization only becomes problematic when the actors in our moral dramas stop playing the roles on which our identification with them depends." When certain women block relief convoys (Minear et al. 1994), butcher one another's children (African Rights 1995b) or engage in suicide bombings (Lindsey 2001), the gender essentialisms underlying the concept of "innocence" render the entire schema of non-combatancy problematic (Mukta 2000). Similarly, when adult men refuse to take up arms, relying on the international community to protect them as civilians, the gap between these gender essentialisms and the cognitive scripts actors must use in order to understand reality can be stretched.

The protection network is not wholly complacent about these implications. Many network officials I spoke with were quick to identify the neglect of civilian men as a problem, both for protection and for the broader process of building genuinely gender-aware approaches in humanitarian assistance:

> You see the pictures of the women and children and they're crying and they're pathetic and sad and everything else, but they're also alive, it was the men who were killed. (Respondent #30, 2002)

> Conscription's often an issue. Officially refugees were not allowed to cross the Afghani border into Pakistan last year, only "vulnerable" groups, only women and children. But in fact the men were perhaps the most vulnerable and the women themselves were most concerned about the men who had the risk of being conscripted to the Taliban at this time. (Respondent #15, 2002)

> I've got nothing against children... in any situation we should look at who has the worst problems. In some situations the worst problems are with children; in others the children have no problems, the worst off are men. (Respondent #1, 2002)

> I think it's a lot to do with communication. If you look at a lot of media reports, press releases talk about "including women and children"... I think we shouldn't do that. Because it gives the message that maybe people are less worthy of attention because they don't happen to be a woman or a child. (Respondent #5, 2002)

But these interviewees seemed either ambivalent about the possibilities of change, given institutional obstacles, or frustrated by the fact that their efforts at change had seemed fruitless.

> I think there's an obsession within the whole so-called humanitarian world about women and children... I have argued before in UNHCR and I often continue to argue that we rewrite our policy papers to change this... but it has been very much in vogue to talk about women, children and the elderly when you talk about vulnerable groups. (Respondent #22, Personal Interview, September 2002, Geneva)

If you want to challenge the idea that all women and children are vulnerable and all men are combatants: how would you package that idea and get it to journalists, public opinion, donor opinion? (Respondent #16, Personal Interview, August 2002, Geneva)

I think it's so easy to continue with that discourse on vulnerable and innocent – not for me but for many actors, UNICEF for example, it's important to get money, it's a discourse a lot of donors use – hammering UNHCR all the time about women and children, and I'm not always sure if they actually know what they're talking about, but it's easy to keep focusing on it. (Respondent #15, 2002)

Moreover, many other protection workers I spoke with saw the operational implications of this discourse to be minimal, the benefits to women and children and to gender-mainstreaming outweighing potential costs to civilian men. A representative of UNITAR, which trains UN peace-keeping staff on gender issues, said:

I think this is a very progressive way of looking at things. But as far as practical steps on the ground, I don't know... the training that we do is basically "women and children for beginners," it's nothing terribly sophisticated, and this is what they [civilian peacekeepers] need. In places we are training peacekeepers from Jordan, from Pakistan. To teach these people gender-mainstreaming while they can still burn their wives at home, you have to start with the old-fashioned concept of teaching that women should be protected. You have to look at the strategic situation. (Respondent #21, 2002)

It is likely that frame transformation would require some consensus within the protection community and within the women's network on the development of a common language that addresses civilian men's protection needs without undermining the emergent awareness of the way that women are affected by armed conflict. As the quotes above suggest, so far there is little evidence of such consensus, even within specific organizations. For example, while the ICRC's Women and War project is working hard to change the idea that women are always vulnerable and men are not, the ICRC's Protection Division has developed a distinction between the notion of "vulnerability" and "risk" that is designed primarily to create a means of discussing civilian men's and boys' needs in conflict situations *without* disrupting the gendered assumption that men are inherently "invulnerable" (Interview, ICRC Protection Officer, May 2002). Both types of efforts suggest a careful negotiation between the perceived need for frame transformation and a keen understanding of the strategic environment.

As previous scholars of norm change have emphasized, existing institutional discourses frame relevant issues in a particular way. These pre-existing frames exert an influence on norm entrepreneurs seeking to map new discourses upon old (Finnemore and Sikkink 1998). Once ideas are configured institutionally in particular ways, they "can have an impact even

128   *'Innocent Women and Children'*

when no one genuinely believes in them as principled or causal statements" (Goldstein and Keohane 1993, 20). Those interested in promoting a particular agenda may be tempted to engage in frame distortion to that end, even if the distortion itself undermines the moral logic of the cause. Moreover, those attempting to correct these "misframings" are also influenced by their presence and salience.

Even among the strongest advocates of "reframing" vulnerability, there is no agreement on *how* to designate adult males as "vulnerable." This is a semantic issue that has more to do with age-old gender discourses underwriting the state-system/war-system than with strategic maneuvering between the protection and women's networks. It is an issue that challenges the very gendered myths of protection on which the war-system rests (Tickner 2001). As one respondent put it, "Gender has always been understood as a women's issue. Is it men who do not want to see themselves as vulnerable?" (Respondent #3, 2002). Some are thinking pragmatically: how to draw attention to men and boys without radically altering the gender paradigm by which war is conducted? But others argue it is this gendered thinking that must be overcome.

Conclusion

The literature on transnational social movements has shown that powerful new ideas emerge and become salient primarily when they can be *and are* decisively linked to pre-existing ideational frames (Barnett 1999; Finnemore and Sikkink 1998; Klotz 1996; Lumsdaine 1993). Their chances of success can be affected by counter-frames, with which they compete in a highly contested normative context (McCarthy 1996; Meyer 1995; Rein and Schon 1993; Risse-Kappen 1994). Norm advocates in international society do not simply "bear" ideas unreflexively (Barnett 1999, 7) but deploy those norms (and sub-norms) as strategic tools to promote their own institutional and normative agenda.

I found that many actors within the civilian protection network were self-conscious in their use of gender discourse and saw its use as a form of principled strategic action. In order to build a broad constituency and to appeal to the presumed gender discourse among constituent groups, the network actors appropriate gender essentialisms as a means of framing the network agenda. The protection of civilians is framed as the protection of "innocent women and children." This discourse has been buttressed by the production of politically useful "facts" that are circulated throughout the protection network and international society. These "facts" bear on the particular vulnerability of women and children to war and a depiction of the problem as a particular feature of post-Cold War society requiring multilateral action.

Advocating for Civilians 129

The humanitarian community is driven by the demands of donor agencies within Western governments who are often beholden to ill-informed constituencies themselves reliant on essentialist discourses to make sense of their world (Aguire 2001; Ignatieff 1998). As a senior representative of World Vision once said, "You can't confuse the public with complex issues" (quoted in Girardet 1993, 46). Despite calls from within the network for higher standards of accuracy (Caversazio 2001), in a context where the media and donor governments favor attention to certain groups or programs, and in which protection organizations are resource-hungry, there is little incentive to alter public discourse if it means foregoing money for programs (Respondent #34, Personal Interview, August 2002, Geneva).

It is unclear whether this frame distortion is actually required to mobilize support, or to what extent it affects civilian protection itself. However, many network actors apparently believe the trade-off is a rational one. They subscribe to the prescription Braumann outlined in 1993 in his essay "When Suffering Makes a Good Story." Braumann emphasized a principled balance between the need to "exploit in the best interests of the victim the potential offered by the popular media" and "demonstrate that what they are doing is founded on principles more solidly based, and hence more demanding, than the appeals to emotions which are so tempting to exploit" (Braumann 1993, 158). Network actors have deliberately distorted their frame for strategic reasons, but they believe the benefits in international attention and resource mobilization outweigh the distortion. They believe they have struck that balance: "We describe in all our objectives particular attention given to women and children. But that doesn't mean we do not give attention to civilian men on the ground, it is whether we emphasize them or not" (Respondent #19, Personal Interview, August 2002, Geneva).

However, while more systematic evaluative research is warranted, available data does not support this optimistic view. A key point made at the ICRC's recent workshops on "Strengthening Protection in War" is that organizations' choices regarding the categories of people assisted will be influenced by the media and donors' proclivities, with a number of side effects, including the possibility that some victims will "fall through the cracks" (Caversazio 2001, 66). While a recent report from the Inter-Agency Standing Committee points out that draft-age men may face particular vulnerabilities, specific programs to address these problems are still lacking (IASC 2002, 175). The ICRC has collected information on "Women and War" but not on "Men and War." Though it is well known that belligerents perceive adult men as combatants, ICRC delegates who disseminate humanitarian law "do not put gender first in our dialogues with the authorities" (Respondent #1, 2002). An official at the US Office for Disaster Assistance in 2002 was unaware of a single assistance program targeting civilian men and boys as such (Respondent #4, 2002). As I describe in the next chapter, ideas are not *simply* symbolic tools: once repeatedly invoked they become part of the way organizations think, and can influence actor practices despite their own best intentions.

Chapter 5

Protecting Civilians in Conflict Zones: Evacuation Operations in the Former Yugoslavia

Larry. No men under sixty, OK?
UNPROFOR General Morillon to UNHCR Officer Hollingworth, Srebrenica, 1993

In the previous chapters I argued that a gender sub-norm exerts a *constitutive* effect on the way in which "civilian protection" rhetoric is deployed in international society. This chapter investigates the causal impact of such gender beliefs on the operational practices of humanitarian agencies. One of the most notable gaps in the framing of civilian protection discourse in the early 1990s was the invisibility of the adult male civilian. To what extent did this discourse exert regulative effects on the way in which protection operations were carried out in the same period? And if it did, in what ways did this intersect with the gendered interpretations of "civilian immunity" by belligerents, as outlined in Chapter 3?

I begin with a brief overview of humanitarian action in world politics, drawing connections between the way in which the protection of civilians is framed and the work that protection organizations actually do. I then make the case that the gender sub-norm can impact humanitarian operations by examining humanitarian evacuation as a protection tactic that emerged in the early 1990s. While protection can take many forms, humanitarian evacuation involves removing civilians from a besieged area in order to spare them the effects of battle (Elliott 1999).[1]

---

1   The term "humanitarian evacuation" has broader connotations. I limit my analysis to mass evacuations of groups from besieged cities, excluding the sort of ad hoc medical evacuation of sick or wounded individuals for which the Sarajevo airlift became famous. Medical evacuation deserves study in its own right, but the manifestations of the civilian protection regime are not likely to be as salient with respect to these operations. They are not strictly civilian protection operations, as war-wounded might also be evacuated. Nor are the subjective perceptions of risk and civilian status in which I am interested necessarily brought to bear in the case of medical evacuation, as the key criteria for these evacuations is life-threatening injury. It would be interesting to replicate this study in the area of medical evacuation, as there is some evidence that prioritizing even among wounded populations may

132   *'Innocent Women and Children'*

The puzzle investigated in this chapter is that, although adult civilian men and boys were the civilians most likely to be summarily killed if a besieged town falls, humanitarian workers typically evacuated only women, children and the elderly from such areas (ICRC News 1999; ICRC News 2001).[2] Tracing the emergence of this form of protection in the Balkan theater during the wars of the Yugoslav secession, I argue that an understanding of gender norms is required to explain such sex/age-selective evacuation procedures.

The analysis presented here is based on historical accounts and diplomatic records, supplemented with a series of in-depth interviews with former UNHCR and ICRC staff between May and December 2002. These organizations were the most actively involved in the former Yugoslavia during the period in question (Minear et al. 1994, 42). More importantly, UNHCR and the ICRC have also engaged in the greatest process of critical self-reflection and analysis regarding the ethics of humanitarian evacuation as a civilian protection mechanism (Caversazio 2001; ICRC 1995; UNHCR 2000b). They also represent hard cases for the neglect of civilian men's issues because of all protection organizations in the former Yugoslavia, UNHCR and the ICRC paid perhaps *more* attention to the plight of men than most (IASC 2002, 175). For example, UNHCR called attention to the forced *refoulement* of draft-age men from Croatia to Bosnia-Herzegovina (Minear et al. 1994, 20); and the ICRC's mandate to work with detainees meant it dealt actively with one key form of violence faced by adult men: detention in concentration camps (Berry 1997). When it came to the threat of sex-selective massacre, however, the response of both these organizations seems paradoxical.

A case study of the 1993 evacuation of Srebrenica illustrates the specific ways in which the gender sub-norm operated so as to exclude men and boys – arguably the most vulnerable civilians – from evacuation convoys. While many examples of humanitarian evacuation are mentioned, the case of the first Srebrenica crisis in 1993 is examined in greater depth for two reasons. First, as the most high profile mass evacuation, there is a fair amount of available evidence on which to base analysis. Second, I am interested in cases where protection workers had some agency in negotiating the terms of evacuation. Emphasizing Srebrenica does mean generalizability is limited: for example, Srebrenica was more politicized than other humanitarian operations, and was larger in scale than many other ad hoc evacuations (Respondent #22, 2002). However, the public nature of the evacuation poses an advantage in examining the manipulation of moral argument and the impact this had on decision-making behavior. Moreover, by tracing the logic

---

proceed according to gender rules (Frohardt, Paul and Minear 1999, 45; Hollingworth 1996, 216); but this is probably a different argument and I do not explore it here.

2   Similar reports from the Caucasus suggest this pattern may be generalizable, although my analysis is limited to the Balkans. See UNHCR Briefing Notes 1999.

Protecting Civilians in Conflict Zones 133

behind this evacuation, some tentative conclusions may be drawn about the conditions under which this logic might apply elsewhere.

Those interviewed included headquarters staff in both UNHCR and the ICRC, and protection workers formerly engaged in field operations in the Balkans between 1991 and 1995, including most of those involved in orchestrating the 1993 evacuation of Srebrenica.[3] A few additional interviews were held with personnel outside these agencies, in particular officials from OCHA and former UNPROFOR personnel. While this does not represent a cross-section of the organizations involved, the data gathered provides a useful supplement to the picture that emerges from written accounts. These interviews were constructed so as to gauge whether sex-selective evacuation strategies could be attributed directly to the gender sub-norm or to more complex strategic factors involved in negotiating access to besieged populations.

Practical Protection in Humanitarian Emergencies

So far this book has dealt with the "protection of civilians" as a set of ideas and moral discourses. But what does this look like in practice? According to one perspective, so long as belligerents uphold civilian immunity norms, the law itself protects (Sassoli and Bouvier 1999). Thus, for example, a number of books on the "protection of civilians" are primarily concerned with laying out the relevant law (Dongen 1991; Sandvik-Nylund 1998). Since belligerents have the responsibility to provide protection in the form of compliance with the law, one role played by humanitarian agencies is to persuade and facilitate warring parties' fulfillment of their treaty obligations. In the past, much protection work involved precisely these sorts of actions. For example, the original "protection" mandate for UNHCR involved legal oversight in countries receiving refugees to make certain that asylum claims were duly processed and asylum seekers' rights upheld (Loescher 2001); and much of the "protection" work engaged in by the ICRC involves quietly reminding belligerents of their responsibilities under the Geneva Conventions (Berry 1997).

But often these efforts are insufficient: compliance does not occur. Where the law is violated and thus affords protection only on paper, "practical

---

3   These include the UNHCR official who negotiated evacuation procedures with the Serb authorities at Srebrenica, the Sarajevo-based UNHCR official engaged in negotiations with the Bosnian authorities, and several UNHCR officials present for the evacuation operations themselves. At the time of this writing I have been unable to establish contact with a number of UNHCR officials who I am told were also involved. The most notable omission from the data set to date is Larry Hollingworth. However, a detailed account of the evacuation appears in his 1996 memoir, on which I have drawn extensively.

protection" must involve more pro-active measures (Caversazio 2001, 9; Frohardt, Paul and Minear 1999). Such activities then take the form of preventive or ameliorative initiatives, encompassing what Weiss and Collins refer to as "humanitarian action." According to these authors, examples of humanitarian action include "diplomacy, emergency relief, and rehabilitation and development projects, designed to alleviate suffering both in the short and long term and to protect human rights" (Weiss and Collins 1996, 219).

These forms of civilian protection emphasize persuasion, diplomacy and consent. They are to be distinguished from *coercive* measures aimed to stop further violations through the use of force and/or to punish perpetrators through post-hoc tribunals. For example, "humanitarian intervention" involves the use of *force* by a state or states not party to a conflict, for the purpose of protecting human rights or enforcing humanitarian law (Murphy 1996; Shi and Shen 2002; Wheeler 2000). In the post-Cold War era, both humanitarian intervention and war crimes tribunals have been implemented without the consent of the belligerents involved, but they often involve other political tradeoffs such as selective application. In the case of humanitarian intervention for example, it is never entirely clear whether saving lives is in fact the driving interest or merely the justification (Mertus 2001). Moreover, there are reasons to question the often indiscriminate use of military force as a tool of "civilian protection" (Crawford 2003; Roberts 1999a; Rogers 2000). Thus, although humanitarian intervention *may* ultimately protect civilians, this is not the same thing as "humanitarian action" in the sense described by Weiss and Collins.

A guiding principle of *non*-forcible humanitarian action (of which the protection of civilians is but a small part)[4] is neutrality: assistance should be given impartially to all victims, and humanitarians should avoid taking sides in a conflict (Kalshoven 1989; Bouchet-Saulnier 2002, 140-143).[5] In fact however, humanitarian action involves numerous political tradeoffs (MacFarlane 2000). Humanitarian agencies are constrained by the need to

---

4   The field of humanitarian action encompasses both assistance (the delivery of relief) and protection (the prevention of human rights abuses); both peace-time development and responses to acute crises (McRae 2001); and disasters both man-made and environmental (Prendergast 1996; Vaux 2001; West 2001). Civilian protection is a relatively small subset of the work the larger humanitarian community does, as it emphasizes war-affected populations specifically (Chesterman 2001; Weiss and Minear 1993).

5   The principle of impartiality is codified in Article 27 of the Fourth Geneva Convention of 1949 and Article 75 of 1977 Additional Protocol I, which states: "persons who are in the power of a Party to the conflict... shall enjoy, as a minimum, the protection provided by this Article without any adverse distinction based upon race, colour, sex, language, religion or belief, political or other opinion, national or social origin, wealth, birth or other status, or on any other similar criteria." Italics added by author.

Protecting Civilians in Conflict Zones 135

negotiate consent with the parties to the conflict. These negotiations often involve concessions or bribes, and nearly always are contingent on relief organizations' appearance of neutrality, occluding denunciation as a tool of drawing attention to human rights violations and sometimes channeling aid to those who do not need it as the price for getting it to others (Anderson 1999; Darst 2003). In the former Yugoslavia, for example, warring parties frequently insisted that equivalent aid be delivered to all ethnic groups, resulting in distribution on the basis of ethnicity rather than need (which was typically higher for some groups than others) (Cutts 1999; Mendiluce 1994).

Humanitarian organizations are simultaneously constrained by pressures from the donor community on whom they are dependent for resources. This pressure encourages the channeling of special assistance to groups deemed particularly vulnerable and to crises of which donor countries' publics are most aware (Caversazio 2001). Predictably, this leaves gaps in programming: "the traditional image of a needy child is a 3-year-old who needs food," lamented a UNICEF official at the ICRC's Seminar on the Protection of Special Categories of Civilian. "So what do you do with a 17-year-old who has committed atrocities? This is also a child in need of assistance." Similarly, the particular emergencies to which aid is channeled depend on the attention of the international community, which fluctuates with the times. This results in the complementarity problem, in which many organizations write grants for particular groups or develop projects in particular regions where donor capital is most concentrated, while others fall through the cracks (de Maio 2000). The intensity and character of the aid thus often reflects the whims of Western publics (Ignatieff 1998; Roberts 1999b). Donor fickleness also creates a demand for quick, visible results over longer-term, slower-yield projects (Weiss and Collins 1996).

Lastly, the behavior of protection organizations is influenced by their own organizational cultures. In the international market for assistance funding, organizations define their mandates and develop internal codes of conduct that both set them strategically apart from one another and define the parameters of their agenda (Snow 2003, 26-27; Cooley and Ron, 2002). Some, such as UNICEF, focus on particular groups; others, such as the World Food Programme (WFP), focus on particular forms of assistance (Bonard 1999). Organizations differ according to the modes of action in which they specialize: Human Rights Watch condemns violations of human rights; the ICRC works behind the scenes to persuade states to avoid such violations; while organizations such as World Vision work to materially alleviate the suffering caused by such violations through relief programs (Minear 2002, 76). Sometimes the "division of labor" between organizations accounts for actions not taken. One UNHCR official formerly deployed in the Balkans told me that UNHCR sometimes overlooked the issue of men's safety because that was assumed to be "the domain of the ICRC" (Respondent #22, 2002).

Finally, organizations differ measurably in their professional codes of conduct. The rift between the ICRC and UNHCR, competing for status as lead agencies during the Balkans crisis, exemplified these distinctions (Berry 1997; Minear et al. 1994). Members of the ICRC, with its culture of professionalism and neutrality, are careful never to break promises made with belligerents, in order to retain trust and access, even if this means abandoning certain vulnerable people in the short term. They are also less willing to make deals that undermine their professional principles. As UNHCR developed its operational policies in the context of a rapidly changing situation in the Balkans, its staff were much more willing to engage in "trickery" and to cut deals in order to save lives: "We think *we're* very principled," one former UNHCR field officer told me. "The ICRC has a different way of doing business" (Respondent #22, 2002).

The interrelationship of material circumstances with identities and values in shaping the behavior of humanitarian institutions is striking (Finnemore and Barnett 1999). The humanitarian community responds to *material* constraints imposed by the socially constructed interests of donors and the demands of warring parties, and to the *social* constraints of their own organizational context. In turn they work to alter the social context by framing humanitarian issues in their calls for appeals, in advocating with warring parties to protect war victims, and in following or redefining their own moral codes. All of these processes require the use of persuasion (Risse 2000; Payne 2001) and the deployment of moral authority (Hall 1997; Hurd 1999), and involve norm-based judgments about appropriate behavior given an actors' mandate and the political context (Jepperson, Wendt and Katzenstein 1996; Slim 1997). This is an environment in which norms – in conjunction with other factors – are likely to play an important role in producing specific outcomes.

How, if at all, does the gender sub-norm affect the way that civilian protection operations manifest on the ground? The evacuation of besieged civilians from cities is one form of protection operation that both exemplifies the various tradeoffs described above and demonstrates the way in which gender assumptions can distort the implementation of these broader norms.

An Empirical Puzzle: Humanitarian Evacuation in the Balkans

With the secession of Slovenia and Croatia from Yugoslavia on June 25, 1991, the Balkan wars began. These included a brief skirmish between Yugoslavia and Slovenia; a longer and bloodier war between Yugoslavia and Croatia; and a civil war within Bosnia-Herzegovina, which had declared independence in October 1991, backed by the Yugoslav National Army (JNA) upon orders from Belgrade (Burg and Shoup 1999).

Protecting Civilians in Conflict Zones 137

Although the fighting in Slovenia was quick and decisive, both the Yugoslav/Croat war and the war in Bosnia were marked by atrocity, and civilians bore the brunt of the violence. The heaviest fighting in Croatia took place in the Krajina region, contiguous with Serbia and densely populated by Croatia's now-persecuted ethnic Serb minority; and along the Dalmatian coast. Croats sought to drive ethnic Serbs eastward through terror tactics, and the JNA responded with siege warfare against Krajina border towns and coastal settlements (Rogel 1998).

The Bosnian Serb Army (BSA) under Radovan Karadzic was drawn into the war late in 1991 after Bosnia-Herzegovina announced its independence. In early 1992, with the war in Croatia winding down, Belgrade began to offer support to the BSA. Because the goal of the BSA was to create ethnically pure territory to remain a part of Serbia, and because the goal of Belgrade was to retain as much land as possible, a settlement was elusive and military tactics became increasingly genocidal (Cigar 1995). Although the BSA would probably have preferred that all Muslims leave voluntarily, when many preferred to fight or stick out the war, terror tactics – later euphemistically called "ethnic cleansing" – became the BSA's strategy of choice (Burg and Shoup 1999). As described in Chapter 4, towns were frequently surrounded, blockaded and besieged for long periods marked by the inhabitants' increasing deprivation, combined with the persistent threat of shelling. The worst atrocities took place after the fall of villages, however: at this time the population was typically either forcibly deported, detained or killed, often after torture, including rape (Honig and Both 1997).[6]

At the onset of the Balkan wars, protection agencies in the region did not have a specific mandate to evacuate civilians from towns per se (UNHCR 2000b).[7] Historically, the war-time evacuation of cities was carried out either by governments, as was the case in World War II, or by warring parties themselves, in accordance with regulations codified in the 1949 Geneva Conventions (Zelinski and Kosinski 1991). Since humanitarian law does provide for evacuating civilian populations from battle zones, there is some precedent under the law for humanitarian workers to assist in such operations (Bouchet-Saulnier 2002, 95-98). However, evacuation by aid agencies as a means of intervening to rescue civilians from the depredations of belligerents had little precedent until the early 1990s. Indeed, the two lead agencies in the region, the UNHCR and the ICRC, were initially engaged

---

6   Although the majority of the known rape victims during the wars in the Balkans were women (Allen 1996; Niarchos 1995; Stigalmeyer 1994), men were also sexually abused during the conflict (Zarkov 2001). In both cases, sexual violence must be understood as a form of torture and a tool of terror (Aafjes and Goldstein 1998).

7   The ICRC does customarily evacuate wounded and sick, civilians and combatants, from war zones as mandated by the First Geneva Convention. See Harroff-Tavel 1993, 195-220.

138   *'Innocent Women and Children'*

simply in the delivery of relief and monitoring and discouraging violations of humanitarian law, respectively (Berry 1997; ICRC 1995; Loescher 2001; Mendiluce 1994).

In the Balkan theater, however, it became increasingly unclear what "protection of civilians" meant in the context of ethnic cleansing tactics (Reiff 1995, 209). Thus, while the ICRC would often arrange for medical evacuations of the wounded (usually in exchange for prisoners elsewhere), mass evacuations of "vulnerable groups" developed only gradually as a response to this inability to protect civilians in situ (Minear et al. 1994).

Typically, protection agencies would be present during a siege for a separate reason. During the course of negotiations with belligerents, the option of removing certain civilians from the area would come up. Humanitarian workers then had to face a complicated choice, influenced by many contextual factors, as to whether to participate in the forced deportation of a civilian population, or to refuse to do so, leaving civilians exposed to the risk of death (UNHCR 2000b, 222). A few small evacuations had taken place early in the war. In some places this involved spur of the moment operations aimed at helping people escape prior to the approach of armed forces;[8] in others, it meant negotiating for a few women and children to get out along with wounded, space permitting. According to Mark Cutts of UNHCR:

> There were other cases where we didn't evacuate people, but told them that if they got to a certain road crossing we could pick them up and give them shelter... sometimes when it was organized locally by the people themselves, we would actually send vehicles to watch – it would seem like we were escorting, but in fact we were monitoring what was going on, driving behind them... we didn't want to be accused of taking people out. (Respondent #22, 2002)

Indeed, operations such as these were immediately controversial. In November 1992, after evacuating 8,000 persons from Bosanski Novi (UNHCR 1992c), High Commissioner Sadako Ogata described the dilemma as follows: "To what extent do we persuade people to remain where they are, when that could well jeopardize their lives and liberties? On the other hand, if we help them to move, do we not become an accomplice to 'ethnic cleansing'?" (quoted in UNHCR 2000b, 222). Yet as the war dragged on, the conundrum of feeding civilians so that they could continue to live under

---

8   Such evacuations were not always as politicized in terms of negotiating access to civilians. In the central Bosnian village of Ahmica in February 1993, UNHCR and UNPROFOR were able to offer transportation to anyone who chose to leave, just before the predominantly Bosniac town was overrun by Croat forces. According to the UNHCR protection official who coordinated the evacuation, "some people chose to go, some people chose to hide in quarries, some people stayed in their homes and got massacred" (Respondent #31, September 2002). The majority of adult men but also some women and older children had opted to stay.

Protecting Civilians in Conflict Zones 139

threat of bombardment was increasingly seen as unacceptable (Frohardt, Paul and Minear 1999, 62). Additionally, "helping people where they were" came to be viewed as a self-serving euphemism that protected European countries from meeting their obligations to provide asylum (Minear et al. 1994, 6).

By 1993, UNHCR had concluded that, controversy aside, helping desperate people to flee to safety was better than the alternative of forcing them to stay in a danger zone. As one UNHCR official put it, "Better to be accused of ethnic cleansing than to go in the village the day after and find bodies" (Respondent #31, 2002). But facing accusations of assisting ethnic cleansing, UNHCR sought to publicly legitimize its actions by emphasizing that only individuals facing an "acute, life-threatening situation" would be removed. "Our responsibility, as we see it, is to alleviate the suffering of vulnerable groups," read a UNHCR field report in December 1993 (UNHCR 1993, xii).

This emphasis on vulnerability of specific groups bears some explanation with respect to the lead agencies. While some organizations such as UNICEF are mandated to target protection toward specific groups, both UNHCR and the ICRC subscribe to the basic humanitarian principle of impartiality: their mandate stressed assisting all victims (Kalshoven 1989; Weller 2000). In cases where resources or opportunities were limited, however, the agencies would fall back on the "reverse-triage" principle of prioritizing the most vulnerable. A UNHCR field manual describes the relationship between these principles in the following words: "Humanitarian assistance should be provided without distinction. Relief must address the needs of all individuals and groups who are suffering, without regard to nationality, political or ideological beliefs, race, religion, sex or ethnicity. Needs assessment and relief activities should be geared toward priority for the most urgent cases" (Wolfson and Wright 1994, 7).

In the latter cases, the goal was to "determine on the basis of an assessment of needs and vulnerability as well as risks to which [civilians] are exposed" (Caversazio 2001, 67). According to Senior UNHCR Protection Officer Wilbert Van Hovell, these were the main criteria for evacuation in particular: protection officials should determine "whether the persons are in an acute, life-threatening situation weighed against various local constraints and possible adverse consequences" (quoted in Minear et al. 1994, 67).

But this emphasis on prioritizing those most vulnerable to death exposes an important puzzle with respect to evacuating towns, for as already demonstrated, those civilians in Bosnia most likely to lose their lives directly as a result of the fall of a besieged town were adult men and older boys. When the BSA took a town, military-age male civilians were typically separated from women, children and the elderly and executed while the latter were permitted to flee (Helsinki Watch/Human Rights Watch 1993).

140   *'Innocent Women and Children'*

This pattern was established early in the war and was blindingly obvious to both journalists (for example, Reiff 1995) and protection workers:

> When you talk about places like the Balkans, there are different kinds of vulnerability... men and boys are the most vulnerable to actually being killed, to actually being tortured and sent to be forcibly recruited... (Respondent #22, 2002)

> What they were interested in, all sides, was they didn't want anybody who could shoot at them getting free to the other side once they had their hands on them... So the operating assumption was that every able-bodied man was a fighter. Each side assumed that every able-bodied man of any other ethnicity was a hostile fighter or would be if he could get a gun. (Respondent #8, 2002)

> Men were seen as potential combatants – they could be cured and come back to fight again. Also perhaps the Serbs believed they deserved to die because they were the enemy. (Respondent #32, Phone Interview, October 2002)

Yet when humanitarian agencies later began to evacuate "vulnerable" civilians en masse from war zones, the evacuees were nearly always women, children and the elderly. Wounded and sick adult men were also often evacuated, particularly by the ICRC, as explicitly laid out in the Geneva Conventions (Mercier 1994; GCIV Article 49). However, able-bodied draft-age male civilians (precisely those civilians most likely to be killed or detained on suspicion of engaging in hostilities) were almost never given safe passage along with their families.

At least two different kinds of mass evacuation scenario occurred in the Balkans. Evacuations of women, children and the elderly during the fall of a town were sometimes carried out by the conquering forces themselves, and there was seldom room to negotiate terms at that point.[9] For example, in 1991 the ICRC arrived during the fall of Vukovar, an eastern Croatian town that had until then survived 80 days of shelling (Neier 1998). The Serb fighters were deporting women, children and the elderly, and killing or arresting the adult men, including many hospital patients (Stover and Peres 1998). ICRC delegates had been permitted in to evacuate wounded and sick from the hospital, but found that the Bosnian Serb forces did not honor the agreement. Rather, women, children and the elderly were being bussed away and both civilian and war-wounded men were being separated, detained and/or shot (Silber and Little 1996, 180). Although the ICRC delegates made efforts to

---

9   As former UNPROFOR officer David Harland explained, "In these cases, there were no able-bodied men to save, because the dominant part would have already dealt with them – either killed them or they ran away. The issue you are interested in, how either the belligerents or the humanitarians made the distinction between combatant/non-combatant, really only came up in the cases of the enclaves, rather than in areas that were actually being overrun" (Respondent #8, 2002).

Protecting Civilians in Conflict Zones

monitor what was happening to men as well as to protest the deportations, they were unsuccessful in preventing a massacre, and it is not clear what else they might have done. They limited themselves in the end to seeing through their mission with respect to the wounded and cannot reasonably be blamed for failing to intervene (Mercier 1994).

A similar situation occurred in 1995 when the eastern Bosnian enclave of Srebrenica was overrun by Serb forces. In this situation, the Dutch UN observers made more blatant errors. For example, they willingly supplied the Serb buses with petrol to evacuate the women and children; they turned adult male civilians who had taken shelter within their compound over to the BSA with certain knowledge of their fate; and they refused to return armaments to the Bosniacs that they might defend themselves (Harland 1999; Honig and Both 1997; Rhode 1998). Moreover, they failed to protect their local employees' families, and UNPROFOR Major Franken signed a document affirming that the evacuation had been carried out in accordance with the Geneva Conventions (Sudetic 1998, 322-23). In these ways they were certainly giving tacit legitimacy to the distinction that the BSA had drawn between the "civilians" (women and children) and the "war criminals" (military-age men) (Jones 2002a; Leeuw 2002; Rhode 1998). But with respect to the evacuation itself, it was neither organized nor carried out by UNPROFOR, and what attempts they did make to influence the demographics of the evacuees were unsuccessful.[10] Given their own extreme vulnerability and abandonment by the international community at a pivotal moment, it is not clear whether any actions they may have taken with respect to the evacuation alone could have saved the lives of most of the thousands who died. In short, the nature of these deportations, and the subsequent massacres, were determined primarily by the belligerents, who, due to military inaction by NATO, had complete control over the situation.

A second type of evacuation scenario suggests far more agency on the part of protection workers, and it is primarily this type that I have examined in some depth. "Pre-emptive" evacuations, such as Srebrenica in March 1993 and Zepa in 1995, present a different set of issues. For example, at Zepa, shortly after the fall of Srebrenica in July, several sets of agreements were concluded among the Zepa authorities, the Bosnian government in Sarajevo, the BSA and UNPROFOR regarding whether and how to evacuate the population in the event of a surrender (Harland 1999, 92-95). Initially, capitulation was perhaps imminent but not already underway. At this point,

---

10 For example, when the Dutchbat Commander requested three Bosniac civilian representatives to draw up their own evacuation plans, they opted to put "a small number of men on each of the buses… to ensure they were safely evacuated." See Harland 1999, 75. Ultimately, these plans were not implemented as promised by the BSA.

142 'Innocent Women and Children'

protection workers were offered a chance to evacuate women, children and the elderly but not draft-age men (Bosnian Action Coalition 1995).

Much concern was expressed by the Bosnian government and local authorities, as well as some observers in the wake of the Srebrenica massacre, about the terms offered by the BSA, which demanded that all draft-age men be taken prisoner, to then be exchanged back to Muslim territory (Rhode 1998, 328). Recognition by these parties of men's specific vulnerabilities was likely heightened by the fact that evidence of the Srebrenica massacre was just coming to light: this led to protracted negotiations aimed at safe passage for adult civilian men as well as other civilians and secondly, for fighters themselves (Respondent #8, 2002). However, UNPROFOR itself did not advocate for the men of Zepa either initially nor as surrender became inevitable (Harland 1999). Indeed, UNPROFOR officials in Sarajevo refused the Bosnian government's request that they guarantee adult men's evacuation to safety (Harland 1999, 95). Thus, as evacuations from Zepa began, men were excluded (Rhode 1998, 332).

This is remarkable considering what was already known about what had happened at Srebrenica a few weeks prior, although a former UNPROFOR official told me, "Zepa fell before the massacre at Srebrenica was really understood properly" (Respondent #8, 2002). In the end, the BSA was distracted from Zepa by events in Banja Luka and withdrew; most of the trapped men of Zepa survived by filtering out of the town and either crossing into Serbia where they surrendered or trekking 50 miles northwest to Muslim-held Tuzla. Compared to the events at Srebrenica that summer, casualties were small. Given historical precedent, however, it is likely that had the BSA persisted in their takeover of Zepa, a large-scale massacre of men and boys would have taken place (Harland 1999).

In short, the civilians most vulnerable to actually being killed after the fall of besieged cities such as Srebrenica and Zepa were adult civilian men and older boys. Protection agencies were mandated with saving the lives of all civilians without distinction, prioritizing the most vulnerable if necessary. Given this mandate and the context, and absent other factors, the most rational policy would have been to insist on safe passage to civilian men and boys first in cases where a takeover was imminent.[11] Yet the leading agencies charged with protecting war-affected civilians in the Balkans consistently did precisely the opposite, even in cases where a town was shortly expected to fall. Why?

Very few commentators on humanitarian evacuation in the Balkans have questioned this operational pattern.[12] The conventional wisdom is

---

11 The assessment of an imminent takeover is important because under ongoing siege conditions, the most vulnerable would be those at risk of deprivation rather than massacre: children, the elderly, pregnant and nursing women and the sick.

12 The notable exception was Adam Jones' (1994) article.

that women, children and the elderly *actually were* the most vulnerable populations and thus were (rightly) prioritized for humanitarian assistance on the basis of their vulnerability (Amnesty International 1998, 1; Mertus 2000, 6). Another, related hypothesis is that most adult men in internal conflicts *actually are* mobilized as combatants, and therefore, whatever fighting men's risk of mortality, "civilian" protection policies apply primarily to other demographic groups (Cockburn 2001, 21). If either explanation is valid, then sex-selective assistance policies would be perfectly rational, given the mandate of civilian protection agencies to: a) protect civilians, rather than combatants and b) to apply a "reverse-triage" approach, assisting the most vulnerable first.

But as already demonstrated, neither of these suggestions conforms to the facts within war-affected regions in general. Bosnia was no exception. There is no evidence that all able-bodied men in the region, but no women, were mobilized. Even with its tradition of universal conscription and peoples' war, mass resistance to conscription characterized the conflict: approximately 700,000 people had fled to avoid conscription at the war's onset, and over 9,000 charges of desertion were initiated in 1992 alone (Wilmer 2002, 157). Those who were under arms included females: as a UNHCR official told me, "some of the most gifted fighters in the region were women" (Respondent #31, 2002).

Regarding vulnerability, women, girls and younger boys were vulnerable in Bosnia to specific forms of attack such as sexual violence, and to exploitation and deprivation that accompanies displacement, as they were more likely than men to flee besieged areas (Mertus 2000).[13] They were also no *less* vulnerable than anyone else to indiscriminate attacks such as shelling. However, as Chapter 3 detailed, in cases where adult men and older boys were singled out for execution, adult women and younger children were the least vulnerable to direct, lethal attack, and it was threat to life that UNHCR presumably used as its criteria for prioritizing evacuation.

In short, neither relative invulnerability nor combatant status explains the neglect of men by the civilian protection community in the Balkans. Can a social constructivist analysis incorporating gender do so? Adam Jones has postulated that the international community routinely overlooks the specific vulnerabilities of civilian men in complex emergencies (Jones 2002a). He discusses the exclusion of men from evacuation convoys as emblematic of this broader problem. Although his treatment of evacuation is primarily descriptive, he suggests that prescriptive gender norms guided the behavior of belligerents, war-affected populations and protection workers alike: "The 'women and children first' rule seems as operative among besieged

---

13 This was particularly the case in Bosnia: see UNHCR/UNICEF/WHO 1992, 5.

144 'Innocent Women and Children'

populations as it once was for ocean-liner passengers abandoning ship" (Jones 2002a).

While I agree with Jones that gender analysis is indispensable to explaining this pattern, his claim requires more systematic assessment. Precisely *how* did gender norms associating women and children with innocence and vulnerability operate so as to channel only certain civilians onto evacuation convoys? This question frames the case study below. Based on a review of written accounts from the former Yugoslavia and a series of in-depth interviews with humanitarian practitioners, I conclude that gender beliefs did operate in practice both as cognitive maps (shaping the preferences of belligerents and the institutional mandates of protection agencies) and as constraints (shaping the options available to protection workers in assisting civilian populations). As demonstrated below by the case of Srebrenica, these two causal pathways converged in the former Yugoslavia to produce effects disastrous to civilians, particularly adult men and male adolescents.

Explaining the Evacuation of Srebrenica, March 1993

The international community remembers the fall of Srebrenica in July 1995 as one of the worst humanitarian catastrophes in the war.[14] Over a series of two weeks, BSA forces overran Srebrenica, a Bosniac-held enclave in eastern Bosnia, which had been placed under putative United Nations protection. As a "safe-area," the enclave had attracted many refugees, but the lightly armed Dutch peacekeepers charged with protecting them were no match for the BSA. After taking the town, Bosnian Serb General Ratko Mladic ordered the women and younger children onto buses while detaining most of the men and boys over twelve. Nearly 8,000 men and boys were later executed, some at Srebrenica and the nearby town of Potocari, others as they fled on foot through the woods (Honig and Both 1997; Rhode 1998).

Two years earlier, in March 1993, many civilians had had an opportunity to escape Srebrenica when it had appeared that the BSA might overrun the enclave. Approximately 9,000 people were evacuated by UNHCR (Hollingworth 1996; Honig and Both 1997; UNHCR 2000b), almost all of them women, children, the elderly and wounded. Although this evacuation was originally designed to take out only particularly ill persons and those at particular risk of starvation, in the end persons of every demographic category except able-bodied adult males were transported to Tuzla on UNHCR trucks. During the evacuation process, males between the ages of

---

14 An unprecedented amount of soul-searching has occurred since the massacre. Several reports under UN auspices have attempted to explain where the international community went wrong, including a 1999 Report by the Secretary-General to the UN Security Council (Harland 1999); and the entire Dutch government resigned in 2002 to atone for the role of Dutch peacekeepers in the incident.

Protecting Civilians in Conflict Zones 145

15 and 60 were explicitly denied access to convoys; those who tried to hide among the hordes of other refugees were removed by UNHCR officials, who refused to be responsible for their protection (Hollingworth 1996, 212).

Srebrenica, which was blockaded and under bombardment, had not yet fallen, so men and boys were arguably not under imminent threat of massacre. However, there were serious concerns that the enclave was shortly to fall, as BSA forces had recently overrun two other enclaves at Konjevic Polje and Cerska (Respondent #27, Phone Interview, October 2002). Moreover, since shelling killed indiscriminately, they stood no less an imminent risk of death or dismemberment than anyone else (Vulliamy 1994, 276). Although many of the able-bodied males of Srebrenica were fighters and some were indeed probably war criminals,[15] many were the same civilian husbands, fathers and older brothers who would end up in mass graves two years later (Respondent #32, 2002). By 1993, protection workers were already aware that once a town fell to the BSA, men and boys were the most likely to be executed. Their mandate was to evacuate the most vulnerable civilians. Why did women, children and the elderly, but not "military-age" civilian men, gain access to UNHCR evacuation convoys out of the enclave?

Hypotheses (see Table 5.1)

Jones' implication, discussed above, is that the gender sub-norm exerted a direct effect on the way that protection workers identified recipients of safe passage. His claim is similar to Goldstein and Keohane's concept of ideas as "road maps," which guide actors' assumptions about consequences in the absence of complete information (Goldstein and Keohane 1993; Yee 1996). In the Balkans case, this would have meant protection workers unreflectively evacuated women and children because they subscribed to the assumption that those alone were "civilians" or "vulnerable." In the absence of clear criteria for distinguishing civilians from combatants, perhaps protection workers relied upon sex and age as proxy variables, limiting their activities to those individuals most likely to be civilians (H1a). We would then expect accounts of such evacuations and interviews with former field workers to reflect the belief that this behavior was unproblematic. It should exhibit a taken for granted character that March and Olsen (1989) describe as a "logic of appropriateness."

---

15 One of the reasons for increasing BSA belligerence near Srebrenica in Spring 1993 was a series of attacks on Serb villages that Spring by Bosniac forces from Srebrenica. According to Honig and Both, "Evidence indicated that Serbs had been tortured and mutilated and others were burned alive when their houses were torched… a great deal of the animosity towards the men of Srebrenica stems from this period" (1997, 79).

146   *'Innocent Women and Children'*

But it would not be necessary for protection workers to subscribe to such a rule in order for the sub-norm on which it is based to affect evacuation procedures. As well as operating directly to shape preferences and perceptions, norms may also exert indirect effects, serving as constraints whether or not a given actor (or his/her community of concern) subscribes to them (Hasenclever et al. 1997, 136; Krasner 1983). As Thomas notes, the "logic of appropriateness" and the "logic of consequences" are not mutually exclusive (Thomas 2001, 37). If some actors in a situation subscribe to a norm, even those who do not may be constrained by it either because they seek the social approval of those who do or because they lack material power to oppose the implementation of the norm.

First, if third parties on whom an actor relies for social approval subscribe to a norm, the actor may be constrained by the desire to maintain approval through conformity to legitimized practices, even those it has not yet "internalized" (Checkel 1999; Finnemore and Sikkink 1998). The protection workers may have responded to an external logic of appropriateness imposed by their expectations of how their behavior would be interpreted by the international community on whom they relied for funding and legitimacy (H2). In this case, the protection workers might not have themselves internalized the "women and children only" rule, and may have even questioned it, but followed it nonetheless, because to do otherwise would have been seen as socially inappropriate by others on whose approval they depended. If these considerations had an effect, we would expect interviewees to describe public relations concerns as a *socially constraining* factor.

Second, the fact that one actor subscribes to a norm can shape the available policy options of another over whom s/he has bargaining leverage. The second actor is then *materially* constrained even if s/he is cognitively and socially indifferent to the norm's effects. Thus, even if protection workers had preferred to evacuate *all* civilians, and even if this had been sanctioned by outside observers, they may have been unable to evacuate the adult men because of the beliefs of either the belligerents in question (H3a), or the war-affected civilians themselves (H3b).

If either the Bosnian Serb Army, or the Bosnian Muslim authorities, or both, opposed the evacuation of adult men because they viewed them as fighters rather than civilians, this may have posed an intractable barrier to negotiating access to such men. The evidence should then bear out the extent to which protection workers attempted to press this issue, what strategies they adopted, and why their efforts ultimately failed. Alternatively, the men themselves may have insisted on staying behind, allowing their families to flee ahead of them; the women indeed may have demanded safe passage only for themselves and their dependent children. If civilian men stayed behind for chivalrous reasons, there should be no evidence that they sought to leave, and there should be evidence that they failed to leave if they had the opportunity (see Table 5.1).

Table 5.1 Hypotheses

H1: Aid workers used sex and age as proxy variables for 'vulnerable civilians.'
  H1a: Aid workers used sex and age as proxy variables for 'civilians.'
  H1b: Aid workers used sex and age as proxy variables for 'vulnerable.'

H2: International actors used sex and age as proxies for 'vulnerable civilians'; aid workers were socially constrained by a desire for approval from their international constituencies.

H3: Local actors used sex and age as proxies for 'civilians'; aid workers were constrained by local actors' demands.
  H3a: Belligerents would only allow women and children to be evacuated.
  H3b: War-affected populations themselves preferred to evacuate only women and children.

Explaining Sex-Selective Evacuation: Cognitive Maps v. Constraints

The data collected show only weak support for Hypothesis 1 as an explanation for sex-selective evacuation: protection workers themselves did not generally subscribe to a "women and children only" rule. Indeed, at Srebrenica in 1993, their first priority was to the sick and wounded, many of whom were adult men. They acquiesced to the demands of belligerents that women and children also be evacuated (Hollingworth 1996). Thus, while gender norms served as cognitive maps guiding the strategies of the *belligerents* (see H3a), they played only a partial role in constructing the evacuation-strategies of protection workers themselves, and this was not decisive. Primarily, the sub-norm affected the behavior of protection workers through the constraints imposed by other actors. Below, I expand upon these findings in turn.

First, to what extent did protection workers construct the civilian population according to sex and age proxies (H1a)? Evidence is mixed as to whether protection workers themselves assumed that all adult men were fighters. Both the UN Srebrenica report and documents within the Dutch government use the terms "military-age men" and "fighters" interchangeably (Harland 1999; Rhode 1998, 336).

> We made agreements constantly with all sides in which we accepted that there was, as in international law, a principle of distinction. But the principle of distinction was not between combatants and non-combatants. It was between *presumptive* combatants and *presumptive* non-combatants. Presumptive combatants being

148 'Innocent Women and Children'

defined as men between the ages of 15 and 60. So there were in 93/94 a series of agreements on freedom of movement in and out of Sarajevo, which we drafted. They excluded men between 15 and 60. (Respondent #8, 2002)

But other evidence suggests that protection workers were fully aware that the civilian population included men. Many protection workers interviewed in this study readily distinguished between combatants and male civilians, and written memoirs of the incidents frequently criticize the BSA's failure to distinguish between combatant and civilian males (Hollingworth 1996; Johnson 1999). Even those interviewees who tended to conflate "civilian" with "women and children" admitted, when prompted, that there were certainly many adult male civilians.

The vast majority of the men [at Srebrenica] were civilians... I don't think necessarily because they refused to fight but because there simply weren't enough arms... few of the men were armed and wearing uniforms. (Respondent #32, 2002)

There was a universal draft in Bosnia, so everyone who had reached the age of 18-40 was legally obligated to serve. However, the draft was 18-40; they killed everyone from 15-60. So they gave themselves a wide margin. (Respondent #8, 2002)

Most protection workers were also fully cognizant of the specific vulnerabilities faced by adult civilian men (H1b). This is borne out both by interview data and the written record (Reiff 1995, 206). While this did not translate into a set of preferences for rules that would address men's vulnerabilities, lack of such preferences was not decisive in producing sex-selective evacuation policy. Nor were the protection officials directly influenced by a belief that the international community expected them to prioritize women and children (H2). Instead, when asked whether UNHCR would have preferred to evacuate all civilians irrespective of sex, most workers agreed that this would have been ideal. Their inability to do so was apparently the result not of it being seen as inappropriate, either by themselves or by the civilian protection network more broadly, but of their freedom of action being *materially constrained* by the other actors involved (H3).

We did try to help men. But that's where we faced the biggest obstacles. A pattern was set up whereby we found we could relatively easily get women and children out. When things were very difficult, moving people out of the enclaves – Zepa, Srebrenica, Gorazde, Bihac – it was women, children, the elderly. There wasn't such a problem with elderly men. (Respondent #22, 2002)

Which external actors were primarily responsible for imposing a regime of discriminatory evacuation protocols based on the gender sub-norm? There

Protecting Civilians in Conflict Zones

is little evidence that the war-affected populations themselves insisted upon the exclusion of men from convoys (H3b). Such a trend might have been expected if civilian authorities also subscribed to the gender sub-norm and wished to maximize the number of "especially vulnerable" who left.

Instead, the general state of disorder that characterizes besieged cities had already led to the breakdown of such social rules within the general population. This was exemplified by behavior at food drop sites, where refugees routinely killed each other over the appropriation of scarce supplies (Hollingworth 1996, 201). Sick and wounded, who would ordinarily receive priority for evacuation even before healthy women and children, were betrayed at the Srebrenica evacuation by hordes of civilians piling onto the buses (Honig and Both 1997, 91). One aid worker explained: "It was really a sort of survival of the fittest, which brought with it a sort of degradation and breakdown of the most elementary and basic social values that people have" (Respondent #27, 2002).

Families' primary concern was with their own welfare, and devising strategies to reduce civilian men's risk of execution was not the least of their worries.[16] Many families refused evacuation in order to stay together, understanding that men's risk of death increased precisely when separated from their families (Respondent #22, 2002). At times during the war, civilian men made efforts to secure their own escape (Harland 1999, 75). The likelihood of their challenging the "women and children only" rule increased with their perception that the fall of a town was imminent.[17] There were some instances of men and boys disguising themselves as women to escape (Rhode 1998).

Yet once a sex-selective evacuation rule had been established, as at Srebrenica in 1993, most men had incentives to comply with the regime.[18] BSA fighters were known for apprehending adult men caught on convoys, and UNHCR officials were willing to enforce the "women and children only"

---

16 The calculus was different for fighting men. Many of them wished to stay in the enclave while their families fled to safety. As Respondent #27 recounted, this was in part what motivated local Bosnian military forces to back down when civilians mobbed the evacuation convoys: many of those allegedly responsible for maintaining order actually had an incentive to allow their own female relatives to get on board.

17 For example, local representatives formulated an evacuation plan that included men at Srebrenica in 1995; and at Zepa the authorities made several attempts to negotiate safe passage for men when it was perceived that the town was lost. See Harland 1999.

18 One UNHCR official overseeing the evacuation described stopping the convoy before the Serb perimeter and informing any men hiding in the trucks that they could not be protected. Of the several hundred people in the first convoy, he saw only four men get out. Later, when the Serbs checked the trucks for adult men, they found and arrested one. This UNHCR official later advocated on behalf of this young man with General Mladic, and he was freed (Respondent #27, 2002).

150   *'Innocent Women and Children'*

rule.[19] As one UNHCR official explained, "They were frightened to accept an evacuation." Instead, men were sometimes able to get out through more covert methods. For example, UNHCR would hire local men as interpreters so that they could move with the protection crews; and UNPROFOR officials often smuggled men out in their Land Rovers (Respondent #22, 2002).

Different families reacted differently to the exclusionary protocols. "One man might be absolutely outraged that he wouldn't be evacuated, nine other men might be happy their families could at least leave," a UNHCR officer told me. Indeed, as the evacuation demographics suggest, for many families, sending away the women and children without the men was seen as acceptable if not optimal. But the conditions that made this choice acceptable were beyond their control. The willingness of women to flee without male relatives did not appear to have been driven by an internalized gender norm but by the structure of the situation. Adult civilian men themselves sought to leave rather than to stay and fight, preferred to leave with their families if possible, and were prevented from doing so on evacuation convoys both by militias and by protection workers enforcing evacuation agreements. While primary data should be collected to corroborate this argument, the available accounts suggest that the besieged population's adherence to gender rules cannot provide an adequate explanation for the sex/age demographics of evacuees.

The evidence supports the view that the belligerents, rather than the civilians themselves, insisted upon the exclusion of "military-age men" from evacuation convoys (H3a). Not only the BSA but also the Bosnian authorities preferred to keep adult men and older boys within the cities. BSA leaders considered the men "war criminals" and intended to execute or detain them en masse when the towns fell. Bosnian authorities needed conscripts to defend the cities (Harland 1999). "The Serbs were happy if it was men only because then they would go into Srebrenica and flatten it... that in turn drove the Bosnian government not to have the civilians evacuated either... in a way to serve as the shields for the men" (Respondent #8, 2002).

BSA and Bosnian government leaders were split on the question of whether to evacuate *other* civilians. The Serb leadership had an incentive to release "presumptive civilians" for three reasons. First, they well understood that the international community considered the deaths of women and children, as presumptive civilians, a greater outrage than those of adult men, and they sought to minimize the public relations cost of overrunning towns: "The less opposition there would be from the international community if

---

19 Larry Hollingworth, who helped oversee the evacuation of Srebrenica, wrote in his memoir: "I stopped the convoy and... made it clear that any males under sixty would be arrested by the Serbs at the check-point and that I would do nothing to help them. There were a couple on board. 'What can we do?' they asked. 'Get off and walk back,' was my reply."

Protecting Civilians in Conflict Zones

there were only military men left" (Respondent #32, 2002; see also Cigar 1995, 133). Second, insofar as their goal was primarily to seize empty land rather than kill people, they preferred that the majority of the civilians choose to leave on their own, facilitating the repopulation of the towns with ethnic Serbs (Respondent #8, 2002). Third, they understood that the evacuation of men's families would both reduce the incentive for men to fight (many were simply defending their families) and would reduce the likelihood of Western intervention, speeding the enclave's fall (Neier 1998, 161).

From the Bosnian authorities' perspective, the calculus was the reverse. To the extent that the suffering of "women and children" kept the international community's attention, it was to their advantage to maintain a wide population base in a particular town (Honig and Both 1997, 92). They also feared the breakdown in morale and reduction in conscripts if families were to leave. However, the key argument *given* for refusing evacuation offers was that it would facilitate ethnic cleansing itself. The Bosnian authorities played into the West's fears of complicity in genocide by fueling the debate that to move people was to do the Serb's dirty work (Respondent #32, 2002). David Harland, who participated in negotiations with the BSA throughout the war and later wrote the UN Secretary-General's Report on the Fall of Srebrenica, explained:

> The Serbs kept saying, we will offer free passage to everybody except men under the age of 60. And the government kept saying no. They wanted to keep the men there. Everybody knew that what was really being fought over was land. The government position was that the women and children – sorry, the non-fighters – would provide some degree of shield to the fighters. And that if you left only the fighters that would leave the fighters more vulnerable (Respondent #8, 2002).[20]

Thus the BSA leadership was responding both to an internalized gender sub-norm by which civilian status was defined according to sex and age, and to the expectation of the international community's interpretation of

---

20 This passage indicates the gradual reflectivity towards avoiding gender essentialisms that emerged during our sustained conversation on the issue of civilian men. Mr. Harland and I both became aware of our tendency to slip into identifying "men" with "fighters" and the fact that this was also the case in UN documents on Srebrenica. He clarified that although the Bosnian government seemed to care very much about not leaving the draftees in Srebrenica vulnerable to attack, it was not civilian men they wanted to protect (in fact they wished to conscript any such men) but soldiers and their claim to the city. In short, Izetbegovic's position was that civilians (defined as women and children) should stay in the enclave to buttress army morale and provide a moral buffer against a loss of the town. The question of non-combatant men's right to flee or particular risk of massacre was not part of the issue: "In none of this do I recall any sort of consideration being given to the people you seem to be interested in, which is non-fighting battle-age men. I don't ever really remember it occurring to anybody that there might be such a category."

152   *'Innocent Women and Children'*

the situation. First, the sub-norm operated as a cognitive map providing the BSA with a means of distinguishing between civilians and combatants: BSA fighters simply constructed all military-age men as combatants and therefore legitimate military targets. According to this logic, women and children, as presumptive civilians, were seen as non-threatening: they might be raped or expelled, but if left alive it was guessed they would not likely rise up against the Serbs.[21] Secondly, the BSA leadership was restrained by its perception of the international community's moral predilections. They expected that the West would be more concerned over women and children than over men, and that sparing women and children from outright massacre could be used as a demonstration of at least marginal compliance with standards of civilized behavior. In this way, the likelihood of forcible intervention by the West would be reduced.

Bosnian authorities, making the same calculation, chose to keep women and children as well as men *in* harm's way in order to provoke the sympathy of the outside world. But because of the same tendency to see those who would intentionally harm women and children as monsters, the Bosnian authorities could only take this argument so far. In part, this explains why, in the end, the Bosnian government acquiesced with the evacuation of "presumptive civilians" despite their initial preferences.[22] Because the BSA monopolized the moral high ground in its stated desire to limit "civilian" casualties, it had more leverage in these negotiations and ultimately the Bosnian authorities gave in to limited evacuation proposals (see Table 5.2).[23]

In short, cognitive maps influenced the preferences of the belligerents; the normative perceptions of the outside world influenced their relative bargaining power. Ultimately, when evacuations were negotiated, adult civilian men were excluded. This satisfied the BSA fighters, who retained their "legitimate targets"; the Bosnian authorities, who retained their pool of potential fighters; and the international community, who could satisfy itself at having "at least" assisted the "most vulnerable."

---

21 In fact, this logic reflected gender assumptions and is faulty: there is evidence that a key motivation of women taking up arms in civil wars or insurgencies, both in Bosnia and in other contexts, is the desire to regain lost social status and get revenge after being raped or widowed by the enemy (Bloom 2005).

22 The perception that a town was shortly to fall also influenced Bosnian officials' willingness to go along with evacuation schemes. See Honig and Both 1997, 93 and Sudetic 1998, 188.

23 The initial evacuation was to include only sick and wounded. To this UNHCR gradually added a few individuals particularly vulnerable to deprivation due to the "survival of the fittest" mentality that had taken hold of the enclave. The Bosnian authorities in Sarajevo put a stop to the mass evacuations, claiming again that it was contributing to ethnic cleansing, when it became clear that other civilians were also leaving.

Protecting Civilians in Conflict Zones 153

Thus protection workers themselves did not intentionally create the conditions under which adult men were abandoned. They were not inherently biased against the protection of male civilians. Rather, protection workers acted in the context of constraints imposed by the belligerents with whom they had to negotiate access to civilian populations (Cutts 1999, 25).

Table 5.2 Belligerents' policy-preference structures regarding evacuation

Bosnian Serb Army:
    1) Evacuate sick and wounded, then women, children, elderly
    2) Evacuate no one

Bosnian government:
    1) *If town still under siege*:
        a) Evacuate no one
        b) Evacuate sick and wounded, then women, children, elderly
        c) Evacuate all civilians without discrimination
    2) *If surrender imminent:*
        a) Evacuate all civilians/safe passage for soldiers
        b) Evacuate no one
        c) Evacuate women, children, elderly/soldiers flee on foot

Explaining Sex-Selective Evacuation: Converging Logics of Appropriateness

So why then did protection workers on the ground *comply* with these demands to evacuate according to discriminatory rules? In particular, why did they do so when the agreement of the war-affected civilians themselves on the legitimacy of these procedures was lacking, placing protection workers in the position of enforcing the belligerents' discriminatory policies against the will of those whom they were there to help? Were they influenced only by a logic of consequences or also by a logic of appropriateness – a tacit agreement with the BSA about the legitimacy of the "women and children only" rule? And if the latter, did this logic of appropriateness manifest as a constraint vis-à-vis. the broader network (H2), or more directly as a cognitive map (H1)?

A useful way to begin analysis is to consider in the abstract what a completely gender-neutral set of preferences for evacuation strategies would

154 'Innocent Women and Children'

have looked like absent the belligerents' demands.[24] If protection agencies were resigned to an evacuation of all civilians, and were completely immune to the "women and children only" rule, and based their evacuation strategies on their preferred outcomes alone, this would have meant evacuating everyone without arms, without distinction. Then, if priority had to be assigned for reasons of space limits or due to a vulnerability assessment, the following criteria would likely have been followed. The agencies would have wished to evacuate sick and wounded first, in accordance with custom laid down in the Geneva Conventions and the practice of civilian protection agencies. Pregnant women would be included in this category as a particularly vulnerable group for medical reasons (Bouchet-Saulnier 2002).

The second two categories to receive priority would have depended for their ranking on an assessment of whether the fall of the town was imminent. If siege conditions were expected to continue for the foreseeable future, children under five and the elderly should be evacuated next, these being most vulnerable to deprivation. Moreover, because the guidelines on the evacuation of children specify that they must be evacuated with their family units, both mothers and fathers, as well as older siblings, should be evacuated along with children under five (Caversazio 2001, 40; Ressler 1992). But, if the fall of the town is likely to occur, placing men and boys at risk of imminent massacre, their escape might be expected to be given preference to the evacuation of small children who at any rate may be able to leave once the siege conditions end.

Arguably, those civilians to receive the least priority for evacuation under such a situation would be healthy adult women without children, who would be no more vulnerable than any one else to indiscriminate attack, no more vulnerable than healthy adult men to deprivation,[25] and less vulnerable than adult men to outright execution.[26] At a minimum, however, adult men and women without children, in a gender-inclusive situation, might have been expected to be accorded the same priority for evacuation (see Table 5.3).

The policy-preference rankings of the protection officials I interviewed seemed to have manifested differently on the ground. The preferred strategy – to evacuate all civilians without distinction – was, as described above, consistent

---

24 It is important to note that this is an abstract exercise: at Srebrenica, in fact, it was not UNHCR's idea to take out the entire civilian population: they began from the position of evacuating the "most vulnerable." Ultimately other able-bodied "presumptive civilians" forced their way onto convoys, at which point the field officers made the call to proceed with the evacuation.

25 However, making this assessment would require an understanding of different adult women's access to food in a given situation, which can often be subject to various forms of discrimination within a war-affected community.

26 However, it must be noted that while adult women without children were not likely to be taken aside and shot, they were vulnerable to sexual assault, and this form of torture was sometimes followed by execution. See Wilmer, 2002.

Protecting Civilians in Conflict Zones 155

with the lack of influence from the gender norm.[27] However, when talking about how to prioritize according to vulnerability, the potential strategies were *not* ranked so as to wholly correspond with the UNHCR's underlying mandate of helping the most vulnerable first.

Table 5.3 Protection agencies' policy-preference structures regarding evacuation: counterfactual v. actual

---

Counter-factual **policy preferences** (based on vulnerability assessment as articulated in UNHCR guidelines, assuming absence of gender norm)

If fall of town imminent, evacuate:
1) All civilians
2) Physically vulnerable
   a. Sick
   b. Wounded
   c. Pregnant/Nursing
3) Execution-risk individuals
   a. Elites (both sexes)
   b. Civilian males
4) Deprivation-risk individuals
   a. Under 5 w/mothers
   b. Elderly
5) Civilian women w/o children

If siege ongoing, evacuate:
1) All civilians
2) Physically vulnerable
   a. Sick
   b. Wounded
   c. Pregnant/Nursing
3) Deprivation-risk individuals
   a. Under 5 w/families
   b. Elderly
4) Execution-risk individuals
   a. Elites (both sexes)
   b. Civilian males
5) Civilian women w/o children

Actual **policy preferences** (as extrapolated from narrative accounts in interviews and memoirs)

If possible, evacuate:
1) All civilians
2) Sick, wounded, pregnant
3) All women, children and elderly

---

27 For example, where it was possible to evacuate villages before warring parties had placed road blocks and thus were in a position to deny escape to men, Mark Cutts of UNHCR reported that "there were times when we assisted whole communities to move, and of course that included men of every age" (Respondent #8, 2002).

156 'Innocent Women and Children'

Sick and wounded were, as predicted, ranked first. But all women, along with children and the elderly were always ranked next: the expectation of an ongoing siege v. an imminent fall did not appear to have altered protection workers' preference structures in negotiations, as it would have given an objective vulnerability assessment.

In short, while protection officials did not subscribe to a "women and children only" rule, they seemed to subscribe to a "women and children first" rule: "In hindsight it stands out [that men were overlooked] but at the time there were so many overwhelming problems, even to save a percentage of the women and children... so you didn't even get to that stage where you could argue on behalf of the men" (Respondent #32, 2002).[28] Moreover, wounded "women and children" took priority over wounded men, as one respondent described with respect to a subsequent helicopter evacuation of war-wounded men from Srebrenica: "They couldn't go out by road so we brought in helicopters. Military-age people had priority at this point, because all the wounded women and children had already been allowed to leave" (Respondent #32, 2002).

Nor were the rules pertaining to the evacuation of children interpreted so as to keep entire family units together. It was assumed that if children were evacuated with their mothers, this was good enough (Hollingworth 1996, 210). According to Manuel Fontaine, who worked with UNICEF evacuating children from Sarajevo, fathers could sometimes get out with children *if* the mother had already been killed or was otherwise absent.[29] In general, however, UNICEF did not consider the issue of men's freedom of movement to be an important part of their mandate, although Fontaine admitted that this perhaps contravened international standards: "In the framework of the Geneva Conventions, if you're not a fighter, you're a civilian, and as such you need to be protected and to move, so that would be an issue obviously. But in a very pragmatic way, what was more important for us was making sure that there would be one adult, and if possible the mother, with the children when they were evacuated" (Respondent #29, 2002).

Most notably, the option of evacuating men and boys while leaving women and children behind was almost entirely absent.[30] To the extent that battle-age men were advocated for, it was in the context of the "all civilians" group or because they fell into a specific category of vulnerable person: civilian men as such were never assigned priority over other groups.

---

28 Italics added by author.

29 The guidelines themselves were not written with the case of mass evacuation in mind, but to prevent well-meaning NGOs from removing unaccompanied children from war-zones to the West arbitrarily (Respondent #26, Phone Interview, October 2002). See Ressler 1992; UNHCR/UNICEF 1992; UNHCR/UNICEF/ICRC 1992.

30 Only one respondent (#20, Personal Interview, August 2002, Geneva) suggested such an option, and this person was speaking in abstract terms, having not personally participated in evacuation operations.

Protecting Civilians in Conflict Zones 157

I don't know of any situation where the UN or the ICRC have taken out people who were "potential combatant" as a category. (Respondent #8, 2002)

I suppose we did put a lot of effort into in some cases men. But it was almost invariably because there was a very special issue of vulnerability related to that man. Even the cases I remember when there were men whom you could argue were of fighting age, they were disabled, older, traumatized, been in hiding, they clearly posed no threat to anybody. (Respondent #22, 2002)

It may rightly be pointed out that even if protection workers had advocated for men and boys' safe passage or, more limitedly, for fathers' evacuation with their families, that the belligerents would probably have said no. The necessity of maintaining an appearance of political neutrality sometimes mitigates against aid workers' advocating for men, who are assumed to be political perpetrators (Frohardt, Paul and Minear 1999, 45).

Similarly, the emphasis on avoiding the issue of men as a means to maintain access to at least some civilians and get at least some past the front lines safely appeared in many respondents' narratives regarding the evacuation process:

At first we talked about taking out seriously wounded, especially women and children who would have no trouble getting past the front lines: the system we worked out was we went around at night and numbered everyone's hand with markers, trying to figure out how we would maximize the number on the trucks without getting attacked by the Serbs. (Respondent #32, 2002)

If the issue was choosing the lesser of two evils in such a context, perhaps evacuating women and children was the best option, and the question of whether protection workers did so for ideational or strategic reasons is surely impossible to resolve. However, if protection workers had other options that they did not even consider, the argument that they were acting at least partly on a logic of appropriateness – a "women and children first rule" stemming from the gender sub-norm – is much stronger.

What might protection workers have done instead? They might have simply refused to evacuate at all. Indeed, if removing women and children contributed to the fall of towns, isolated men and boys in preparation for massacre, and reduced the incentive of the international community to intervene, then it is possible that keeping the women and children with the men might have saved their lives. It does not appear that UNHCR considered this option. According to David Harland, when the Izetbegovic government attempted to block evacuation for precisely this reason, UNHCR negotiators attempted to convince them to allow the women and children out (Respondent #8, 2002).

Yet withdrawing from protection initiatives to protest violations of international rules has many precedents within the protection community.

158   *'Innocent Women and Children'*

For example, the ICRC withdrew from several operations in Bosnia when its own workers came under attack (Minear et al. 1994); UNHCR eventually withdrew protection to refugee camps in Zaire when it became clear they were being used as sanctuaries for armed elements (Loescher 2001, 311); and UNHCR initially opposed evacuation because of the concern that it would contribute to genocide (UNHCR 2000b). More analogously, when belligerents insist upon services going only to certain groups, there are cases in which aid agencies have withdrawn services entirely until they could be distributed in an impartial manner. For example, Oxfam and CARE withdrew aid from boys' schools to protest the exclusion of girls under the Taliban (Mertus 2000). So why was the option of protesting civilian men's exclusion from evacuation by refusing to cooperate not on the UNHCR's menu of choices?

Simply put, excluding men was not considered a form of gender discrimination or a violation of humanitarian rules regarding the impartial distribution of assistance. Although the Geneva Conventions prohibit "adversely distinguishing" between civilians on the basis of sex when implementing humanitarian law, this concept is understood only to apply to discrimination against women (Krill 1985; Lindsey 2001). In a personal interview, ICRC Legal Advisor Antoine Bouvier stated, "It's a bit far-fetched to consider [sex-selective evacuation] adverse distinction." Other protection workers I spoke to suggested that the BSA's insistence on detaining the men was reasonable, and at any rate, just a part of war:

> Evacuation was… simply not an option for [the men], tragic though that was… (Respondent #26, Phone Interview, October 2002)

> Frankly in the case of Bosnia, most men were at least potentially fighters, so every man had to be accounted for… (Respondent #28, Phone Interview, October 2002)

> The Serbs felt they had to detain or interrogate all the men, and quite justifiably so, I think. (Respondent #34, Personal Interview, August 2002, Geneva)

Of course, had the protection workers considered the option of taking a stand with respect to this issue, they may still have chosen to save as many lives as possible, and, given the situation, this choice would probably have been defensible. Even with the benefit of hindsight and reflection in the context of the interview, several protection workers I spoke to insisted that the choice made by UNHCR was probably the right one.

> The closer you are to the field the less principled you become and the more pragmatic. I was a negotiator, I was one of the least principled ones. In my experience I was always on the side of saying, "If they create a situation of terror in which ethnic cleaning is taking place, we aren't facilitating anything by taking anyone away. The guilt for that lies with those who are shelling the place in the

Protecting Civilians in Conflict Zones 159

first place. We are simply saving lives. If they can agree among themselves that group x can be evacuated then I will evacuate group x. If they can't agree among themselves, group x will die along with group y and z." That was always my view. And I broadly think that to have been correct even as I look back upon it. (Respondent #8, 2002)

I am absolutely convinced we saved lives. For all of us who were working then there, everything you did was controversial. But at the end of the day you just had to look at whether you could contribute to saving lives or not. And I'm convinced that is what we were doing. If you had seen the determination of the people who were there, the level of frustration and anger and hurt and despair, you would have had a very hard time leaving them behind. (Respondent #27, 2002)

I don't know if it means that the men would not have been killed, because they would have been separated out anyway. It seemed like the right thing to do, it's easy to convince yourself. It doesn't often happen that 7,000 men get killed. (Respondent #22, 2002)

These quotes suggest that even if UNHCR had actively considered refusing to evacuate, they may well have gone ahead in the end. Indeed, at the point at which crowds of women and children forced their way onto the convoys, the question was moot: evacuating the desperately sick meant also taking all those others whom the BSA would allow out (Hollingworth 1996, 211). But the point here is that even prior to that, *this option was not considered.*

Conclusion

None of us thought about it at this level of sophistication. Events were moving very fast. You just were buzzing from one thing or another, there was very little introspection or reflection... the assumption was that somehow the sides were willing to do something to mitigate the effect of the war on the civilian/non-belligerent/whatever population. And the way they would do that is by creating a few clear categories of people who could benefit from say freedom of movement. And able-bodied men were always excluded from that. (Respondent #8, 2002)

On the basis of this evidence it is clear that a logic of appropriateness resulted in ambivalence toward the protection of adult male civilians, but it is harder to disentangle whether this logic operated primarily at the cognitive level or as a social constraint. Many respondents expressed a sense that their mandate did not include advocacy for adult men to the same extent as for the women and children. The denial of adult civilian men's and boys' right to flee in Bosnia was taken for granted by many protection workers as an unfortunate but understandable aspect of the situation.

But this sense of ambivalence was often mixed. Some respondents retrospectively admitted men should have been given greater attention,

160 'Innocent Women and Children'

but justified UNHCR's actions by reference to the international constraints. (Even these respondents failed to suggest that men and boys should have been evacuated first.) The interconnection between these causal pathways is evident in the following quote:

> When you start prioritizing, any way you go, there are certain categories that are easy to deal with. There's the vulnerable, but then there are the vulnerable who are politically easy. Elderly people, young children who need an operation, pregnant women, that's easy… There is not a good understanding of how vulnerable men are… Most of us on the ground there understood [men were vulnerable], but we lived with it. I think it was unfortunately the reality and we knew we could get women and children out, so why not get them out. (Respondent #22, 2002)

This evidence suggests that the manner in which actors process information and frame moral decision-making is not always so distinguishable from the broader social milieu in which they act. The gender sub-norm embedded within the protection principle was reproduced by and thus ensnared actors within particular protection agencies. For example, when protection agencies questioned the ethics of evacuating civilians, their concern rested with the question of moving anyone at all, not that of discriminating against certain civilians.[31]

Framing the dilemma in this way mirrored the debate over the ethics of humanitarian evacuation at the international level (UNHCR 2000b, 222). For example, UNHCR Special Envoy Jose-Maria Mendiluce told journalist David Reiff, "We found ourselves in the morally impossible position of furthering the goal of ethnic cleansing in order to save people's lives" (Reiff 1995, 212). The dilemma was expressed at all levels within the network as one of abetting or choosing not to abet ethnic cleansing. Yet one of the key ways that sex-selective evacuation worked to the advantage of the BSA was in removing those civilians whose deaths would most likely attract the opprobrium of the international community. In evacuating "women and children" as synonymous with the "civilian population," protection agencies replicated the notion that the remaining population was composed of "fighters" and legitimized Serb targeting of those individuals (Respondent #8, 2002).

This twin dilemma, abandoning the most vulnerable while legitimizing their massacre, was not articulated in the debate on whether evacuation was tantamount to ethnic cleansing. Indeed, it was precisely the ability to claim that they had at least "saved the innocent" that enabled UNHCR to resolve its queasiness about "aiding genocide." Taking a stand after the 1993 evacuation of Srebrenica, Special Envoy Mendiluce said, "We may denounce ethnic cleansing, but when you have thousands of women and children at

---

31 Only one interviewee identified leaving men behind as a second moral dilemma (Respondent #27, Phone Interview, October 2002).

risk who want desperately to be evacuated, it is my responsibility to save their lives" (UNHCR 2000b, 222).

Given these findings, a combination of the "cognitive maps" and "social constraints" pathways makes the most sense in explaining this acquiescence to the belligerents' demands. This convergence might be better expressed as what Finnemore and Barnett have described as the "power of international organizations" – equally applicable to advocacy networks. In "classifying" the world, "fixing meanings" and "diffusing norms," networks of moral meaning in international society delimit the parameters of acceptable action, and even the ways in which it is possible to think about acting, in a given milieu (Finnemore and Barnett 1999). Yet as these authors point out, organizations can become trapped in their own classification schemes and exhibit "pathologies," or strategic behavior inconsistent with their mandate. This may be neither wholly a result of individual cognitive bias nor of rationality under external social constraints, but the combined effect of snaring actors within an institutional discourse ill-fitted to the strategic context. "Once in place, an organization's culture, understood as the rules, rituals and beliefs that are embedded in the organization, has important consequences for the way individuals who inhabit that organization make sense of the world" (Finnemore and Barnett 1999, 719).

The civilian protection network had, early in the Bosnian war, promulgated a conception of "especially vulnerable groups" that reflected gender discourse within international society, rather than an assessment varying by context. Certain agencies within the network, UNHCR in particular, were simultaneously engaged in an intensive public relations campaign to draw attention to the Balkans crisis, legitimize their own civilian protection initiatives, and secure a redefined role in post-Cold War international society (Loescher 2001). This meant highlighting successes and carefully avoiding publicity fiascos in order to keep international funding pouring in. The rhetoric of "women and children" in need of rescue resonated with international ethics, and with the frames used by the women's movement: these became part of the agency's self-image and mandate. Such discourse also fed back into and reproduced the gender sub-norm within the civilian protection principle.

In this context it would never have occurred to protection agencies to evacuate men and boys first, even if they had had the chance. Nor would it have been appropriate, given this sub-norm, to put the lives of women and children at risk in order to advocate for adult males. As one UNHCR official said, "when it came to men and adolescent boys, we recognized we probably wouldn't get boys out, we knew we wouldn't get men out, so we didn't try" (Respondent #22, 2002).

Sex-selective evacuation rules were material constraints imposed by the warring parties. BSA and Bosnian government forces interpreted civilian immunity according to a logic of gender: both in mapping the civilian/combatant distinction and in calculating the parameters within which the international community was likely to interpret and enforce the civilian immunity norm. But as actors within the network, protection officials at Srebrenica were also influenced by the gender sub-norm as they considered how to act in the context of these constraints. Gendered notions of "vulnerability" made it easier to acquiesce, given the manner in which donors and onlookers would likely interpret their actions either way. The result was that the physical security of many children and women was improved, at the cost of their husbands' and fathers' lives.

Chapter 6

"Un-Gendering" Civilian Protection, Engendering Change

This study has demonstrated that gender beliefs influence both the moral framework according to which the civilian protection regime has developed historically and the manner in which civilian protection operations manifest in situations of armed conflict. When the civilians in question are female or young (and especially females *with* young), states and other warring parties are less likely to directly target them with lethal violence; they are less likely to justify their actions when they do; and they are more likely to condemn such actions by others. Transnational advocates of the civilian protection norm are likely to employ images of women and children in their appeals, reports, condemnations and press releases because of the assumed persuasive power of these representations. And international and non-governmental organizations dealing operationally with the protection of civilians are more likely to earmark programs for women, along with children and other "presumed civilian" groups, and to prioritize them over adult males in the implementation of their civilian-focused initiatives. I argue that all of this undermines the very humanitarian norms at stake.

From a theoretical perspective, this project advances explanatory scholarship on gender by demonstrating how such analysis looks when integrated into conventional constructivist epistemologies. There is a notion in the IR community that gender studies is a feminist preserve, but I hope to have demonstrated that gender analysis is equally relevant to scholars motivated by other agendas than overcoming gender hierarchies per se or working in primarily post-positivist frameworks. This does not render my position "anti-feminist," as some would argue (see Whitworth 2004), but it does mean that I see value in a serious engagement with sympathetic non-feminists about the importance of gender as a category of analysis across axiological divides in IR theory and in foreign policy-making. If my argument is persuasive, I hope to see other mainstream constructivists incorporating gender as a variable into their own analyses. This in turn may generate a more vibrant dialogue between IR feminism and conventional IR than has been evident in recent years.

My argument also advances literature on norms in world politics by exposing the manner in which gender assumptions can "stow away" within seemingly sex-neutral categories such as the "innocent civilian," thereby

164 'Innocent Women and Children'

generating prescriptive "gender rules" that undermine the moral logic of the original norm itself. Thus, in contrast to their well-known role as explicit norm-entrepreneurs, international organizations and transnational advocacy networks may also find themselves captured by implicit norms or "sub-norms," either unwittingly or as part of their strategic framing process.[1] These norms may then work through organizational culture so as to undermine operational imperatives, as at Srebrenica. Analysts of traditional themes in international relations theory will need to pay close attention to gender as well as other implicit normative systems in order to adequately explain the phenomena with which they are concerned.

From a practical perspective, the empirical findings suggest that the "innocent civilian" is a gendered concept and that thinking about civilian protection according to gender stereotypes can inhibit effective policy. I have argued that the gender sub-norm adversely affects the implementation of the immunity norm, but that it is not constitutive of the norm itself. Importantly, this leaves open the possibility that altering these gender assumptions could strengthen, rather than nullify, the immunity norm.

If this claim is accurate, it is not only possible but desirable to "ungender" the regime principles in order to achieve norm effects more consistent with the regime's moral logic. Thus, I conclude with the modest suggestion that the protection community work to correct for this gender bias, both in the ways they frame civilian protection and in their operational practices. At a minimum, this would need to involve a self-conscious change in normative discourse, particularly within the civilian protection network. For example, the ICRC would be wise to implement the recommendations of its own "Women and War" project, which include actively countering these stereotypes in the dissemination process (Lindsey 2001, 63-64).

This would serve the civilian protection agenda in three important ways. Most obvious and perhaps most importantly from a humanitarian law perspective, it could save the lives of civilian men who might otherwise be targeted as "potential combatants." This in itself would be a major victory for the protection of civilians. If we are to take the humanitarian principle of impartiality seriously, adult civilian males and older boys are entitled to no less protection than other civilians, and a failure to protect them is a failure of civilian protection policy more generally. Thus, currents in humanitarian discourse and policy supportive of recognizing male civilians' particular needs and interests seem to me to be a step in the right direction (IASC 2002; Lindsey 2001).

However, these efforts must be mainstreamed into policies designed to disseminate humanitarian law. Strong efforts to delegitimize the use of sex as a proxy for civilian/combatant could undermine that claim made by belligerents that every battle-age man is a legitimate target (Bruderlein

---

1 I am thankful to Lisa Martin for this point.

2001). These efforts might not generate immediate compliance, but they would constitute a gradual shift away from the legitimation of the gender sub-norm, at least on the part of human rights advocates.[2]

Secondly, extending greater protection to civilian men and boys could have effects beneficial to the rest of the civilian population. First, there is a fair amount of evidence that civilian children and women become more vulnerable in wartime when their men go missing (Aafjes and Goldstein 1998, 17; Bop 2002, 27; Date-Bah et al. 2001, 6-7; Lindsey 2001, 29; Shoemaker 2001, 19). Testimonies of war-affected women often emphasize the trauma of family dissolution due to the separation from male relatives (for examples from Bosnia, see Mrvic-Petrovic 1995). Thanks to the efforts of the international women's network and the gradual shift to gender-sensitive programming, there are now programs in place to address these vulnerabilities: to provide support and medical care to survivors of sexual violence; to secure livelihoods for displaced women; to provide psycho-social services for widows and their children; to trace separated family members and to identify the dead (Mertus 2001; Ward 2002).

To take seriously these problems faced by survivors of armed conflict, however, perhaps it makes sense for the "protection" agenda to address the socio-cultural factors that lead men to disappear in the first place. Certainly, some adult men and older boys will voluntarily take up arms in wartime. But the fate of those who are executed, arbitrarily detained or forcibly conscripted might be improved by norms that take seriously the civilian status of adult men in wartime. The protection community could do more to promote such norms. Generating data on the number of men who remain in the civilian sector, emphasizing the specific risks to which they are exposed *as men* rather than as generic human beings, and emphasizing the right of civilian men to be protected – in negotiations with belligerents and in public discourse on war-affected civilians – would be a fine start.

It should not be assumed that war-affected civilian children and women will necessarily be better off in every way if their adult male relatives are present with them in the midst of conflict or during flight. We know that some of the greatest threats to women in wartime come from within their communities, rather than from without (Enloe 2000; Gardam and Jervis 2001,

---

2 Another means of un-gendering the distinction principle would be to highlight women's participation as agents of armed conflict, and generate clearer, more gender-sensitive policies with respect to female combatants. While this does not involve civilian protection as such and thus has not been explored here, it is the case that female combatants and ex-combatants have been and still are one of the most underserved categories in humanitarian assistance (Mazurana and McKay 2003). Their invisibility reproduces the distinction principle as a gender construct. Greater attention to their presence and needs would also highlight the fact that sex is not an adequate proxy variable for "civilian" or "combatant" in a way that could strengthen the distinction principle.

166   *'Innocent Women and Children'*

102). For example, family violence skyrockets in times of war (for example, Nikolic-Ristanovic 1996). This is particularly true among refugee or displaced populations, where traditional male roles have evaporated (Bennett et al. 1995, 10-13; Meertens 2001), or among men who have returned to their families after having been traumatized by violence (Kumar 2001, 11). There is a glaring gap in psycho-social programming for war-affected civilian men in humanitarian settings (Ward 2002; World Health Organization 2000). A number of scholars have recently called for gender-sensitive psycho-social programming that targets male victims of gender-based wartime violence, as well as efforts to promote meaningful identities for displaced male family members. As Barbara Harrell-Bond argues, "If you want to help women, help men."[3]

There are concerns within the gender-mainstreaming community that programming for civilian men would undermine the advancement of women (Chant and Gutmann 2001). However, I suspect that protecting men as well as women from gender-based violence and its effects is likely to strengthen, not undermine, gender-mainstreaming efforts. There is evidence that allowing men a space to talk about their own victimization validates male trauma and draws men into gender-mainstreaming initiatives (Lang 2002; UNHCR 2001b, 9). Reducing barriers to the discussion of the gender-based violence which men face in wartime could be a valuable step both in helping men face the impact of gendered hierarchies on their own interests as well as those of women, but also in reducing the salience of militarized masculinity, in which the acceptance of both men's violence against men and wartime violence against women is grounded (Enloe 2000). Arguably, this could benefit the entire civilian population. It would enhance gender-awareness among both war-affected civilians and humanitarian practitioners. As recent studies have demonstrated and this research confirms, such gender-awareness is crucial to the effective protection of civilians – children, women and men. Conceivably it could also benefit peace-building efforts, by promoting non-militarized identities for men and protecting those adult males who refuse to take up arms in times of war.[4]

Finally, at a meta-normative level, the case studies here suggest that efforts to advocate for males as civilians, and thus "un-gender" the concept of the civilian, would strengthen the protection regime by clarifying its moral precepts. Although humanitarian law is clear both on how civilians are to be treated and how they are to be identified – as those not taking direct part

---

3   Quoted by Doreen Indra, in Indra 1999a, 62.

4   However, "peace" is a loaded concept: we must be careful not to assume that all war-affected civilians will benefit equally from the transition from conflict to "peace" (DeLaet 2005; Enloe 1993; Meintjes, Pillay and Turshen 2001; Rehn and Sirleaf 2002). Sustaining gender-sensitive assistance policies into post-conflict situations may be vital to the creation of "positive" rather than "negative" peace (Kumar 2001).

in hostilities – many actors on the ground interpret principles too broadly to provide adequate protection for civilians. For example, they may define "participation in hostilities" as encompassing those who feed or house combatants. One respondent to the ICRC's *People on War* study (ICRC 1999a, 32) stated, "Somebody can hold a submachine gun and somebody only a ladle. But it doesn't mean a cook is less responsible than a soldier." A related problem is that when the principles are interpreted narrowly (invoking the gender sub-norm), evidence of women and children taking part in hostilities is taken to mean that the entire concept of immunity must be outdated. This logic, which is often used as an excuse for indiscriminate targeting, can be refuted through a systematic effort to change the perception that sex and age are coterminous with the category "civilian."

In this context, it would appear that the actors within the civilian protection regime may be fighting a losing battle to indoctrinate belligerents with the laws of war unless they also work to decisively "un-gender" the distinction principle. This means doing more than simply emphasizing the proper criteria by which distinction is to be made in practice. It also means engaging in decisive efforts at frame transformation.

Frame transformation involves, as a first step, commissioning and disseminating systematic gender-sensitive research on the experience of civilian men in times of war. Jones has suggested that the UN establish a "male-focused equivalent" of the Special Rapporteur of the Commission on Human Rights on Violence Against Women, "The Special Rapporteur for Gender-Based Violence Against Men could serve as the catalyst for educational and activist efforts aimed at sensitizing both publics and governments to the special vulnerabilities of battle-age males in conflict," along with other forms of gender-based violence affecting males (Jones 2002a, 12).

Secondly, frame transformation requires explicit and self-conscious efforts to delegitimize the sex-selective targeting of men, such as have proliferated through the protection community with respect to sexual violence since the early 1990s. For agencies like the UNHCR, engaged in "practical protection," it means a refusal to be complicit in policies that deny unarmed civilian males the same opportunities for protection as those of unarmed civilian women. For the ICRC, which aims to disseminate norms, it means distributing educational materials and training modules that specifically address the responsibility of warring parties to avoid targeting civilian men in particular. It might begin by adding a page on "draft-age males" to its civilian protection webpage, alongside the current categories of "women," "children," "elderly," "displaced" and "refugees" (Protecting Civilians in Wartime 2003).

It is important to acknowledge the limits of the argument made here. This study has aimed to scratch the surface of and generate interest in an understudied topic rather than to cover it in depth. If I have succeeded, I will have raised more conceptual and substantive questions than I have answered, questions that might best be carried forth through a respectful engagement between IR feminists and social constructivists along the positivist/post-positivist continuum in international relations theory, and by policy-oriented scholarship on the protection of civilians as well.

One of the central gaps in this study from a social constructivist perspective is that I have emphasized the regulative role of norms to the near exclusion of the ways in which they interact with actor identities (see Kowert and Legro 1996, 452). In other words, I have avoided an investigation of the way that individual gender identities bound up in protector/protected relationships function, focusing instead on how institutional discourses and language constrain actors' interpretation of norms. This has left certain open questions with respect to the role of individual actors within the protection network as transmitters of these gender discourses.

To give an example, one male respondent I spoke with laughed nervously when asked to comment on the vulnerability of adult male civilians. For the purposes of this project, the methodologically significant aspect of this reply was his response itself (that you cannot really consider young men vulnerable since they can always pick up a gun). But the *way* in which he replied and the anxiety it engendered for him is also interesting. Studies such as Cohn's (1993) or Leeuw's (2002) that take seriously the genealogies of specific individuals and track the way in which their gender identities interact with their institutional positions, affecting their language practices, institutional power and political choices, would add insights that this analysis does not aim to capture.

Additionally, it would be useful for constructivists to connect with feminist investigations of the way in which the ostensible protection of "women and children" is used in international society to demarcate self and other. Kinsella (2005) has described how international humanitarian law posits distinctions between "civilized" states and those presumably beyond the pale, generating international hierarchies and regulating actor identities as well as prescribing codes of conduct. We see neo-colonial versions of the same phenomena when Western and non-Western states confront one another over which state best protects "its" women. Feminists such as Hunt (2002), Tickner (2002) and Enloe (1993) are keen to track the ways in which such discourse obscures the needs of actual women and children; constructivists will want to consider the conditions under which such gender discourse is or is not salient as a form of identity marker between nations and activated, perhaps, by different sorts of issues in world politics.

Scholars studying international norms of armed conflict should also more critically assess the various ways in which the "protection of women and children" is invoked in international society. Several feminists have already pointed to the dangerous tendency for "protected" categories to be cast as dependent (Steihm 1982; Tickner 2001). Others have pointed to the use of gendered "protection" myths to legitimize policies that buttress "national" security in the name of "women and children" but undermine the human security of actual children and their families (Enloe 2000; Hunt 2002). Both these trends are evident in post-war Iraq, a war fought ostensibly to protect Iraqi "women and children" from a dictator, but after which women are less secure than before and have been largely excluded from reconstruction efforts and emerging structures of governance. Those who understand the gendered dynamics of the public/private divide know that "protection" from others can be a form of racket in which the protector, assigned a role of dominance and assumed to use it responsibly, is in fact licensed to exploit or harm those to whom s/he is presumably responsible. To give a recent example, evidence that humanitarian workers and peacekeepers routinely exploit girl children and women for sexual services in conflict zones has prompted commentators to ask, "who protects from the protectors?" (Naik 2002).

On the other hand, "protection" at its best is a progressive concept, one invoking caring, stewardship and relations of consideration to those in subordinate positions. While protection relationships have the potential indeed to lock in those hierarchies, they could also be conceptualized as fluid. Perhaps for this reason gendered "protection" discourse is being simultaneously invoked by some feminist-friendly initiatives, such as Save the Children's "Every Mother Every Child" campaign, to draw the attention of the powerful donor states to issues such as reproductive health. Feminists will need to keep an eye on such initiatives and find ways to systematically assess whether or not they are likely to backfire. It is not at all clear, for example, whether the Congressional "Protection of Women and Children in Armed Conflict Act," supported by the Women's Commission for Refugee Women and Children, is essentially a whitewash that locks in a victim view of war-affected women or whether it is a trope that can be used to hold the US responsible for initiatives that can promote gender equity in conflict situations.

Phenomena such as the above point to the ways in which ideas and discourses constitute resources for the powerful and mask hierarchies between differentiated groups. As Barnett and Duvall argue (2005, 1), constructivists, keen to distinguish themselves from the realist emphasis on power as a variable, have been slow to explicitly consider the way that power works in and through their theories. Prugl and Locher, sketching possible areas in which feminism and constructivism might learn from one another, also point to IR feminists' explicit understanding of power as a fundamental part of the social fabric, rather than simply a set of material or ideational resources. For example, "central to feminist investigations of identity in IR has been the suggestion that identities do not only create interests and meanings (as constructivists... argue) but also relationships of superiority and inferiority" (Locher and Prugl 2001b, 80). Taking this argument seriously, Barnett and

Duvall (2005) have generated a taxonomy of power from a variety of implicit approaches characteristic of different areas of IR theory. They differentiate forms of power according to whether they involve regulative or constitutive effects, and whether they are exercised directly by one actor over another or through diffuse institutional arrangements.

It would be interesting to revisit the question of the gendered immunity norm through such a theoretical lens. Like other constructivists, I have clearly been talking about power – "the production, in and through social relations of effects that shape the capacities of actors to determine their own circumstances and fate" (Barnett and Duvall 2005, 2). The exercise of armed violence and/or mercy is a form of what Barnett and Duvall would call "compulsory power." Sadako Ogata's appeals for strong states to assist "vulnerable" groups involved acts of compulsory (shaming) power with respect to international society, but also of more diffuse institutional power with respect to civilians, since the language through which she framed the issue of protection conditioned their existence by legitimizing non-action on behalf of civilian men. Likewise, the social structure (such as a structure that divides the war-affected population into presumed participants and non-participants) constitutes actors' structural positions (such as the civilian) and hence their interests, identities and social capacities (such as the ability to claim to be immune from attack, and to have attackers respond to that claim). Diffuse discourses are also implicated in producing and reproducing the social structure in which these meanings make sense, in part by constructing and naturalizing hierarchies between rights-bearers based on assumptions about gender roles.

Some of the most interesting questions this study raises regarding the manifestation of power in world politics are about how these forms of power interrelate. Barnett and Duvall's depiction of structural power seems to leave little room to understand actors' ability to alter their structural positions by choice. In the case of civilian/combatant distinction (as a set of binary structural positions), a person can switch positions simply by picking up or putting down a weapon. Is there a systematic way that we might understand the behavior of actors (war-affected civilians themselves, as they blur into the category "belligerent," as that blurs into the category "humanitarian" through the category "peacekeeper") in the context of these structures interacting with material constraints?

Clearly there are webs of power relationships that defy easy categorization. If the act of forcing males off evacuation convoys is an exercise of power over civilians' ability to control their fate by humanitarian workers, how do we best understand the kinds of power that constrained the aid workers to agree to act in these ways? If the ability to successfully make a rights claim is a form of power, can we make the argument that recipients of mercy are relatively more "powerful" than those who are denied mercy, when to be at someone's mercy is often itself understood as an absence of power? Are we to conclude that "women and children" are relatively more powerful than civilian men in times of war? To what extent can we separate the ability of civilian men to "determine their own circumstances and fate" from the circumstances and fate of the civilian women who are affected by their disappearance?

We need to understand how actors are embedded in these webs of power relationships and how they interact. Feminist theory indeed has much to teach constructivism in this regard, but IR feminists must be prepared for such a dialogue to yield perhaps uncomfortable insights such as the above and to contradict seeming feminist givens such as the idea that power is something "women don't have" (Locher and Prugl 2001a, 88). Surely a more complex understanding of social relations, in which gender relations is but one of many referents, would yield a more nuanced view. The case studies presented in this book suggest that this is the case, but a careful examination of their implication for the theorization of power in world politics remains to be undertaken.

Substantively, also, there is much more to learn about the regulative role of the gender sub-norm identified here. For example, in terms of protection operations, it is difficult to generalize from the somewhat atypical case of Srebrenica to other complex emergency situations. Therefore, comparative work evaluating the extent to which the "women and children first" rule affects operations in different contexts would build on this preliminary analysis. Under what conditions are belligerents less inclined to use sex as a proxy for "combatant?" Are adult male civilians more likely to be spared in cases where fewer men are mobilized, or is a critical mass of female combatants the pivotal factor in reducing the salience of gender as a cognitive map? How do the strategies and opportunities of protection workers differ in cases where belligerents' gender assumptions are not so deterministic, and to what extent are they constant, based on the public relations demands of the greater protection network? Other protection initiatives, such as measures taken to separate armed elements from "bona fide" refugees, may also provide glimpses of the way in which "distinction" is operationalized in humanitarian settings, and the extent to which gender sub-norms underwrite its implementation (Hamilton 2002).

Another point I have touched upon but inadequately explored is the extent to which the gendered basis for civilian immunity in the network norms themselves is undergoing change as a result of the strain imposed by the complex emergencies of the 1990s. Much has happened since 1993. Civilian protection agencies learn from their catastrophes. The gender-mainstreaming process within the protection community has awakened theorists and practitioners to the dangers of casting women as passive victims rather than agents of change in conflict and post-conflict contexts (Moser and Clark 2001). While there still exist no protection initiatives targeting civilian men as such, and while gender-based violence continues to be defined in

172   *'Innocent Women and Children'*

reference to women only, both the ICRC and OCHA have recently begun to tentatively acknowledge men's particular vulnerabilities as civilians (Lindsey 2001; IASC 2002). I suspect this is a step in the right direction, but we will need to more systematically assess the results of such efforts in order to confirm or disconfirm that suspicion. It would be interesting to track these attempts at reframing "vulnerability" and examine the extent to which they flounder or, if successful, produce additional gendered side-effects.

This sort of analysis might be best undertaken by methodologies associated with critical theory (Linklater 1996; Cox 1986). Critical theorists examine the interrelationship between material resources, institutions and ideas to identify possible leverage points for bringing about change in world politics. Both Whitworth's (1994) and Steinstra's (1994) work on international organizations demonstrate how to make inferences about the conditions under which norm change can occur. There is currently a debate afoot in the humanitarian assistance community regarding the relative merits of perpetuating gender essentialisms in protection discourse, at the expense of mainstreaming gender analysis, or explicitly drawing attention to men's vulnerability, possibly at the expense of women. Real-world actors would benefit greatly from some systematic research that assessed the potential for overcoming this dilemma.

Finally, if we want to take seriously the issue of gender-based violence against men in armed conflict as a human rights issue from a policy perspective, our research agenda must go beyond the limited focus of this project. The case studies here have focused on the failure of international society to adequately condemn the sex-selective execution of males or to take pro-active steps to prevent the separation of men from their families in conflict situations. But execution is only one form of gender-based abuse against men and boys in wartime. There are other such understudied practices that are implicated both in the harms to which the rest of the civilian population is exposed, and to the normative/institutional context in which such violations are legitimized.

To give one example, forced recruitment of adult men deprives civilian men of their liberty and civilian families of their male kin, while reproducing the sex-gender structures that naturalize the gender sub-norm addressed here (Carpenter, 2006). While forced recruitment of children is condemned, the forced recruitment of adults, a practice largely targeted at males, is still considered legitimate and is neither condemned nor addressed by civilian protection organizations (Respondent #30, 2002). For example, the United States Committee for Refugees (USCR) considered the question of whether the asylum regime extended to draft evaders during the breakup of the former Yugoslavia. Its report pointed out that "deserters generally engender little sympathy in the asylum context... the *UN Handbook on Procedures for Determining Refugee Status...* holds that states have a sovereign right to conscript their citizens" (USCR 1992, 21-24). Some protections exist in the refugee regime for draft evaders "who fear persecution on political grounds" (UNHCR 2002) or who are fleeing a conflict characterized by massive humanitarian law violations (USCR 1992), but the act of forcible recruitment itself is not considered a form of political repression or slavery, and the concept of "gender-based persecution" as grounds for asylum has been applied primarily to the kinds of persecution faced by women.

The absence of a strong norm against forced conscription as a form of gender-based violence should be analyzed both by scholars interested in norm dynamics and by those seeking to strengthen both human rights and gender-mainstreaming initiatives within international society. Similar work could be undertaken to understand rape narratives that obfuscate sexual violence targeted at males, to take seriously the secondary victimization of men through violence directed at female relatives, and to understand better how conflict and post-conflict situations may serve as sites for renegotiating norms and social hierarchies. This research should take place so as to complement, rather than undermine, existing feminist research on women and armed conflict.

It is laudable that international institutions increasingly recognize the importance of human security as part of the global security agenda. But as Lindner (2002) argues, human security cannot be achieved by accommodating older norms that contradict the principle of universal human rights. Regarding the protection of civilians specifically, if this protection is to serve its intended purpose, it must not take place at the expense of fundamental humanitarian principles, such as impartiality among victims. Tradeoffs will at times be made, but this should occur through a thoughtful and systematic moral process (Slim 1997). Decisions about who receives protection should no more be based on sex than on religion, race or nationality. Michael Ignatieff is right when he claims that "our pity is structured by history and culture" (1998, 287) but rather than indicting the possibility of an impartial humanitarianism, his words might be understood as a warning to recognize this fact so as to overcome it. The doctrine of human rights and humanitarianism suggests a world in which our willingness to help and to speak out is structured, instead, by objective facts and an impartial ethical logic; on the basis of human need rather than culturally constructed affinity, or lack thereof.

Bibliography

Aafjes, Astrid and Ann Tierney Goldstein, Gender Violence: The Hidden War Crime (Washington, DC: Women, Law and Development International, 1998).

Additional Protocol I to the Geneva Conventions of 12 August 1949 (Geneva: International Committee of the Red Cross, 1977).

Additional Protocol II to the Geneva Conventions of 12 August 1949 (Geneva: International Committee of the Red Cross, 1977).

African Rights, Death, Despair and Defiance (London: African Rights, 1995a).

African Rights, Rwanda – Not So Innocent: When Women Become Killers (London: African Rights, 1995b).

Aguire, Mariano, "The Media and the Humanitarian Spectacle." In Reflections of Humanitarian Action: Principles, Ethics and Contradictions, edited by the Humanitarian Studies Unit (London: Pluto Press, 2001), pp. 157-176.

Ahlstrom, Christer, Casualties of Conflict: Report for the World Campaign for the Protection of Victims of War (Sweden: Department of Peace and Conflict Research, Uppsala University, 1991).

Ali, Tariq, ed., Masters of the Universe: NATO's Balkan Crusade (NY: Verso Books, 2000).

Allen, Beverly, Rape Warfare: The Hidden Genocide in Bosnia-Herzegovina (Minneapolis: University of Minnesota Press, 1996).

American Association for the Advancement of Science. (2000) Policy or Panic? The Flight of Ethnic Albanians from Kosovo, March-May 1999. Available online at http://hrdata.aaas.org/kosovo/policyorpanic.

Amnesty International, Human Rights Abuses Against Women in Kosovo Province (London: Amnesty International, 1998).

Anderson, David, ed., Facing My Lai: Moving Beyond the Massacre (Lawrence: University of Kansas, 1999).

Anderson, John, "Israel Committed War Crimes in West Bank, Rights Group Says." Washington Post, November 4, 2002.

Anderson, Mary, Do No Harm: How Aid Can Support Peace – Or War (Boulder: Lynne Reinner, 1999).

Anderson, Mary, Ann Howarth and Catherine Overholt, A Framework for People-Oriented Planning in Refugee Situations Taking Account of Women, Men and Children (Geneva: UNHCR, 1992).

Andreopoulos, George, "The Age of National Liberation Movements." In Laws of War: Constraints on Warfare in the Western World, edited by

176   *'Innocent Women and Children'*

Michael Howard, George Andreopoulos and Mark Shulman (New Haven: Yale University Press, 1994) pp. 191-213.

Anscombe, Elizabeth, "War and Murder." In War and Morality, edited by Richard Wasserstrom (Belmont: Wadsworth Publishing Company, 1970), pp. 42-53.

Anonymous, "Arafat Asks Bombers to Spare Israeli Women and Children." Sydney Morning Herald. May 26, 2003. Available online at http://www.smh.com.au/articles/2003/05/25/1053801275924.html

Ardery, Breck, "UN/Mandela/Burundi." Voice of America. September 29, 2000. Available online at http://www.fas.org/man/dod-101/ops/war/2000/09/war-000929-afburundi2.htm.

Arkin, William, "Operation Allied Force: 'The Most Precise Application of Air Power in History.'" In War Over Kosovo: Politics and Strategy in a Global Age, edited by Andrew Bacevich and Eliot Cohen (NY: Columbia University Press, 2001), pp. 1-37.

Askin, Kelly, War Crimes Against Women: Prosecution in International War Crimes Tribunals (The Hague: Martinus Nijhoff Publishers, 1997).

Baines, Erin, "Gender Construction and the Protection Mandate of the UNHCR: Responses from Guatemalan Women." In Gender Politics and Global Governance, edited by Mary Meyer and Elisabeth Prugl (NY: Rowman and Littlefield Publishers, 1999), pp. 245-259.

Baines, Erin, "Body Politics and the Rwandan Crisis." Third World Quarterly, 24(3) (2003), pp. 479-493.

Baines, Erin, Vulnerable Bodies: Gender, the UN and the Global Refugee Crisis (Aldershot: Ashgate Publishing, 2004).

Ball, Stephen, Prosecuting War Crimes and Genocide (Lawrence: University Press of Kansas, 1999).

Barnett, Michael, "Culture, Strategy and Foreign Policy Change: Israel's Road to Oslo," European Journal of International Relations 5(1) (1999), pp. 5-36.

Barnett, Michael, Eyewitness to a Genocide: The United Nations and Rwanda (Ithaca, NY: Cornell University Press, 2002).

Barnett, Michael and Robert Duvall, "Introduction: Power and Global Governance." In Power and Global Governance, edited by Michael Barnett and Robert Duvall (Cambridge: Cambridge University Press 2005).

Barstow, Anne, ed., War's Dirty Secret: Rape, Prostitution and Other Crimes Against Women (Cleveland, Ohio: The Pilgrim Press, 2000a).

Barstow, Anne, "Introduction." In War's Dirty Secret: Rape, Prostitution and Other Crimes Against Women, edited by Anne Barstow (Cleveland, Ohio: The Pilgrim Press, 2000b), pp. 1-10.

Barstow, Anne, "The U.N.'s Role in Defining War Crimes Against Women." In War's Dirty Secret: Rape, Prostitution and Other Crimes Against Women, edited by Anne Barstow (Cleveland, Ohio: The Pilgrim Press, 2000c), pp. 234-244.

Bibliography

Beaumont, Peter, "Warlords Hear Karzai Vow To Build an Era of Peace." London Observer, December 23, 2001. Available online at http://observer.guardian.co.uk/afghanistan/story/0,1501,624306,00html

Beer, Francis, Peace Against War: The Ecology of International Violence (San Francisco: W.H. Freeman and Company, 1981).

Beigbeder, Yves, New Challenges for UNICEF: Children, Women and Human Rights (NY: Palgrave Macmillan, 2002).

Benjamin, Judy and Khadija Fancy, The Gender Dimensions of Internal Displacement: Concept Paper and Annotated Bibliography (NY: Women's Commission for Refugee Women and Children, 1998).

Bennett, Olivia, Jo Bexley and Kitty Warnock, eds., Arms to Fight, Arms to Protect: Women Speak Out About Conflict (London: Panos, 1995).

Benthall, Jonathan, Disasters, Relief and the Media (London: I.B. Tauris and Co., 1993).

Berry, Nicholas, War and the Red Cross: The Unspoken Mission (NY: St. Martin's Press, 1997).

Best, Gregory, Humanity in Warfare: The Modern History of the International Law of Armed Conflicts (London: Methuen, 1983).

Blanning, T., "Liberation or Occupation? Theory and Practice in the French Revolutionaries' Treatment of Civilians Outside France." In Civilians in the Path of War, edited by Mark Grimsley and Clifford Rogers (Lincoln: University of Nebraska Press, 2002), pp. 111-136.

Blom, Ida, "Gender and Nation in International Comparison." In Gendered Nations: Nationalisms and Gender Order in the Nineteenth Century, edited by Ida Blom et al. (NY: New York University Press, 2000), pp. 3-26.

Blom, Ida, Catherine Hall and Karen Hagemann, eds., Gendered Nations: Nationalisms and Gender Order in the Nineteenth Century (NY: New York University Press, 2000).

Bloom, Mia, Dying To Kill: The Allure of Suicide Terror (NY: Columbia University Press).

Bonard, Paul, Modes of Action Used by Humanitarian Players: Criteria for Operational Complementarity (Geneva: ICRC, 1999).

Bop, Codou, "Women in Conflicts: Their Gains and Their Losses." In The Aftermath, edited by Sheila Meintjes et al. (London: Zed Books, 2002), pp. 19-34.

Bosnian Action Coalition, "Bosnian Town of Zepa Falls to Serb Nationalists." This Week in Bosnia-Herzegovina, July 25, 1995. Available online at http://www.applicom.com/twibih/95archive/TWiBH-950725.txt. Accessed October 20, 2002.

Bouchet-Saulnier, Francoise, The Practical Guide to Humanitarian Law (Lanham: Rowman and Littlefield, 2002).

Bourke, Joanna, An Intimate History of Killing: Face to Face Killing in Twentieth Century Warfare (London: Basic Books, 1999).

178   *'Innocent Women and Children'*

Braumann, Rony, "When Suffering Makes a Good Story." In Life, Death and Aid: The Medicines Sans Frontieres Report on World Crisis Intervention, edited by Francois Jean (London: Routledge, 1993), pp. 149-158.

Braybon, Gail and Penny Summerfield, Out of the Cage: Women's Experience in Two World Wars (London: Pandora, 1987).

Bringa, Tone, Being Muslim the Bosnian Way (Princeton, NJ: Princeton University Press, 1995).

Brown, Sarah, "Feminism, International Theory and International Relations of Gender Inequality." Millennium: Journal of International Studies. 17(3) (1998), pp. 461-475.

Brownmiller, Susan, "Making Female Bodies the Battlefield." In Mass Rape: The War Against Women in Bosnia-Herzegovina, edited by Alexandra Stigalmeyer (Lincoln: University of Nebraska Press, 1994), pp. 180-182.

Bruderlein, Claude, "The End of Innocence: Humanitarian Protection in the 21st Century." In Civilians In War, edited by Simon Chesterman (Boulder: Lynne Reinner, 2001), pp. 221-236.

Buchanan, David, "Gendercide and Human Rights." Journal of Genocide Research 4(1) (2002), pp. 95-108.

Buckley, William, ed., Kosovo: Contending Voices on Balkan Interventions (Grand Rapids, MI: Eerdmans Publishing Co., 2000).

Bunch, Charlotte, "Women's Rights as Human Rights: Towards a Re-Vision of Human Rights." Human Rights Quarterly 12(4) (1990), pp. 486-500.

Bunch, Charlotte and Niamh Reilly, Demanding Accountability: The Global Campaign and Vienna Tribunal for Women's Human Rights (Rutgers, NJ: Center for Women's Global Leadership, 1994).

Burg, Steven and Paul S. Shoup, The War in Bosnia-Herzegovina (NY: M.E. Sharpe, 1999).

Butalia, Urvashi, "Women and Communal Conflict: New Challenges for the Women's Movement in India." In Victims, Perpetrators or Actors? Gender, Armed Conflict and Political Violence, edited by Caroline Moser and Fiona Clark (London: Zed Books, 2001), pp. 99-114.

Butler, Judith, Bodies That Matter: On the Discursive Limits of 'Sex' (NY: Routledge, 1993).

Buzan, Barry, "From International System to International Society: Structural Realism and Regime Theory Meet the English School." International Organization 47(3) (1993), pp. 327-52.

Cain, Kenneth, "The Rape of Dinah: Human Rights, Civil War in Liberia, and Evil Triumphant." Human Rights Quarterly 21(1) (1999), pp. 265-307.

Calic, Mari-Janine, "Kosovo in the Twentieth Century: A Historical Account." In Kosovo and the Challenge of Humanitarian Intervention, edited by Albrecht Schnable and Ramesh Thakur (Tokyo: United Nations University Press, 2000), pp. 19-31.

Campbell, Kenneth, Genocide and the Global Village (London: Palgrave, 2001).

Bibliography

Caprioli, Mary, "Feminist IR Theory and Quantitative Methodology: A Critical Analysis." International Studies Quarterly, 6(2) (2004), pp. 253-269.

Carpenter, Charli, "Surfacing Children: Limitations of Genocidal Rape Discourse." Human Rights Quarterly 22(2) (2000), pp. 428-477.

Carpenter, Charli, "Gender Theory in World Politics: Contributions of a Non-Feminist Standpoint." International Studies Review 4(3)(2002a):153-166.

Carpenter, Charli, "Beyond Gendercide: Incorporating Gender into Comparative Genocide Studies." International Journal of Human Rights 6(4) (2002b), pp. 77-101.

Carpenter, Charli, "'Women and Children First': Gender, Norms and Humanitarian Evacuation in the Balkans 1991-1995." International Organization 57(4) (2003a), pp. 661-694.

Carpenter, Charli, "Stirring Gender into the Mainstream: Feminism, Constructivism and the Uses of Theory." International Studies Review 5(3) (2003b), pp. 297-300.

Carpenter, Charli, "Recognizing Gender-Based Violence Against Civilian Men and Boys in Conflict Situations." Security Dialogue 37(1) (2006), pp. 103-124.

Carr, Caleb, The Lessons of Terror: A History of Warfare Against Civilians (NY: Random House, 2002).

Carver, Terrell, "Men and IR/Men in IR." In Gendering the International, edited by Louiza Odysseios and Hakan Seckinelgin (NY: Palgrave Macmillan, 2002), pp. 86-105.

Carver, Terrell, "Gender/Feminism/IR." International Studies Review 5(3) (2003), pp. 288-290.

Carver, Terrell, Molly Cochran and Judith Squires, "Gendering Jones: Feminisms, IRs, and Masculinities." Review of International Studies 24(2) (1998), pp. 283-297.

Caversazio, Sylvie Giossi, Strengthening Protection in War: A Search for Professional Standards (Geneva: ICRC, 2001).

Chalk, Frank, "Hate Radio in Rwanda." In Path of a Genocide: The Rwanda Crisis From Uganda to Zaire, edited by Howard Adelman and Astri Suhrke (New Bruswick: Transaction Publishers, 1999), pp. 93-110.

Chalk, Frank and Kurt Jonassohn eds., The History and Sociology of Genocide (New Haven: Yale University Press, 1990).

Chant, Sylvia and Matthew Gutmann, Mainstreaming Men into Gender and Development: Debates, Reflections and Experiences (London: OXFAM, 2001).

Charlesworth, Hilary, "Human Rights as Men's Rights." In Women's Rights, Human Rights: International Feminist Perspectives, edited by Andrea Wolper and J.S. Peters (NY: Routledge, 1995), pp. 103-113.

180 'Innocent Women and Children'

Charlesworth, Hilary and Christine Chinkin, The Boundaries of International Law (UK: Manchester Press, 2000).

Charlesworth, Hilary, Christine Chinkin and Shelley Wright, "Feminist Approaches to International Law." In International Rules: Approaches from International Law and Relations, edited by Robert Beck et al. (NY: Oxford University Press, 1996), pp. 253-285.

Checkel, Jeffrey, "The Constructivist Turn in IR Theory." World Politics 50(2) (1998), pp. 324-348.

Checkel, Jeffrey, "Norms, Institutions, and National Identity in Contemporary Europe." International Studies Quarterly 43(1) (1999), pp. 83-114.

Chesterman, Simon, "Introduction." In Civilians in War, edited by Simon Chesterman (Boulder: Lynne Reinner, 2001), pp. 1-8.

Chomsky, Noam, A New Generation Draws the Line: Kosovo, East Timor and the Standards of the West (NY: Verso Books, 2001).

Christian Century, "Famine Threatens Ethiopia Again." Anonymous Article, May 3, 2000.

Cigar, Norman, Genocide in Bosnia (College Station: Texas A&M University Press, 1995).

Clark, Howard, Civil Resistance in Kosovo (Sterling, VA: Pluto Press, 2000).

CNN. (2002) "Bush Offers Condolences to Afghan People." Anonymous Article, 2 July. Available online at http://www.cnn.com/2002/US/07/02/bush.afghan.deaths/index.html. Accessed October 20, 2002.

Cockburn, Cynthia, The Space Between Us: Negotiating Gender and National Identities in Conflict (London: Zed Books, 1998).

Cockburn, Cynthia, "The Gendered Dynamics of Armed Conflict and Political Violence." In Victims, Perpetrators or Actors? Gender, Armed Conflict and Political Violence, edited by Caroline Moser and Fiona Clark (London: Zed Books, 2001), pp. 13-29.

Cockburn, Cynthia and Dubravka Zarkov, eds., The Post-War Moment: Militaries, Masculinities and International Peacekeeping (London: Lawrence and Wishart, 2002).

Cohen, Roberta and Francis Deng, Masses in Flight: The Global Crisis of Internal Displacement (Washington, DC: Brookings Institution Press, 1998).

Cohen, Stanley, States of Denial: Knowing About Atrocities and Suffering (Cambridge, UK: Polity Press, 2001).

Cohn, Carol, "Clean Bombs and Clean Language." In Women, Militarism and War, edited by Jean-Bethke Elshtain and Sheila Tobias (Savage, MD: Rowman and Littlefield, 1993), pp. 33-55.

Cohn, Carol, "Gays in the Military: Texts and Subtexts." In The 'Man' Question in International Relations, edited by Marysia Zalewski and Jane Parpart (Boulder: Westview Press, 1998), pp. 129-149.

Cohn, Carol, Helen Kinsella and Sheri Gibbings, "Women, Peace and Security: Resolution 1325." International Feminist Journal of Politics 6(1) (2004), pp. 130-140.

Coleman, James, Foundations of Social Theory (Cambridge: Belknap Press, 1990).

Coll, Alberto, "Kosovo and the Moral Burdens of Power." In War Over Kosovo, edited by Andrew Bacevich and Eliot Cohen (NY: Columbia University Press, 2001), pp. 124-154.

Connell, Robert, Gender and Power (Cambridge: Polity Press, 1987).

Connell, Robert, The Men and the Boys (Berkeley: University of California Press, 2000).

Cooke, Miriam, "WO-man, Retelling the War Myth." In Gendering War Talk, edited by Miriam Cooke and Angela Woollacott (Princeton, NJ: Princeton University Press, 1993), pp. 177-204.

Cooke, Miriam and Angela Woollacott, eds., Gendering War Talk (Princeton, NJ: Princeton University Press, 1993).

Cooley, Alexander and James Ron, "The NGO Scramble: Organizational Insecurity and the Political Economy of Transnational Action." International Security 27(1) (2002), pp. 5-29.

Cornell, Dan and Frank Smyth, "New Leaders and New Hopes." Boston Globe, March 22, 1998.

Council of Europe. (1993) Resolution 1011 on the Situation of Women and Children in the Former Yugoslavia. Available online at http://assembly. coe.int/Documents/AdoptedText/TA93/ERES1011.HTM. Accessed October 25, 2003.

Cox, Robert, "Social Forces, States and World Orders: Beyond IR Theory." In Neorealism and Its Critics, edited by Robert Keohane (NY: Columbia University Press, 1986), pp. 204-255.

Crane, Conrad, "Contrary to Our National Ideals: American Strategic Bombing of Civilians in World War II." In Civilians in the Path of War, edited by Mark Grimsley and Clifford Rogers (Lincoln: University of Nebraska Press, 2002), pp. 219-250.

Crawford, Neta, "Just War Theory and the U.S. Counter-terror War." In Perspectives on Politics 1(1) (2003), pp. 5-26.

Crisp, Jeff, "Who Has Counted the Refugees?" In Humanitarian Action: Social Science Connections, edited by Stephen Lubkemann, Larry Minear and Thomas Weiss (Providence, RI: Thomas J. Watson Institute for International Studies, Brown University, 1999), pp. 33-62.

Cummins, Chip, "Human Rights Group to Estimate Civilians Killed in U.S. Campaign." Wall Street Journal, February 7, 2002. Available online at http://www.commondreams.org/headlines02/0207-03.htm. Accessed October 21, 2003.

Cutts, Mark, "The Humanitarian Operation in Bosnia, 1992-1995: Dilemmas of Negotiating Humanitarian Access." Journal of Humanitarian Assistance

(1999). Available from http://www.jha.ac/articles/u008.pdf. Accessed October 2002.

Daalder, Ivo and Michael Ottenlon, Winning Ugly (Washington: Brookings Institute Press, 2000).

Danner, Mark, "Endgame in Kosovo: Ethnic Cleansing and American Amnesia." In Kosovo: Contending Voices on Balkan Interventions, edited by William Buckley (Grand Rapids, MI: William Eerdmans, 2000), pp. 56-72.

Darst, Robert, "The Samaritan's Dilemma in International Environmental Politics." Paper presented to the Annual Meeting of the International Studies Association, Portland, Oregon, 2003.

Date-bah, Eugenia et al., Gender and Armed Conflicts. Working Paper 2, In Focus Programme on Crisis Response and Reconstruction (Geneva: International Labor Organization, 2001).

Declaration on the Protection of Women and Children in Emergency and Armed Conflict, General Assembly Resolution 3318(XXIX), December 14, 1974.

De Maio, Jacques, The Challenges of Complementarity (Geneva: ICRC, 2000).

De Preux, J., "Special Protection of Women and Children." In *International Review of the Red Cross*, 307 (1985), pp. 292-302.

DeLaet, Debra, "Gender, Truth-Telling and Sustainable Peace." In Telling the Truths: Peace Building and Truth Telling, edited by Tristan A. Borer (Indianapolis: University of Notre Dame Press, 2005).

DeMars, William, "Contending Neutralities: Humanitarian Organizations and War in the Horn of Africa." In Transnational Social Movements and Global Politics, edited by Jackie Smith, Charles Chatfield and Ron Pagnucco (NY: Syracuse University Press, 1997), pp. 101-122.

Demjaha, Agon, "The Kosovo Conflict: A Perspective From Inside." In Kosovo and the Challenge of Humanitarian Intervention, edited by Albrecht Schnabel and Ramesh Thakur (Tokyo: United Nations University Press, 2000), pp. 32-43.

Deutz, Andrew, "Gender and International Human Rights." Fletcher Forum 17(2) (1993), pp. 33-52.

Di Stefano, Christine, Configurations of Masculinity: A Feminist Perspective on Modern Political Theory (NY: Cornell University Press, 1991).

Dombrowski, Nicole, ed., Women and War in the Twentieth Century: Enlisted With or Without Consent (NY: Garland Publishing, 1999).

Dongen, Yvonne, The Protection of Civilian Populations in Times of Armed Conflict (Amsterdam: Thesis Publishers, 1991).

Duster, Troy, "Conditions for a Guilt-Free Massacre." In Sanctions For Evil, edited by Newitt Sanford and Craig Comstock (San Francisco: Jossey-Bass Publishers, 1972), pp. 25-36.

Dyer, Gwynne, War (NY: Crown Publishers, 1985).

Economic and Social Council (ECOSOC). Resolution 1998/26. "Mainstreaming a Gender Perspective into all Policies and Programs in the United Nations System." UN Doc E/Res/1998/26.

Ehrenreich, Barbara, Blood Rites: The Origins and History of the Passions of War (NY: Metropolitan Books, 1997).

El-Bushra, Judy, "Transforming Conflict: Some Thoughts on a Gendered Understanding of Conflict Processes." In States of Conflict: Gender, Violence and Resistance, edited by Susie Jacobs et al. (London: Zed Books, 2000), pp. 66-86.

Elliott, H. Wayne, "Evacuation of Civilians from the Battlefield." In Crimes of War, edited by Roy Gutman and David Reiff (NY: W.W. Norton, 1999), pp. 139-141.

Elshtain, Jean-Bethke, Women and War (NY: Basic Books, 1987).

Elshtain, Jean-Bethke and Sheila Tobias, eds., Women, Militarism, and War: Essays in History, Politics and Social Theory. (Savage, Maryland: Rowman & Littlefield, 1990).

Enloe, Cynthia, Bananas, Beaches and Bases: Making Feminist Sense of International Politics (Berkeley: University of California Press, 1989).

Enloe, Cynthia, The Morning After: Sexual Politics After the Cold War (Berkeley: University of California Press, 1993).

Enloe, Cynthia, "All the Men are in the Militias, All the Women are Victims: The Politics of Masculinity and Femininity in Nationalist Wars." In The Women and War Reader, edited by Lois Ann Lorentzen and Jennifer Turpin (NY: New York University Press, 1999), pp. 50-62.

Enloe, Cynthia, Maneuvers: The International Politics of Militarizing Women's Lives (Berkeley: University of California Press, 2000).

Erdem, Suna, "Iraqi Army Deserters Go North to Escape Mutilation." Reuters World Report, October 31, 1994.

Fain, Jessica, "Letter to the Editor." Newsweek, July 12, 1999.

Fairness and Accuracy in Reporting. (2001) "Civilian Casualties Not News." Anonymous Article, 8 November. Available online at http://www.fair.org/activism/fox-civilian-casualties.html. Accessed October 20, 2002.

Feil, Scott, Preventing Genocide: How the Early Use of Force Might Have Succeeded in Rwanda (Washington, D.C.: Carnegie Commission on Preventing Deadly Conflict, 1998).

Ferroggiaro, William, (2001) "The US and the Genocide in Rwanda 1994." Available through George Washington University's National Security Archive website. Online at http://www.gwu.edu/~nsarchiv/. Accessed November 25, 2003.

Fierke, Karin, "Multiple Identities, Interfacing Games: The Social Construction of Western Action in Bosnia." European Journal of International Relations 2(4) (1996), pp. 467-497.

Finnemore, Martha, National Interests in International Society. (NY: Cornell University Press, 1996a).

184 'Innocent Women and Children'

Finnemore, Martha, "Constructing Norms of Humanitarian Intervention." In The Culture of National Security, edited by Peter Katzenstein (NY: Columbia University Press, 1996b), pp. 154-185.

Finnemore, Martha, "Rules of War and Wars of Rules: The International Red Cross and the Restraint of State Violence." In Constructing World Culture: International Nongovernmental Organizations Since 1875, edited by John Boli and George Thomas (Stanford, CA: Stanford University Press, 1999).

Finnemore, Martha and Michael Barnett, "The Politics, Power and Pathologies of International Organizations." International Organization 53(4) (1999), pp. 699-732.

Finnemore, Martha and Kathryn Sikkink, "International Norm Dynamics and Political Change." International Organization 52(4) (1998), pp. 887-918.

Finnis, John, "The Ethics of War and Peace in the Catholic Natural Law Tradition." In The Ethics of War and Peace, edited by Terry Nardin (Princeton, NJ: Princeton University Press, 1996), pp. 15-39.

Fisher, Siobhan, "Occupation of the Womb: Forced Impregnation as Genocide." Duke Law Journal 46(1) (1996), pp. 91-133.

Fisk, Robert, "War in the Balkans – Families Blasted in 'Just Another Mistake.'" The Independent, April 30, 1999. Available online at http://www.ius.bg.ac.yu/apel/fisk.htm. Accessed October 21, 2003.

Florini, Ann, "The Evolution of International Norms." International Studies Quarterly 40(3) (1996), pp. 363-389.

Florini, Ann, ed., The Third Force: The Rise of Transnational Civil Society (Washington: Carnegie Endowment for International Peace, 2000).

Flynn, Gregory and Henry Farrell, "Piecing Together the Democratic Peace: The CSCE, Norms and the 'Construction' of Security in Post-Cold War Europe." International Organization 53(3) (1999), pp. 505-535.

Ford, John, "The Morality of Obliteration Bombing." In War and Morality, edited by Richard Wasserstrom (Belmont: Wadworth Publishing Company, 1970), pp. 15-41.

Forrest, Alan, "Conscription as Ideology: Revolutionary France and the Nation in Arms." In The Comparative Study of Conscription in the Armed Forces, edited by Lars Mjoset and Stephen Van Holde (Amsterdam: Elsevier Science, 2002), pp. 95-116.

Frohardt, Mark, Diane Paul and Larry Minear, Protecting Human Rights: The Challenge to Humanitarian Organizations. Thomas J. Watson Jr. Institute for International Studies, Occasional Paper #35 (Providence, RI: Brown University, 1999).

Fullenwider, Robert, "War and Innocence." In International Ethics, edited by Barry Cohen et al. (Princeton: Princeton University Press, 1985), pp. 90-97.

Gardam, Judith, Non-Combatant Immunity as a Norm of International Humanitarian Law (Dordrecht: Martinus Nijhoff Publishers, 1993).

Bibliography 185

Gardam, Judith and Hilary Charlesworth, "Protection of Women in Armed Conflict." Human Rights Quarterly 22(1) (2000), pp. 148-166.

Gardam, Judith and Michelle Jervis, Women, Armed Conflict and International Law (The Hague: Kluwer Law International, 2001).

Garnett News Service, "Coleman Joins Calls for Action in Bosnia." Anonymous Article, April 23, 1993.

Gasser, Hans, "Protection of the Civilian Population." In The Handbook of Humanitarian Law in Armed Conflicts, edited by Dieter Fleck (NY: Oxford University Press, 1995), pp. 209-288.

Geertz, Clifford, Negara: The Theatre State in Nineteenth-Century Bali (Princeton: Princeton University Press, 1980).

Gendercide Watch. (2003a). Online at http://www.gendercide.org. Updated October 12, 2003. Accessed November 4, 2003.

Gendercide Watch. (2003b). "Case Study: Colombia." Online at http://www.gendercide.org/case_colombia.html. Accessed January 30, 2004.

Ghobarah, Hazem, Paul Huth and Bruce Russett, "Civil Wars Kill and Maim People – Long After the Shooting Stops." American Political Science Review 97(2) (2003), pp. 189-202.

Girardet, Edward, "Public Opinion, the Media and Humanitarianism." In Humanitarianism Across Borders: Sustaining Civilians in Times of War, edited by Thomas Weiss and Larry Minear (Boulder: Lynne Reinner 1993), pp. 39-53.

Goldberg, Elissa and Don Hubert, "Case Study: The Security Council and the Protection of Civilians." In Human Security and the New Diplomacy, edited by Rob McRae and Don Hubert (Montreal: McGill-Queen's University Press, 2001), pp. 223-230.

Goldberg, Pamela, "Where in the World is There Safety for Me? Women Fleeing Gender-Based Persecution." In Women's Rights, Human Rights: International Feminist Perspectives, edited by Julie Peters and Andrea Wolper (NY: Routledge, 1995), pp. 345-355.

Goldstein, Joshua, War and Gender (Cambridge, MA: Cambridge University Press, 2001).

Goldstein, Judith and Robert Keohane, "Ideas and Foreign Policy: An Analytical Framework." In Ideas in Foreign Policy: Beliefs, Institutions and Political Change, edited by Judith Goldstein and Robert Keohane (NY: Cornell University Press, 1993), pp. 3-30.

Goodwin-Gill, Guy and Ilene Cohn, Child Soldiers: A Study on Behalf of the Henry Dunant Institute (Oxford: Oxford University Press, 1994).

Goonsekere, Savitri, "Women's Rights and Children's Rights: The U.N. Conventions as Compatible and Complementary International Treaties." (Florence: UNICEF Innocenti Centre, 1992).

Gordenker, Leon and Thomas Weiss, "Pluralizing Global Governance: Analytical Approaches and Dimensions." In NGOs, the U.N. and Global

186   *'Innocent Women and Children'*

Governance, edited by Leon Gordenker and Thomas Weiss (Boulder: Lynne Reinner, 1996), pp. 17-50.

Gordon, Linda, "Family Violence, Feminism and Social Control." In Gender Violence: Interdisciplinary Perspectives, edited by Laura O'Toole and Jessica Schiffman (NY: New York University Press, 1997), pp. 314-330.

Gourevitch, Philip, We Wish to Inform You That Tomorrow We Will Be Killed With Our Families (NY: Farrar, Strauss and Giroux, 1998).

Grant, Rebecca and Kathleen Newland, eds., Gender and International Relations (Bloomington: Indiana University Press, 1991).

Grimsley, Mark, "'Rebels' and 'Redskins': U.S. Military Conduct Toward White Southerners and Native Americans in Comparative Perspective." In Civilians in the Path of War, edited by Mark Grimsley and Clifford Rogers (Lincoln: University of Nebraska Press, 2002), pp. 137-162.

Grimsley, Mark and Clifford Rogers, eds., Civilians in the Path of War (Lincoln: University of Nebraska Press, 2002).

Grossman, David, On Killing: The Psychological Cost of Learning to Kill in War and Society (Boston: Back Bay Books, 1995).

Guidry, John, Michael Kennedy and Mayer Zald, eds., Globalizations and Social Movements: Culture, Power and the Transnational Sphere (Ann Arbor: University of Michigan Press, 2000).

Gutman, Roy and David Reiff, eds., Crimes of War: What the Public Should Know (NY: W.W. Norton and Company, 1999).

Haas, Peter, "Introduction: Epistemic Communities and International Policy Coordination." International Organization 46(1) (1992), pp. 1-36.

Habermas, Jurgen, "Hannah Arendt's Communications Concept of Power." In Power, edited by Stephen Lukes (NY: New York University Press, 1986).

Hagemann, Karen, "A Valorous Volk Family: The Nation, the Military and the Gender Order in Prussia in the Time of the Anti-Napoleonic Wars, 1806-1815." In Gendered Nations: Nationalisms and Gender Order in the Long Nineteenth Century, edited by Ida Blom, Karen Hagemann and Catherine Hall (NY: Oxford University Press, 2000).

Hall, Rodney Bruce, "Moral Authority as a Power Resource." International Organization 51(4) (1997), pp. 591-622.

Hamilton, Bernice, Political Thought in the 16th Century (Oxford: Clarendon, 1963).

Hamilton, Heather, "Refugee Women, UNHCR and the Great Lakes Crisis." Available online at http://www.pressroom.com/~hbhamilton/srp.html. Accessed December 10, 2002.

Hamilton, Heather, "Rwanda's Women: The Key to Reconstruction." Journal of Humanitarian Assistance, posted January 2000. Available online at http://www.jha.ac/greatlakes/b001.htm. Accessed October 20, 2003.

Hammock, John and Joel Charny, "Emergency Response as Morality Play: The Media, the Relief Agencies, and the Need for Capacity Building." In

Bibliography 187

From Massacres to Genocide: The Media, Public Policy and Humanitarian Crises (Washington, DC: Brookings Institution Press, 1996).

Hampson, Francoise, "Military Necessity." In Crimes of War, edited by Roy Gutman and David Reiff (NY: W.W. Norton, 1999), pp. 251-252.

Harff, Barbara, "Empathy for Victims of Massive Human Rights Violations and Support for Government Intervention: A Comparative Study of American and Australian Attitudes." Political Psychology 8(1) (1987), pp. 1-19.

Harkavy, Robert and Stephanie Neumann, Warfare and the Third World (London: Palgrave, 2001).

Harland, David, Report of the Secretary General Pursuant to General Assembly Resolution 53/35: The Fall of Srebrenica, UN Doc A/54/549, 1999.

Harroff-Tavel, Marion, "Action Taken by the International Committee of the Red Cross in Situations of Internal Violence." International Review of the Red Cross 294 (1993), pp. 195-220.

Harroff-Tavel, Marion, "Promoting Norms to Limit Violence in Crisis Situations: Challenges, Strategies and Alliances." International Review of the Red Cross, 322 (1998), pp. 5-20.

Hartigan, Richard, The Forgotten Victim: A History of the Civilian (NY: Transaction Publishers, 1983).

Hartle, Anthony, "Discrimination." In Moral Constraints on War, edited by Bruce Coppieters and Nick Fotion (Lanham, MI: Lexington Books, 2002).

Hasenclever, Andreas, Peter Mayer and Volker Rittberger, Theories of International Regimes (Cambridge: Cambridge University Press, 1997).

Hearn, Jeff and David Morgan, eds., Men, Masculinities and Social Theory (London: Unwin Hyman, 1990).

Helms, Elssa, "Women as Agents of Ethnic Reconciliation? Women's NGOs and International Intervention in Postwar Bosnia-Herzegovina." Women's Studies International Forum 26(1) (2003), pp. 15-33.

Helsinki Watch, War Crimes in Bosnia-Herzegovina (NY: Human Rights Watch, 1992/1993).

Hersh, Seymour, Cover-Up: The Army's Secret Investigation of the Massacre at My Lai 4 (NY: Random House, 1972).

Higate, Paul, "Traditional Gendered Identities: National Service and the All-Volunteer Force." In The Comparative Study of Conscription in the Armed Forces, edited by Lars Mjoset and Stephen Van Holde (Amsterdam: Elsevier Science, 2002), pp. 229-236.

Hollingworth, Larry, Merry Christmas Mr. Larry (London: William Heineman, 1996).

Holmes, Richard, Acts of War: The Behavior of Men in Battle (NY: Free Press, 1986).

Honig, Jan Willem and Norbert Both, Srebrenica: Record of a War Crime (NY: Penguin Books, 1997).

Hooper, Charlotte, "Hegemonic Masculinities in Transition: The Case of Globalization." In Gender and Global Restructuring, edited by Marianne Marchand and Anne Sisson Runyan (NY: Routledge, 2000), pp. 59-73.

Hooper, Charlotte, Manly States: Masculinities, International Relations and Gender Politics (NY: Columbia University Press, 2001).

Horowitz, Donald, Ethnic Groups in Conflict (Berkeley: University of California Press, 1985).

Hranski, Hrvoje, "We Could Have Done More, We Could Have Done Better: Belgian PM Apologizes for Failing in Rwanda." Ottowa Citizen, April 8, 2000.

Hudson, Valerie and Andrea den Boer, "A Surplus of Men, a Deficit of Peace: Security and Sex Ratios in Asia's Largest States." International Security 26(4) (2002), pp. 5-38.

Hughes, Lisa, "Can International Law Protect Child Soldiers?" Peace Review, 12(3) (2000), pp. 399-406.

Human Rights Watch, Shattered Lives: Sexual Violence During the Rwandan Genocide and its Aftermath (NY: Human Rights Watch, 1996).

Human Rights Watch, War Without Quarter: Colombia and International Humanitarian Law (NY: Human Rights Watch, 1998).

Human Rights Watch, Leave None to Tell The Story: Genocide in Rwanda (NY: Human Rights Watch, 1999a).

Human Rights Watch, A Week of Terror in Drenica: Humanitarian Law Violations in Kosovo (NY: Human Rights Watch, 1999b). Available online at http://www.hrw.org/reports/1999/kosovo. Accessed December 11, 2002.

Human Rights Watch, Civilian Deaths in the NATO Air Campaign: The Crisis in Kosovo (NY: Human Rights Watch, 2000a). Available online at http://www.hrw.org/reports/2000/NATO/NATbm200-01.htm. Accessed November 26, 2002.

Human Rights Watch, Kosovo: Rape as a Weapon of Ethnic Cleansing (NY: Human Rights Watch, 2000b). Available online at http://www.hrw.org/reports/2000/fry/. Accessed October 24, 2003.

Human Rights Watch, Under Orders: War Crimes in Kosovo (NY: Human Rights Watch, 2001). Available online at http://www.hrw.org/reports/2001/kosovo/#Acknowledgements. Accessed October 24, 2003.

Human Rights Watch, "Precipice: Insecurity in Northern Afghanistan." HRW Briefing Paper, June, (2002).

Hunt, Krista, "The Strategic Co-optation of Women's Rights: Discourse in the 'War on Terrorism'." International Feminist Journal of Politics 4(1) (2002), pp. 116-121.

Hurd, Ian, "Legitimacy and Authority in International Politics." International Organization 53(2) (1999), pp. 379-408.

Ignatieff, Michael, "The Stories We Tell: Television and Humanitarian Aid." In Hard Choices: Moral Dilemmas In Humanitarian Intervention, edited by Jonathan Moore (NY: Rowman and Littlefield, 1998), pp. 287-302.

Igric, Gordana, "Kosovo Rape Victims Suffer Twice." In Mother Jones, June 18, 1999. Available online at http://www.motherjones.com/total_coverage/kosovo/victims.html. Accessed October 21, 2003.

Independent International Commission on Kosovo, The Kosovo Report: Conflict, International Response, Lessons Learned (NY: Oxford University Press, 2000).

Indra, Doreen, ed., Engendering Forced Migration (NY: Berghahn Books, 1999a).

Indra, Doreen, "Not a 'Room of One's Own': Engendering Forced Migration Knowledge and Practice." In Engendering Forced Migration, edited by Doreen Indra (NY: Berghahn Books, 1999b), pp. 1-23.

Inter-Agency Standing Committtee (IASC). (1999) "Policy Statement for the Integration of a Gender Perspective in Humanitarian Assistance." Included in the IASC SWG Gender and Humanitarian Assistance Resource Kit, available on CD-ROM from the UNOffice for the Coordination of Humanitarian Affairs.

IASC Sub-Working Group on Gender and Humanitarian Assistance. (2001) Gender and Humanitarian Assistance Resource Kit. Available on CD-ROM from the UN Office for the Coordination of Humanitarian Affairs or online at http://www.reliefweb.int/ocha_ol/civilians/women_war/index.html.

IASC, Growing the Sheltering Tree: Protecting Rights Through Humanitarian Action (NY: UNICEF/IASC, 2002).

International Committee of the Red Cross, Protocols Additional to the Geneva Conventions of 12 August 1949 (Geneva: ICRC, 1977).

ICRC. Annual Report (Geneva: ICRC, 1995).

ICRC. The People on War Report (Geneva: ICRC, 1999a).

ICRC. Arms Availability and the Situation of Civilians in Armed Conflict (Geneva: ICRC, 1999b).

ICRC News, "Yugoslavia/Kosovo: ICRC Assists Civilians Caught up in Clashes." March 11, 1999. Available online at http://www.cidi.org/humanitarian/icrc/99/0009.html. Accessed October 24, 2003.

ICRC News, "Former Yugoslav Republic of Macedonia: Over 300 Civilians Evacuated." June 23, 2001. Available online at http://www.cidi.org/humanitarian/icrc/01/ixl22.html. Accessed October 24, 2003.

ICRC. Official website for the International Committee of the Red Cross. Online at http://www.icrc.org. Accessed November 3, 2003.

Ipsen, Knut, "Combatants and Non-Combatants." In The Handbook of Humanitarian Law in Armed Conflicts, edited by Dieter Fleck (NY: Oxford University Press, 1995), pp. 65-101.

190   *'Innocent Women and Children'*

Jackson, Robert, The Global Covenant: Human Conduct in a World of States (Oxford: Oxford University Press, 2000).

Jacobs, Susie, Ruth Jacobson and Jennifer Marchbank, eds., States of Conflict: Gender, Violence and Resistance (London: Zed Books, 2000).

Jain, A., J. Belsky and K. Crnic, "Beyond Fathering Behaviors: Types of Dads." Journal of Family Psychology 10(4) (1996), pp. 431-42.

Jarvis, Darryl, International Relations and the Challenge of Post-modernism: Defending the Discipline (Columbus: University of South Carolina Press, 2000).

Jepperson, Richard, Alexander Wendt and Peter Katzenstein, "Norms, Identity and Culture in National Security." In The Culture of National Security, edited by Peter Katzenstein (NY: Columbia University Press,1996), pp. 33-78.

Joachim, Jutta, "Shaping the Human Rights Agenda: The Case of Violence Against Women." In Gender Politics in Global Governance, edited by Mary Meyer and Elisabeth Prugl (Lanham, MD: Rowman and Littlefield Publishers, 1998), pp. 142-160.

Joachim, Jutta, "Framing Issues and Seizing Opportunities: the UN, NGOs and Women's Rights." International Studies Quarterly 47(2) (2003), pp. 247-274.

Johnson, James Turner, Ideology, Reason and the Limitation of War: Religious and Secular Concepts 1200-1740 (Princeton, NJ: Princeton University Press, 1975).

Johnson, James Turner, Just War Tradition and the Restraint of War (Princeton: Princeton University Press, 1981).

Johnson, James Turner, The Holy War Idea in Western and Islamic Traditions (University Park, PN: Pennsylvania State University Press, 1997).

Johnson, James Turner, Morality and Contemporary Warfare (New Haven: Yale University Press, 1999).

Jones, Adam, "Gender and Ethnic Conflict in Ex-Yugoslavia." Ethnic and Racial Studies 17(1) (1994), pp. 115-134.

Jones, Adam, "Does Gender Make the World Go Round? Feminist Critiques of International Relations." Review of International Studies 22(4) (1996), pp. 405-429.

Jones, Adam, "Pity the Innocent Men." Globe and Mail, February 20, 1999.

Jones, Adam, "Gendercide and Genocide." Journal of Genocide Studies 2(2) (2000), pp. 185-212.

Jones, Adam, "Genocide and Humanitarian Intervention: Incorporating the Gender Variable." Journal of Humanitarian Assistance (2002a). Available online at http://www.jha.ac/articles/a080.htm. Accessed June 24, 2003.

Jones, Adam, "Gendercide and Genocide in Rwanda." Journal of Genocide Studies 4(1) (2002b), pp. 65-94.

Jones, Adam, ed.,. Gendercide and Genocide (Nashville: Vanderbilt University Press, 2004).

Bibliography

Jones, Bruce and Charles Cater, "From Chaos to Coherence? Toward a Regime for Protecting Civilians in War." In Civilians in War, edited by Simon Chesterman (Boulder, CO: Lynne Reinner Press, 2001) pp. 237-262.

Jones, Edward and Thane Pittman, "Toward a General Theory of Strategic Self-Presentation." In Psychological Perspectives on the Self, Volume 1, edited by Jerry Suls (Hillsdale, NJ: Lawrence Erlbaum Associates, 1982).

Judah, Tim, "A History of the Kosovo Liberation Army." In Kosovo: Contending Voices on Balkan Intervention, edited by William Joseph Buckley (Grand Rapids, MI: Eerdmans Publishing Company, 2000), pp. 108-115.

Junod, Marcel, Warrior Without Weapons (London: Cape, 1951).

Kalshoven, Fritz, "Impartiality and Neutrality in Humanitarian Law and Practice." International Review of the Red Cross 273 (1989), pp. 516-35.

Kalshoven, Fritz and Liesbeth Zegveld, Constraints on the Waging of War (Geneva: International Committee of the Red Cross, 2001).

Karawan, Ibrahim, "The Muslim World: Uneasy Ambivalence." In Kosovo and the Challenge of Humanitarian Intervention, edited by Albrecht Schnabel and Ramesh Thakur (Tokyo: United Nations University Press, 2000), pp. 215-222.

Kashnikov, Boris, "NATO's Intervention in the Kosovo Crisis: Whose Justice?" In Moral Constraints on War, edited by Bruno Coppieters and Nick Fotion (NY: Lexington Books, 2002), pp. 229-246.

Katzenstein, Peter, ed., The Culture of National Security (NY: Columbia University Press, 1996).

Keagan, John, A History of Warfare (NY: Alfred Knopf, 1993).

Keck, Margaret and Kathryn Sikkink, Activists Beyond Borders: Advocacy Networks in International Politics (Ithaca: Cornell University Press, 1998).

Kelly, Liz, "Wars Against Women: Sexual Violence, Sexual Politics and the Militarised State." In States of Conflict, edited by Susie Jacobs et al. (London: Zed Books, 2000), pp. 45-65.

Kelly, Rita Mae, Jane Bayes, Mary Hawkesworth, Brigitte Young, eds., Gender, Globalization and Democratization (Lanham, MD: Rowman and Littlefield, 2001).

Kelsay, John, Islam and War (Louisville: Westminster/John Knox Press, 1993).

Keohane, Robert, "International Relations Theory: Contributions of a Feminist Standpoint." In Gender in International Relations, edited by Rebecca Grant and Kathleen Newland (Bloomington: Indiana University Press, 1991), pp. 41-50.

Keohane, Robert, "Beyond Dichotomy: Conversations Between International Relations and Feminist Theory." International Studies Quarterly 42(1) (1998), pp. 193-198.

192   *'Innocent Women and Children'*

Kerber, Linda, "May All Our Citizens Be Soldiers and All Our Soldiers Citizens: The Ambiguities of Female Citizenship in the New Nation." In Women, Militarism, and War: Essays in History, Politics and Social Theory, edited by Jean-Bethke Elshtain and Sheila Tobias (Savage, Maryland: Rowman & Littlefield, 1990), pp. 87-103.

Kesic, Obrad, "Women and Gender Imagery in Bosnia: Amazons, Sluts, Victims, Witches and Wombs." In Gender Politics in the Western Balkans, edited by Sabrina Ramet and Branka Magas (University Park, PA: Pennsylvania State University Press, 1999), pp. 187-202.

Kestnbaum, Meyer, "Citizen-Soldiers, National Service and the Mass Army: The Birth of Conscription in Revolutionary Europe and North America." In The Comparative Study of Conscription in the Armed Forces, edited by Lars Mjoset and Stephen Van Holde (Amsterdam: Elsevier Science, 2002), pp. 117-144.

Khagram, Sanjeez, James Riker and Kathryn Sikkink, eds., Restructuring World Politics: Transnational Social Movements, Networks and Norms (Minneapolis, MN: University of Minnesota Press, 2002).

Kidron, Michael and Dan Smith, The New State of War and Peace Atlas (NY: Grafton Books, 1991).

Kier, Elizabeth, "Homosexuals in the U.S. Military: Open Integration and Combat Effectiveness." International Security 23(2) (1998), pp. 5-39.

King, Gary, Robert Keohane and Sidney Verba, Designing Social Inquiry: Scientific Inference in Qualitative Research (Princeton, NJ: Princeton University Press, 1994).

Kinsella, Helen, "To Fight Has Always Been the Man's Habit: Engendering the Innocent." Presentation at the Conference on Gender, War, and the Military, Center for International Security and Cooperation, Stanford University, 2001.

Kinsella, Helen, "Women, Peace and Security: Securing Gender at the United Nations." Paper presented at the American Political Science Association Annual Meeting, Boston, MA, 2002.

Kinsella, Helen, "For a Careful Reading: The Conservativism of 'Gender Constructivism'." International Studies Review 5(3) (2003), pp. 294-297.

Kinsella, Helen, "Securing the Civilian: Gendering Grotius." In Power and Global Governance, edited by Michael Barnett and Robert Duvall (Cambridge: Cambridge University Press, 2005).

Klinghoffer, Arthur Jay, International Dimensions of Genocide in Rwanda (New York: New York University Press, 1998).

Klotz, Audie, Norms in International Relations: The Struggle Against Apartheid (NY: Cornell University Press, 1996).

Kostovicova, Denisa, "Kosovo's Parallel Society: The Successes and Failures of Nonviolence." In Kosovo: Contending Voices on Balkan Intervention, edited by William Joseph Buckley (Grand Rapids, MI: Eerdmans Publishing Company, 2000), pp. 142-148.

Kowert, Paul and Jeffrey Legro, "Norms, Identity and their Limits: A Theoretical Reprise." In The Culture of National Security, edited by Peter Katzenstein (NY: Columbia University Press, 1996), pp. 451-497.

Krasner, Stephen, "Structural Causes and Regime Consequences: Regimes as Intervening Variables." In International Regimes, edited by Stephen Krasner (NY: Cornell University Press, 1983), pp. 1-21.

Kratochwil, Fredrich and John Gerard Ruggie, "International Organization: A State of the Art on the Art of the State." International Organization 40(4) (1986), pp. 753-775.

Krill, Francoise, "The Protection of Women in International Humanitarian Law." International Review of the Red Cross 249 (1985), pp. 337-363.

Kumar, Krishna, "Civil Wars, Women and Gender Relations: An Overview." In Women and Civil War: Impact, Organizations and Action, edited by Krishna Kumar (Boulder: Lynne Reinner, 2001), pp. 5-77.

Kuper, Leo, Genocide and Its Political Use in the Twentieth Century (London: Penguin, 1981).

Laffey, Mark and Jutta Weldes, "Beyond Belief: Ideas and Symbolic Technologies in the Study of International Relations." European Journal of International Relations 3(2) (1997), pp. 193-237.

Lake, David and Robert Powell, "International Relations: A Strategic Choice Approach." In Strategic Choice and International Relations, edited by David Lake and Robert Powell (Princeton, NJ: Princeton University Press, 1999), pp. 3-38.

Lang, James, "Introduction." In Partners in Change: Working with Men to End Gender-Based Violence, edited by Alan Grieg et al., (Santo Domingo: INSTRAW, 2002), pp. 1-9.

Lapid, Yosef, "Theorizing the National in International Relations Theory: Reflections on Neorealism and Neoliberalism." In International Organizations: A Reader, edited by Friedrich Kratochwil and Edward Mansfield (NY: Harper Collins, 1994), pp. 20-31.

Leeuw de, Marc, "A Gentleman's Agreement: Srebrenica in the Context of Dutch War History." In The Postwar Moment, edited by Cynthia Cockburn and Dubravka Zarkov (London: Lawrence and Wishart, 2002), pp. 162-182.

Legro, Jeffrey, "Which Norms Matter? Revisiting the 'Failure' of Institutionalism." International Organization 51(1) (1997), pp. 31-63.

Lemarchand, Rene, "The Rwanda Genocide: Eyewitness Accounts." In Century of Genocide, edited by Samuel Totten, William Parsons and Israel Charny (NY: Garland Publishing, 1997), pp. 408-423.

Lentin, Ronit, ed., Gender and Catastrophe (London: Zed Books, 1997a).

Lentin, Ronit, "Introduction: Engendering Genocides." In Gender and Catastrophe, edited by Ronit Lentin (London: Zed Books, 1997b), pp. 2-17.

194   *'Innocent Women and Children'*

Lerner, Gerda, The Creation of Patriarchy (NY: Oxford University Press, 1986).

Levi, Margaret, Consent, Dissent and Patriotism (Cambridge: Cambridge University Press, 1997).

Lindner, Evelin Gerda, "Gendercide and Humiliation in Human Rights and Honor Societies." Journal of Genocide Research 4(1) (2002), pp. 137-155.

Lindsey, Charlotte, Women Facing War (Geneva: ICRC, 2001).

Linklater, Andrew, "The Achievements of Critical Theory." In International Theory: Positivism and Beyond, edited by Steve Smith, Ken Booth and Marysia Zalewski (Cambridge: Cambridge University Press, 1996), pp. 279-298.

Liu Institute, Human Security Report 2005: War and Peace in the 21st Century (Canada: University of British Columbia, 2005).

Livington, Stephen, "Media Coverage of the War: An Empirical Assessment." In Kosovo and the Challenge of Humanitarian Intervention, edited by Albrecht Schnabel and Ramesh Thakur (Tokyo: United Nations University Press, 2000), pp. 360-384.

Locher, Birgit and Elisabeth Prugl, "Feminism: Constructivism's Other Pedigree." In Constructing International Relations: The Next Generation, edited by Karen Fierke and Knud Erik Jorgensen (NY: M.E. Sharpe, 2001a), pp. 76-92.

Locher, Birgit and Elisabeth Prugl, "Feminism and Constructivism: Worlds Apart or Sharing the Middle Ground?" International Studies Quarterly 45(1) (2001b), pp. 111-130.

Loescher, Gill, The UNHCR and World Politics: A Perilous Path (Oxford: Oxford University Press, 2001).

Lorentzen, Lois Ann and Jennifer Turpin, eds., The Women and War Reader (NY: New York University Press, 1998).

Lumsdaine, David, Moral Vision in World Politics: The Foreign Aid Regime 1949-1989 (Princeton, NJ: Princeton University Press, 1993).

Maas, Peter, Love Thy Neighbor: A Story of War (New York: A.A. Knopf, 1996).

MacFarlane, Neil, Politics and Humanitarian Action. Occasional Paper #41 (Thomas J. Watson Institute for International Studies and United Nations University, 2000).

MacKinnon, Catherine, "Rape, Genocide and Women's Human Rights." In Mass Rape: The War Against Women in Bosnia-Herzegovina, edited by Alexandra Stigalmeyer (Lincoln: University of Nebraska Press, 1994), pp. 183-196.

March, Candida, Ines Smyth and Maitrayee Mukhpadhyay, A Guide to Gender-Analysis Frameworks (London: OXFAM, 1999).

March, James and Johan Olsen, Rediscovering Institutions: The Organizational Basis of Politics (NY: Free Press, 1989).

Marchand, Marianne, "Different Communities/Different Realities/Different Encounters: A Reply to J. Ann Tickner." International Studies Quarterly 42(1) (1998), pp. 199-204.

Marchand, Marianne and Anne Sisson Runyan, eds., Gender and Global Restructuring: Sightings, Sites and Resistances (NY: Routledge, 2000).

Mavrodes, George, "Conventions and the Morality of War." In International Ethics, edited by Charles Beitz, Marshall Cohen, Thomas Scanlon and A. John Simmons (Princeton, NJ: Princeton University Press, 1985), pp. 75-89.

Mayar, Tamar, "Gender Ironies of Nationalism: Setting the Stage." In Gender Ironies of Nationalism, edited by Tamar Mayar (London: Routledge, 1999), pp. 1-24.

Mazurana, Dyan, "International Peacekeeping Operations: To Neglect Gender is to Risk Peacekeeping Failure." In Cockburn and Zarkov, eds., The PostWar Moment: Militaries, Masculinities and International Peacekeeping (London: Zed Books, 2002), pp. 41-50.

Mazurana, Dyan and Susan McKay, "Girls in Fighting Forces in Northern Uganda, Sierra Leone, and Mozambique: Policy and Program Recommendations." (Unpublished Manuscript: University of Wyoming and University of Montana, 2003).

McAdam, Doug, John McCarthy and Mayer Zald, Comparative Perspectives on Social Movements: Political Opportunities, Mobilizing Structures and Cultural Framings (Cambridge, MA: Cambridge University Press, 1996).

McAskie, Carolyn, "Gender, Humanitarian Assistance and Conflict Resolution." (2000) Available online at http:// www.un.org/ womenwatch/daw/csw/Mcaskie.htm. Accessed May 22, 2003.

McCarthy, John, "Constraints and Opportunities in Adopting, Adapting and Inventing." In Comparative Perspectives on Social Movements, edited by Doug McAdam, John McCarthy and Mayer Zald (Cambridge: Cambridge University Press, 1996), pp. 141-151.

McKeogh, Colm, Innocent Civilians: The Morality of Killing in War (NY: Palgrave, 2002).

McMahan, Jeff, "Realism, Morality and War." In The Ethics of War and Peace, edited by Terry Nardin (Princeton, NJ: Princeton University Press, 1996), pp. 78-92.

McNeill, William, Polyethnicity and National Unity in World History (Toronto: Toronto University Press, 1986).

McRae, Rob, "Human Security in a Globalized World." In Human Security and the New Diplomacy, edited by Rob McRae and Don Hubert (Montreal: McGill-Queen's University Press, 2001), pp. 14-27.

Meertens, Donny, "The Nostalgic Future: Terror, Displacement and Gender in Colombia," In Victims, Perpetrators or Actors? edited by Caroline Moser and Fiona Clark (London: Zed Books, 2001), pp. 133-148.

Meintjes, Sheila, Anu Pillay and Meredeth Turshen, eds., The Aftermath: Women in Post-Conflict Transformation (London: Zed Books, 2001).

Mekata, Motoko, "Building Partnerships Toward a Common Goal: Experiences of the International Campaign to Ban Landmines." In The Third Force, edited by Ann Florini (Washington: Carnegie Endowment for International Peace, 2000), pp. 143-177.

Mendiluce, Jose Maria. "War and Disaster in the Former Yugoslavia." (United States Committee for Refugees 1994) Available online at http://www.refugees.org/world/articles/yugoslavia_wrs94.htm.

Mercier, Michele, Crimes Without Punishment: Humanitarian Action in the Former Yugoslavia (London: Pluto Press, 1994).

Mertus, Julie, "Women in the Service of National Identity." Hastings Women's Law Journal 5(1) (1994), pp. 5-23.

Mertus, Julie, Kosovo: How Myths and Truths Started a War (Berkeley: University of California Press, 1999).

Mertus, Julie, War's Offensive on Women: Humanitarian Action in Bosnia, Kosovo and Afghanistan (San Francisco: Kumarian Press, 2000).

Mertus, Julie, "Legitimizing the Use of Force in Kosovo." In Ethics and International Affairs 15(1) (2001), pp. 133-150. Available online at http://www.cceia.org/pdf/mertus.pdf. Accessed December 10, 2002.

Meyer, David, "Framing National Security: Elite Public Discourse on Nuclear Weapons During the Cold War." Political Communication 12 (1995), pp. 173-192.

Meyer, Mary and Elisabeth Prugl, eds., Gender Politics in Global Governance (London: Rowman and Littlefield, 1999).

Miller, Laura and Charles Moskos, "Humanitarians or Warriors? Race, Gender and Combat Status in Operation Restore Hope." Armed Forces and Society 21(4) (1995), pp. 615-637.

Minear, Larry, The Humanitarian Enterprise: Dilemmas and Discoveries (San Francisco: Kumarian Press, 2002).

Minear, Larry, Jeffrey Clark, Roberta Cohen, Dennis Gallagher, Iain Guest and Thomas Weiss, Humanitarian Action in the Former Yugoslavia: The U.N.'s Role 1991-1993 (Providence: Thomas Watson Institute for International Studies, 1994).

Mische, Patricia, "Women, Men and Systems of Security: From a War System Toward a Just Peace System?" In Dilemmas of War and Peace, edited by Dick Ringler (Madison, WI: University of Wisconsin/Annenberg CPB, 1989), pp. 297-323.

Mjoset, Lars and Stephen Van Holde, eds., The Comparative Study of Conscription in the Armed Forces (Amsterdam: Elsevier Science, 2002a).

Mjoset, Lars and Stephen Van Holde, "Killing for the State, Dying for the Nation: An Introductory Essay on the Life Cycle of Conscription into Europe's Armed Forces." In The Comparative Study of Conscription

Bibliography 197

in the Armed Forces, edited by Lars Mjoset and Stephen Van Holde (Amsterdam: Elsevier Science, 2002b), pp. 3-94.

Moeller, Susan, Compassion Fatigue: How the Media Sell Famine, Disease, War and Death (NY: Routledge, 1999).

Moller, Bjorn, "Conscription and Its Alternatives." In The Comparative Study of Conscription in the Armed Forces, edited by Lars Mjoset and Stephen Van Holde (Amsterdam: Elsevier Science, 2002), pp. 277-306.

Morris, Patricia, Weaving Gender in Disaster and Refugee Assistance. Report of the February 12, 1998 Seminar on Gender Integration in Disaster and Refugee Assistance (Washington, DC: InterAction, 1998).

Moser, Caroline and Fiona Clark, eds., Victims, Perpetrators or Actors? Gender, Armed Conflict and Political Violence (London: Zed Books, 2001).

Mrvic-Petrovic, Natasa, "Separation and Dissolution of the Family." In Women, Violence and War, edited by Vesna Nikolic-Ristanovic (Budapest: Central European University Press, 1995), pp. 135-150.

Mueller, John, "The Banality of Ethnic War." International Security 25(1) (2000), pp. 42-70.

Mukta, Parita, "Gender, Community, Nation: The Myth of Innocence." In States of Conflict: Gender, Violence and Resistance, edited by Susie Jacobs et al. (London: Zed Books, 2000), pp. 163-178.

Murphy, Craig, "Seeing Women, Recognizing Gender, Recasting International Relations." International Organization 50(3) (1996), pp. 513-538.

Murphy, Craig, "Six Masculine Roles in International Relations and Their Interconnection: A Personal Investigation." In The 'Man' Question in International Relations, edited by Marysia Zalewski and Jane Parpart (Boulder: Westview Press, 1998), pp. 93-108.

Murphy, Sean, Humanitarian Intervention: The United Nations in an Evolving World Order (Philadelphia: University of Pennsylvania Press, 1996).

Murray, Christopher and Alan Lopez, The Global Burden of Disease: A Comprehensive Assessment of Morality and Disability from Diseases, Injuries and Risk Factors in 1990 and Projected to 2020 (Cambridge, MA: Harvard University Press, 1996).

Nabulsi, Karma, "Evolving Conceptions of Civilians and Belligerents: One Hundred Years After the Hague Peace Conferences." In Civilians and War, edited by Simon Chesterman (Boulder: Lynne Reinner, 2001), pp. 9-24.

Nadelmann, Ethan, "Global Prohibition Regimes: The Evolution of Norms in International Society." International Organization 44(4) (1990), pp. 479-526.

Nagel, Thomas, "War and Massacre." In International Ethics, edited by Barry

Cohen et al. (Princeton: Princeton University Press, 1985), pp. 53-74.

Naik, Asmita, "Protecting Children from the Protectors: Lessons from West Africa." Forced Migration Review, 2002. Available online at www.fmreview.org/FMRpdfs/FMR15/fmr15.7.pdf.

Neier, Aryeh, War Crimes: Brutality, Genocide, Terror and the Struggle for Justice (NY: Times Books, 1998).

Neuffer, Elisabeth, The Key To My Neighbor's House (NY: Picador, 2002).

Newsweek "Letters to the Editor." June 28, 1999, pp. 16-18.

Niarchos, Catherine, "Women, War and Rape: Challenges Facing the International Tribunal for the Former Yugoslavia." Human Rights Quarterly 17(4) (1995), pp. 649-690.

Nickerson, Hoffman, The Armed Horde: 1793-1939: The Rise, Survival and Decline of the Mass Army (NY: Putnam's Sons, 1940).

Nikolic-Ristanovic, Vesna, "War and Violence Against Women." In The Gendered New World Order, edited by Jennifer Turpin and Lois Lorentzen (NY: Routledge, 1996), pp. 195-210.

Niva, Steve, "Tough and Tender: New World Order Masculinity and the Gulf War." In The 'Man' Question in International Relations, edited by Marysia Zalewski and Jane Parpart (Boulder: Westview Press, 1998), pp. 109-128.

Nordstrom, Carolyn, "Girls and War Zones: Troubling Questions." In Engendering Forced Migration, edited by Doreen Indra (NY: Bergahn Books, 1999), pp. 63-82.

Norman, Richard, Ethics, Killing and War (Cambridge: Cambridge University Press, 1995).

Office for the Coordination of Humanitarian Affairs (OCHA). (2000). "Child Rights are Women's Rights, Says UNICEF Afghanistan." Cited on Assistance Afghanistan Site http://www.pcpafg.org/news/Afghan_News/Year2000/2000_12_11/. Accessed October 24, 2003.

OCHA, Reaching the Vulnerable (Geneva: OCHA, Copy on file with the author, 2001).

OCHA, "Report on OCHA/ISS Humanitarian Policy Workshop: The Protection of Civilians in Armed Conflict – Humanitarian Challenges in Southern Africa." (OCHA, 2002). Available online at http://www.reliefweb.int/ocha_ol/civilians/Workshops/index.htm. Accessed October 29, 2003.

Office of Foreign Disaster Assistance, USAID Field Operations Guide for Disaster Assessment and Response (Washington, DC: OFDA, 1994).

Office of the High Commissioner for Human Rights (OHCHR), MidTerm Review of the 2000 UN Consolidated Inter-Agency Appeals. Copy on file with author (2000).

Onuf, Nicholas, "Constructivism: A User's Manual." In International Relations in a Constructed World, edited by Vendulka Kubalkova et al. (London: M.E. Sharpe, 1998), pp. 58-78.

Bibliography

Opton, Edward Jr., "It Never Happened and Besides They Deserved It." In *Sanctions for Evil*, edited by Newitt Sanford and Craig Comstock (San Francisco: Jossey-Bass Publishers, 1972), pp. 49-70.

Orford, Anne, "The Politics of Collective Security." *Michigan Journal of International Law* 17(2) (1996), pp. 373-409.

Organization for Security and Cooperation in Europe (OSCE). (1999) Young Men of Fighting Age in Kosovo/Kosova as Seen, as Told. Available online at http://www.osce.org/kosovo/documents/reports/hr/part1/ch15. htm. Accessed September 26, 2003.

Palmer-Fernandez, Gabriel, "The Targeting of Civilian Populations in War." In *Encyclopedia of Applied Ethics*, vol. 1. (San Diego, CA: Academic Press, 1998), pp. 509-525.

Parker, Geoffrey, "Early Modern Europe." In Michael Howard et al., *The Laws of War* (New Haven, CT: Yale University Press, 1994), pp. 40-58.

Payne, Rodger, "Persuasion, Frames and Norm Construction." *European Journal of International Relations* 7(1) (2001), pp. 37-61.

Peers, William, *The My Lai Inquiry* (NY: W.W. Norton and Company, 1979).

Penhaul, Karl, "Colombia's Communist Guerrillas Take on Feminine Face." *Boston Globe*, January 7, 2001.

Penn, Michael and Rachel Nardos, *Overcoming Violence Against Women and Girls: The International Campaign to Eradicate a Worldwide Problem* (NY: Rowman and Littlefield, 2003).

Peterson, V. Spike, ed., *Gendered States: Feminist (Re)Visions of International Relations Theory* (Boulder: Lynne Reinner, 1992a).

Peterson, V. Spike, "Introduction." In *Gendered States: Feminist (Re)Visions of International Relations Theory*, edited by V. Spike Peterson (Boulder: Lynne Reinner, 1992b), pp. 1-30.

Pettman, Jan, *Worlding Women: A Feminist International Politics* (London: Routledge, 1996).

Physicians for Human Rights, *War Crimes in Kosovo: A Population-Based Assessment of Human Rights Violations of Kosovar Albanians by Serb Forces* (London: Physicians for Human Rights, 1999). Available online at http://www.phrusa.org/past_news/kexec.html.

Pine, Art, "U.N. Forces Fire on Somali Crowd, Fueling U.S. Debate." *Los Angeles Times*, September 10, 1993.

Pleck, J., *The Myth of Masculinity* (Cambridge: MIT Press, 1981).

Pope, Stephen, "The Politics of Apology and Slaughter in Rwanda." *America*, March 6, 1999.

Prendergast, J., *Frontline Diplomacy: Humanitarian Aid and Conflict in Africa* (Boulder: Lynne Reinner, 1996).

President George Bush, July 31, 1991. Press Briefing. Available online at http://bushlibrary.tamu.edu/papers/1991/91072300.html. Accessed October 24, 2003.

Price, Richard, The Chemical Weapons Taboo (Ithaca: Cornell University Press, 1997).

Price, Richard, "Reversing the Gun Sights: Transnational Civil Society Targets Land Mines." International Organization 52(3) (1998), pp. 613-644.

Price, Richard, "Transnational Civil Society and Advocacy in World Politics." In World Politics 55 (July) (2003), pp. 579-606.

Protecting Civilians in Wartime. International Committee of the Red Cross Webpage Available at http://www.icrc.org/Web/eng/siteeng0.nsf/htmlall/civilian_population? OpenDocument. Accessed November 6, 2003.

Protection of Civilians. Office for the Coordination of Humanitarian Affairs Online Webpage. Available at http://www.reliefweb.int/ocha_ol/civilians/. Accessed November 6, 2003.

Prugl, Elisabeth, The Global Construction of Gender (NY: Columbia University Press, 1999).

Prunier, Gerard, The Rwanda Crisis: History of a Genocide (NY: Columbia University Press, 1997).

Radio Free Europe, "Afghanistan: Investigation Launched into U.S. Air Strike Against Civilians." (2002) Transcript available online at http://www.rferl.org/nca/features/2002/07/02072002155753.asp. Accessed October 21, 2003.

Rahe, Paul, "Justice and Necessity: The Conduct of the Spartans and the Athenians in the Peloponnesian War." In Civilians in the Path of War, edited by Mark Grimsley and Clifford Rogers (Lincoln: University of Nebraska Press, 2002), pp. 1-32.

Rehn, Elizabeth and Ellen Johnson Sirleaf, Women, War and Peace: The Independent Experts' Assessment of the Impact of Armed Conflict on Women and Women's Role in Peace-Building, (NY: UNIFEM, 2002).

Reiff, David, Slaughterhouse: Bosnia and the Failure of the West (NY: Simon and Schuster, 1995).

Rein, Martin and Donald Schon, "Reframing Policy Discourse." In The Argumentative Turn in Policy Analysis and Planning, edited by Frank Fischer and John Forester (Durham: Duke University Press, 1993), pp. 145-166.

Reliefweb. "US Congress should put women and children first in setting priorities for humanitarian assistance in war zones." Available online at http://wwww.reliefweb.int/w/Rwb.nsf/0/0914c1383bb5e11d85256dc00077fadc?OpenDocument. Accessed October 25, 2003.

Remy, John, "Patriarchy and Fratriarchy as Forms of Androcracy." In Men, Masculinities and Social Theory, edited by Jeff Hearn and David Morgan (London: Unwin Hyman, 1990), pp. 43-54.

Ressler, Everett, Evacuation of Children from Conflict Areas: Considerations and Guidelines (Geneva: UNHCR/UNICEF, 1992).

Rhode, David, Endgame: The Betrayal and Fall of Srebrenica (Boulder: Westview, 1998).

Ricchiardi, Sherry, "War Children: The Highly Personal Spin." In Sharing the Front Lines and the Back Hills, edited by Yael Danieli (Amityville, NY: Baywood Publishing, 2001), pp. 303-304.

Richards, Paul, "Militia Conscription in Sierra Leone: Recruitment of Young Fighters in an African War." In The Comparative Study of Conscription in the Armed Forces, edited by Lars Mjoset and Stephen Van Holde (Amsterdam: Elsevier Science, 2002), pp. 255-276.

Risse, Thomas, "Let's Argue! Communicative Action in World Politics." International Organization 54(1) (2000), pp. 1-39.

Risse, Thomas, Stephen Ropp and Kathryn Sikkinik, eds., The Power of Human Rights: International Norms and Domestic Change (Cambridge, UK: Cambridge University Press, 1999).

Risse-Kappen, Thomas, "Ideas Do Not Float Freely: Transnational Coalitions, Domestic Structures and the End of the Cold War." International Organization 48(2) (1994), pp. 185-214.

Ritter, Gretchen, "Of War and Virtue: Gender, American Citizenship and Veterans Benefits After World War II." In The Comparative Study of Conscription in the Armed Forces, edited by Lars Mjoset and Stephen Van Holde (Amsterdam: Elsevier Science, 2002), pp. 201-228.

Roberts, Adam, "NATO's 'Humanitarian War' Over Kosovo." Survival, 41(3) (1999a), pp. 102-123.

Roberts, Adam, "Humanitarian Principles in International Politics in the 1990s." In Reflections on Humanitarian Action, edited by the Humanitarian Studies Unit (London: Pluto Press, 1999b), pp. 23-54.

Roberts, Adam, "Humanitarian Issues and Agencies as Triggers for International Military Action." In Civilians in War, edited by Simon Chesterman (Boulder: Lynne Reinner, 2001), pp. 177-196.

Rogel, Carol, The Breakup of Yugoslavia and the War in Bosnia (Westport, CT: Greenwood Press, 1998).

Rogers, A.P.V., "Zero-Casualty Warfare." International Review of the Red Cross 837 (2000), pp. 165-181.

Rosenblatt, Lionel, "The Media and the Refugee." In From Massacres to Genocide, edited by Robert Rotberg and Thomas Weiss (Washington, DC: Brookings Institution Press, 1996), pp. 136-148.

Ruggie, John Gerard, "Territoriality and Beyond: Problematizing Modernity in International Relations." International Organization 47 (1993), pp. 159.

Ruggie, John Gerard, "What Makes the World Hang Together: Neo-Utilitarianism and the Social Constructivist Challenge" International Organization 52(4) (1998), pp. 855-85.

Rummell, R.J., Death by Government (New Brunswick, NJ: Transaction Publishers, 1994).

Russell, Graeme, "Adopting a Global Perspective on Fatherhood." In A Man's World? Changing Men's Practices in a Globalized World, edited by Bob Lease and Keither Pringle (London: Zed Books, 2001), pp. 53-68.

Sandoz, Yves, Claude Pilloud, Jean de Preux, Bruno Zimmerman, Philippe Eberlin, Hans-Peter Gasser, Claude Weiger, Sylvie Junod, Commentary on the Additional Protocols (Dordrecht: Martinus Nijhoff Publishers, 1987).

Sandvik-Nylund, Monika, Caught in Conflicts: Civilian Victims, Humanitarian Assistance and International Law (Abo: Institute for Human Rights, 1998).

Sassoli, Marco and Antoine Bouvier, How Does Law Protect in War? Cases, Documents and Teaching Materials on Contemporary Practice in International Humanitarian Law. (Geneva: ICRC, 1999).

Save the Children, State of the World's Mothers: Mothers and Children in War and Conflict (Westport, CT: Save the Children, 2002).

Scott, Shirley, International Law in World Politics: An Introduction (Boulder: Lynne Reinner, 2004).

Seager, J., State of Women of the World Atlas, 2nd ed. (London: Penguin, 1997).

Searle, John, The Social Construction of Reality (NY: Free Press, 1995).

Segal, Lynne, Slow Motion: Changing Masculinities, Changing Men (London: Virago, 1990).

Shannon, Vaughn, "Norms Are What States Make of Them." International Studies Quarterly 44(2) (2000), pp. 293-316.

Shi, Yinhong and Shen Zhixiong, "After Kosovo: Moral and Legal Constraints on Humanitarian Intervention." In Moral Contraints on War: Principles and Cases, edited by Bruno Coppieters and Nick Fotion (NY: Lexington Books, 2002).

Shinoda, Hideaki, "The Politics of Legitimacy in International Relations: The Case of NATO's Intervention in Kosovo." (2000) Available online at www.theglobalsite.ac.uk/press/010shinoda.htm, accessed December 10, 2002.

Shiras, Peter, "Big Problems, Small Print: A Guide to the Complexity of Humanitarian Emergencies and the Media." In From Massacres to Genocide, edited by Robert Rotberg and Thomas Weiss (Washington, DC: Brookings Institution Press, 1996), pp. 93-114.

Shoemaker, JoLynn, "Women and Wars Within States: Internal Conflict, Women's Rights and International Security." Civil Wars 4(3) (2001), pp. 1-34.

Shoumaff, Alex, "The Warlord Speaks." The Nation, April 4, 1994.

Sikkink, Kathryn, "Restructuring World Politics: The Limits and Asymmetries of Soft Power." In Restructuring World Politics: Transnational Social Movements, Networks and Norms, edited by Sanjeev Khagram, James Riker and Kathryn Sikkink (Minneapolis, MN: University of Minnesota Press, 2002), pp. 301-318.

Bibliography

Silber, Laura and Allen Little, Yugoslavia: Death of a Nation (NY: Penguin Books, 1996).

Simons, Marlene, "Verdict is Due in Major Trial on War Crimes in Bosnia." NY Times, August 2, 2001.

Sivard, Ruth, World Military and Social Expenditures 1991, 14th Edition (Washington: World Priorities, 1991).

Skjelsbaek, Inger, "Is Femininity Inherently Peaceful? The Construction of Femininity in the War." In Gender, Peace and Conflict, edited by Inger Skjelsbaek and Dan Smith (London: Sage, 2001), pp. 47-67.

Skjelsbaek, Inger and Dan Smith, "Introduction." In Gender, Peace and Conflict, edited by Inger Skjelsbaek and Dan Smith (London: Sage, 2001), pp. 1-13.

Slapsak, Svetlana, "The Use of Women and the Role of Women in the Yugoslav War." In Gender, Peace and Conflict, edited by Inger Skjelsbaek and Dan Smith (London: Sage, 2001), pp. 161-183.

Slim, Hugo, "Doing the Right Thing: Relief Agencies, Moral Dilemmas and Moral Responsibility in Political Emergencies and War." Disasters 21(3) (1997), pp. 244-257.

Small, Melvin and David Singer, Resort to Arms: International and Civil War, 1816-1980 (Beverly Hills: Sage, 1982).

Smith, Dan, War, Peace and Third World Development (Oslo: International Peace Research Institute, 1994).

Smith, Dan, The State of War and Peace Atlas. (Oslo: International Peace Research Institute, 1997).

Smith, Dan, "The Problem of Essentialism." In Gender, Peace and Conflict, edited by Inger Skjelsbaek and Dan Smith (London: Sage, 2001), pp. 32-46.

Smith, Jackie, Charles Chatfield and Ron Pagnucco, eds., Transnational Social Movements and Global Politics: Solidarity Beyond the State (Syracuse, NY: Syracuse University Press, 1997).

Smith, Steve, "'Unacceptable Conclusions' and the 'Man' Question: Masculinity, Gender and International Relations." In The 'Man' Question in International Relations, edited by Marysia Zalewski and Jane Parpart (Boulder: Westview Press, 1998), pp. 54-72.

Smythe, Tony and Devi Prasad, Conscription: A World Survey (London: War Resisters International, 1968).

Snow, David and Robert Benford, "Master Frames and Cycles of Protest." In Frontiers in Social Movement Theory, edited by Aldon Morris and Carol Mueller (New Haven, CT: Yale University Press, 1992), pp. 133-155.

Snow, David, Burke Rochford Jr., Steven Worden and Robert Benford, "Frame Alignment Processes, Micromobilization and Movement Participation." American Sociological Review 51(4) (1986), pp. 464-481.

Snow, Donald, Cases in International Relations: Portraits of the Future (NY: Addison Wesley Longman, 2003).

Spruyt, Hendrik, The Sovereign State and its Competitors (Princeton, NJ: Princeton University Press, 1994).

Stacey, Robert, "The Age of Chivalry." In Laws of War: Constraints on Warfare in the Western World, edited by Michael Howard, George Andreopoulus and Mark Shulman (New Haven, CT: Yale University Press, 1994), pp. 27-39.

Stauber, John and Sheldon Rampton, Toxic Sludge Is Good For You: Lies, Damn Lies and the Public Relations Industry (Monroe, ME: Common Courage Press, 1995).

Steans, Jill, Gender and International Relations: An Introduction (NJ: Rutgers University Press, 1998).

Steihm, Judith, "The Protected, the Protector, the Defender." Women's International Studies Forum 5(3) (1982), pp. 367-376.

Steinstra, Deborah, Women's Movements and International Organizations (NY: St. Martin's Press, 1994).

Steinstra, Deborah, "Of Roots, Leaves and Trees: Gender, Social Movements and Global Governance." In Gender Politics and Global Governance, edited by Mary Meyer and Elisabeth Prugl (NY: Rowman and Littlefield, 1998), pp. 260-272.

Stigalmeyer, Alexandra, Mass Rape: The War Against Women in Bosnia-Herzegovina (Lincoln: University of Nebraska Press, 1994).

Stover, Eric and Gilles Peres, The Graves: Srebrenica and Vukovar (Zurich: Scalo Press, 1998).

Sudetic, Chuck, Blood and Vengeance (New York: W.W. Norton, 1998).

Swidler, Ann, "Culture in Action: Symbols and Strategies." American Sociological Review 51(2) (1986), pp. 273-286.

Sylvester, Christine, Feminist Theory and International Relations in a Post-Modern Era (Cambridge: Cambridge University Press, 1994).

Sylvester, Christine, Feminist International Relations: An Unfinished Journey (Cambridge: Cambridge University Press, 2002).

Tannenwald, Nina, "The Nuclear Taboo: The United States and the Normative Basis of Nuclear Non-Use." International Organization 53(3) (1999), pp. 433-468.

Tarrow, Sidney, Power in Movement: Social Movements, Collective Action and Mass Politics in the Modern State (Cambridge: Cambridge University Press, 1994).

Tarrow, Sidney, "States and Opportunities: The Political Structuring of Social Movements." In Comparative Perspectives on Social Movements, edited by Doug McCarthy et al. (Cambridge: Cambridge University Press, 1998), pp. 41-61.

Taylor, Christopher, Sacrifice as Terror: The Rwandan Genocide of 1994 (Oxford: Berg Press, 1999).

Tessler, Mark et al., "Gender, Feminism and Attitudes Toward International Conflict: Exploring Relationships with Survey Data from the Middle East." World Politics 49(2) (1997), pp. 250-281.

Thakur, Ramesh, "Global Norms and International Humanitarian Law: An Asian Perspective." International Review of the Red Cross 841 (2001), pp. 19-44.

Thomas, Ward, The Ethics of Destruction: Norms and Force in International Relations (NY: Cornell University Press, 2001).

Thompson, Karen Brown, "Women's Rights are Human Rights." In Restructuring World Politics, edited by Sanjeev Khagram et al. (Minneapolis, MN: University of Minnesota Press, 2002), pp. 96-123.

Tibi, Bassam, "War and Peace in Islam." In The Ethics of War and Peace, edited by Terry Nardin (Princeton, NJ: Princeton University Press, 1996), pp. 128-145.

Tickner, J. Ann, Gender in International Relations (NY: Columbia University Press, 1992).

Tickner, J. Ann, "You Just Don't Understand: Troubled Engagements Between Feminists and IR Theorists." International Studies Quarterly 41(4) (1997), pp. 611-632.

Tickner, J. Ann, Gendering World Politics (NY: Columbia University Press, 2001).

Tickner, J. Ann, "Feminist Perspectives on 9/11." International Studies Perspectives 3(4) (2002), pp. 333-350.

Tickner, J. Ann, "What is Your Research Program? Some Feminist Answers to IR Methodological Questions." International Studies Quarterly, 49(1) (2005), pp. 1-22.

True, Jacqui, "National Selves and Feminine Others." Fletcher Forum 17(2) (1993), pp. 75-90.

True, Jacqui and Michael Minstrom, "Transnational Networks and Policy Diffusion: The Case of Gender Mainstreaming." International Studies Quarterly 45(1) (2001), pp. 27-58.

Turpin, Jennifer and Lois Lorentzen, eds., The Gendered New World Order (NY: Routledge, 1996).

Turshen, Meredith, "Women's War Stories." In What Women Do In Wartime, edited by Meredith Turshen and Clotilde Twagiramariya (London: Zed Books, 1998), pp. 1-26.

Turshen, Meredith and Clotilde Twagiramariya, What Women Do In Wartime (London: Zed Books, 1998).

United Nations. (1994a) Statement by the President of the Security Council. 17 February. UN Doc. S/PRST/1994/8.

UN. (1994b) Statement by the President of the Security Council. 7 April. UN Doc. S/PRST/1994/16.

UN. (1994c) Statement by the President of the Security Council. 30 April. UN Doc. S/PRST/1994/21.

206 'Innocent Women and Children'

UN. (1994d) Statement by the President of the Security Council. 14 July. UN Doc. S/PRST/1994/34.

UN. (1994e) Statement by the President of the Security Council. 10 August. UN Doc. S/PRST/1994/42.

United Nations, Secretary-General's Office, Daily Press Briefing, April 3, 1997.

UN. (1998) Secretary General's Report on the Situation in Africa. 13 April. UN Doc. S/1998/318.

UN. (1999a) Security Council, 3968th Meeting. 21 January. UN Doc. S/PV.3968.

UN. (1999b) Security Council, 3980th Meeting. 22 February. UN Doc. S/PV.3980.

UN. (1999c) Security Council, 3980th Meeting. 22 February. UN Doc. S/PV.3980 (Resumption 1).

UN. (1999d) Statement by the President of the Security Council. 19 January. UN Doc. S/PRST/1999/2.

UN. (1999e) Security Council 3988th Meeting. 24 March. UN Doc. S/PV.3988.

UN. (1999f) Security Council, 3989th Meeting. 26 March. UN Doc. S/PV.3989.

UN. (1999g) Report of the Secretary-General to the Security Council on the Protection of Civilians in Armed Conflict. 8 September. UN Doc S/1999/957.

UN. (1999h) Security Council. 3977th Meeting. 12 February 1999. UN Doc S/PV.3977.

UN. (1999i) Security Council. 3978th Meeting. 12 February 1999. UN Doc S/PV.3978.

UN. (1999j) Letter Dated January 18, 1999 from the Charge D'Affaires A.I. of the Permanent Mission of Yugoslavia to the United Nations Addressed to the Secretary-General. UN Doc. S/1999/56.

UN. Report of the Secretary-General to the Security Council on the Protection of Civilians in Armed Conflict. (NY: United Nations 2001). UN Doc. S/2001/331.

UN Security Council, Women, Peace and Security: Study for the Secretary-General Pursuant to Security Council Resolution 1325 (NY: United Nations, 2002). UN Doc. S/2002/1154.

United Nations Children's Emergency Fund (UNICEF), Human Rights for Children and Women: How UNICEF Helps Make Them a Reality (NY: UNICEF, 1999).

United Nations Department of Public Information (DPI). Statement by Angela King, Special Advisor on Gender Issues and the Advancement of Women at the DPI/NGO Briefing on Women: Violence, Peace and Security. November 9, 2000. Available online at: http://www.un.org/dpi/ngosection/king.html. Accessed January 31, 2004.

Bibliography

United Nations High Commissioner for Refugees (UNHCR), Situation Update No. 2, 18 February (Geneva: UNHCR, 1992a).

UNHCR, UNHCR Update (Geneva: UNHCR, 1992b).

UNHCR, UNHCR Update, 13 August (Geneva: UNHCR, 1992c).

UNHCR, UNHCR Update, December (Geneva: UNHCR, 1993).

UNHCR, UNHCR Update, February (Geneva: UNHCR, 1994a).

UNHCR, "Situation Worsens in Besieged Gorazde Pocket." UNHCR Update, April 10 (1994b).

UNHCR, "Ogata Appeals for Immediate End to Violence in Kosovo." UNHCR Update, June 11, 1998.

UNHCR, "Georgia: Chechen Airbridge Evacuation Complete." Briefing Notes, December 17, 1999.

UNHCR, Statistics and Registration: A Progress Report (Geneva: UNHCR, 2000a).

UNHCR, State of the World's Refugees (Geneva: UNHCR, 2000b).

UNHCR, Women, Children and Older Refugees: The Sex and Age Distribution of Refugee Populations With a Special Emphasis on UNHCR Priorities (Geneva: UNHCR Population Data Unit, 2001a).

UNHCR, Prevention and Response to Sexual and Gender-Based Violence in Refugee Situations: Inter-Agency Lessons Learned – Conference Proceedings, 27-29 March (Geneva: UNHCR, 2001b).

UNHCR, Protecting Refugees: Questions and Answers (Geneva: UNCHR, Brochure on file with author, 2002).

UNHCR/UNICEF, Joint Statement on The Evacuation of Children from the Former Yugoslavia. 13 August (Geneva: UNHCR, 1992).

UNHCR/UNICEF/ICRC, Further Considerations Regarding the Evacuation of Children from the Former Yugoslavia. 16 December (Geneva: UNHCR, 1992).

UNHCR/UNICEF/WHO, Emergency Report: Displacement in the Former Yugoslavia (Geneva: United Nations, 1992).

United States Committee for Refugees (USCR), Yugoslavia Torn Asunder: Lessons for Protecting Refugees from Civil War (Washington, DC: USCR, 1992).

USCR, "More Male Refugees Than Previously Thought." (Washington, DC: USCR 2002). Available online at http://www.refugees.org/world/articles/males_rr00_2.htm. Accessed September 26, 2003.

US Defense Department. (1994) "Discussion Paper: Office of the Deputy Assistant Secretary of Defense for Middle East/Africa Region." Available online at http://www.gwu.edu/~nsarchiv/NSAEBB/NSAEBB53/rw050194.pdf. Accessed November 25, 2003.

US National Archives and Records Administration. (1994) "Weekly Compilation of Presidential Documents." Archived online at http://www.gpoaccess.gov/wcomp/search.html. Accessed November 25, 2003.

US State Department. (1994a) "US State Department Daily Press Briefings." Archived online at http://dosfan.lib.uic.edu/ERC/briefing/daily_briefings/1994/index.html#9404. Accessed November 25, 2003.

US State Department. (1994b) "Talking Points for UNAMIR Withdrawal." April 15. Cable Number 099440. Copy on file with author.

US State Department. (1994c) "Rwanda – Geneva Convention Violations." Memorandum to Assistant Secretary of State for African Affairs George Moose and Department of State Legal Advisor Conrad Harper. May 18. Available online at http://www.gwu.edu/~nsarchiv/NSAEBB/NSAEBB53/rw051894.pdf. Accessed November 25, 2003.

US State Department. (1994d) "Draft Legal Analysis." May 16, 1994. Available online at http://www.gwu.edu/~nsarchiv/NSAEBB/NSAEBB53/rw051694.pdf. Accessed November 25, 2003.

US State Department. (1994e) "Has Genocide Occurred in Rwanda? Action Memorandum to Secretary of State Warren Christopher." May 21. Available online at http://www.gwu.edu/~nsarchiv/NSAEBB/NSAEBB53/rw052194.pdf. Accessed November 25, 2003.

Vattel, Emmerich de, The Law of Nations, or the Principles of Natural Law Applied to the Conduct and to the Affairs of Nations and of Sovereigns. Trans. Charles G. Fenwick. (Washington, DC: Carnegie Institute, 1916, 1758).

Vaux, T., The Selfish Altruist: Relief Work in Famine and War (London: Earthscan, 2001).

Vickers, Miranda, "Kosovo: The Illusive State." In Kosovo: Contending Voices on Balkan Intervention, edited by William Joseph Buckley (Grand Rapids, MI: Eerdmans Publishing Company, 2000), pp. 97-100.

Vulliamy, Ed, Seasons in Hell: Understanding Bosnia's War (NY: St. Martin's Press, 1994).

Walker, R.B.J., Inside/Outside: International Relations as Political Theory (Cambridge: Cambridge University Press, 1993).

Walzer, Michael, Just and Unjust Wars (NY: Basic Books, 1977).

Ward, Jeanne, If Not Now, When? Addressing Gender-based Violence in Refugee, Internally Displaced and Post-Conflict Settings (NY: Reproductive Health for Refugees Consortium, 2002).

Warkentin, Craig, Reshaping World Politics: NGOs, the Internet, and Global Civil Society (Lanthan, NH: Rowman and Littlefield Publishers, 2001).

Weber, Cynthia, "Good Girls, Little Girls, Bad Girls," Millennium: Journal of International Studies, 23(2) (1994), pp. 337-348.

Weiss, Thomas, Military-Civilian Interactions: Intervening in Humanitarian Crises (Lanham, MD: Rowman and Littlefield Press, 1999).

Weiss, Thomas and Cindy Collins, Humanitarian Challenges and Intervention: World Politics and the Dilemmas of Help (Boulder: Westview Press, 1996).

Bibliography

Weiss, Thomas and Larry Minear, eds., Humanitarianism Across Borders: Sustaining Civilians in Times of War (Boulder: Lynne Reinner, 1993).

Weller, Marc, "The Relativity of Humanitarian Neutrality and Impartiality." Journal of Humanitarian Assistance (2000). Available online at http:www.jha.ac/articles/a029.htm. Accessed June 24, 2003.

Wendt, Alexander, "Anarchy Is What States Make of It: The Social Construction of Power Politics." International Organization 46(2) (1992), pp. 391-425.

Wendt, Alexander, Social Theory of International Politics (Cambridge: Cambridge University Press, 1999).

West, Candice and Fenstermaker, Sarah, "Power, Inequality and the Accomplishment of Gender: An Ethnomethodological View." In Theory on Gender, Feminism on Theory, edited by Paula England (NY: Aldine de Gruyter, 1993), pp. 151-174.

West, K., Agents of Altruism: The Expansion of Humanitarian NGOs in Rwanda and Afghanistan (Aldershot, UK: Ashgate, 2001).

Wheeler, Nicholas, Saving Strangers: Humanitarian Intervention in International Society (NY: Oxford University Press, 2000).

Whitworth, Sandra, Feminism and International Relations: Towards a Political Economy of Gender in Interstate and Non-governmental Institutions (London: Macmillan, 1994).

Whitworth, Sandra, Men, Militarism and UN Peacekeeping: A Gendered Analysis (Boulder: Lynne Reinner, 2004).

Williams, Colin, "The Question of National Congruence." In Political Geography: A Reader, edited by John Agnew (London: Arnold Publishing, 1997), pp. 336-347.

Wilmer, Franke, The Social Construction of Man, the State and War: Identity, Conflict and Violence in the Former Yugoslavia (London: Routledge, 2002).

Wing, Adrien Katherine and Sylke Merchan, "Rape, Ethnicity and Culture: Spirit Injury from Bosnia to Black America." Columbia Human Rights Law Review, 25(1) (1993), pp. 1-48.

Wolfson, Stephen and Neill Wright, A UNHCR Handbook for the Military on Humanitarian Operations (Geneva: UNHCR, 1994).

Women's Commission for Refugee Women and Children, "Bill to Provide Vital Protection to Women and Children in Armed Conflict." (2003) Available online at http://www.womenscommission.org/newsroom/press_releases/0506.html. Accessed January 7, 2004.

Wood, D., Conflict in the Twentieth Century. Adelphi Paper No. 48 (London: Institute for Strategic Studies, 1968).

World Health Organization, What About Boys? A Literature Review on the Health and Development of Adolescent Boys (Geneva: WHO Department of Child and Adolescent Health and Development, 2000).

World Socialist Website, "What Does the Bombing of Kosovar Refugees Say about NATO's 'Humanitarian' War?" Editorial, April 16, 1999. Online at http://www.ess.uwe.ac.uk/Kosovo/Kosovo-controversies7.html.

Yee, Albert, "The Causal Effects of Ideas on Policies." International Organization 50(1) (1996), pp. 69-108.

Yuval-Davis, Nira, Gender and Nation (London: Sage, 1997).

Zacher, Mark, "The Territorial Integrity Norm: International Boundaries and the Use of Force." International Organization 55 (2) (2001), pp. 215-250.

Zald, Mayer, "Culture, Ideology and Strategic Framing." In Comparative Perspectives on Social Movements, edited by Doug McAdam, John McCarthy and Mayer Zald (Cambridge: Cambridge University Press, 1996), pp. 261-274.

Zalewski, Marysia, "Well, What is the Feminist Perspective on Bosnia?" International Affairs 71(2) (1995), pp. 339-356.

Zalewski, Marysia, "All These Theories Yet the Bodies Keep Piling Up." In International Theory: Post-Positivism and Beyond, edited by Smith et al. (Cambridge: Cambridge University Press, 1996), pp. 340-353.

Zalewski, Marysia and Jane Parpart, The 'Man' Question in International Relations (Boulder: Westview, 1998).

Zarkov, Dubravka, "War Rapes in Bosnia: On Masculinity, Femininity and the Power of Rape Victim Identity." Tijschrift voor Criminologie 39(2) (1997), pp. 140-151.

Zarkov, Dubravka, "The Body of the Other Man: Sexual Violence and the Construction of Masculinity, Sexuality and Ethnicity in the Croatian Media." In Victims, Perpetrators or Actors?, edited by Caroline Moser and Fiona Clark (London: Zed Books, 2001), pp. 69-82.

Zarkov, Dubravka, "Srebrenica Trauma: Masculinity, Military and National Self-Image in Dutch Daily Newspapers." In The Postwar Moment, edited by Cynthia Cockburn and Dubravka Zarkov (London: Zed Books, 2002), pp. 183-203.

Zehfuss, Maja, Constructivism in International Relations: The Politics of Reality (Cambridge: Cambridge University Press, 2002).

Zelinski, Wilbur and Leszek Kosinski, "The Emergency Evacuation of Cities: A Cross-National Historical and Geographical Study." (NY: Rowman and Littlefield, 1991).

Index

aerial bombing
  civilian immunity 49
  women and children 63
Afghanistan
  Khost incident 68–9
  Orugzan incident 68–9
agenda-setting 104–25
Amnesty International 95–6
assassination norm 47
asylum 172–3

Baldwin, Stanley 49
Balkan Wars 136–8
  evacuations by armed forces 139–41
  humanitarian evacuations 137–9,
    139–43
belligerents
  advocacy with 108–9
  decision-making processes 16
  women as 121–2, 124–5, 126
Bosnia-Herzegovina *see also* Balkan
    Wars; Srebrenica; Yugoslavia;
    Zepa
  humanitarian intervention 74–5
  sex-selective massacres 65–6
  sexual abuse 65
  war victims, women and children as
    18–19
Bosniacs 64, 145
Bosnian Serb Army (BSA) 1, 65–6
  ethnic cleansing 137–8
  male civilians, justification of
    treatment 67–8
boys *see* men; women and children
BSA *see* Bosnian Serb Army

children *see also* women and children
  innocence and vulnerability 33
citizenship 49–50
civilian immunity 2, 10–11, 29–30
  aerial bombing 49
  clerics 41

combatancy 30
compliance with norm 59–67
distinction principle 40–42, 45
gender beliefs 20, 22
gender essentialisms 22, 26
gender norms 43–4
gender sub-norm 26–7, 41–4, 164
gendered application of 9, 13, 171–2
interpretation of 59
military culture 48–52
as moral good 29
norm 57
political authority 47
principle 10–11, 29–30, 113
side effects of war 9
state-building 27
women 44
civilian protection 113 *see also* civilian
    protection network; civilian
    protection regime; protection
abuse of 168–9
advocates 16
compliance with law 133
forced recruitment 172–3
gender beliefs 3, 163
gender essentialisms 172
gender sub-norm 89, 145, 160
human rights 173
humanitarian action 134
impartiality 164
journalists 110
Kosovo intervention 36, 81–2
and males 8–9
misframing of discourse 93
moral language concepts 14
nationalism 55–7
NATO 81–2
in practice 133–6
principle 30–31
United Nations 36–40

212   *'Innocent Women and Children'*

Office for the Coordination
of Humanitarian Affairs
(OCHA) 36–7
withdrawal from 157–8
civilian protection network 96–103 *see
also* civilian protection; civilian
protection regime; protection
civil society 113–18
civilians 95
gender 97–103
tropes 20–21
governments 95
donor 113–18
media 109–13
non-state entities 95–6
normative discourse 164
partnerships 118–25
rhetoric on civilian casualties 114
women's network 120–21
women's rights 118–25
civilian protection regime 10–11, 94 *see
also* civilian protection; civilian
protection network; protection
actors 27
gender discourses 31–40
norms 56–7
principles 19, 28–31
ungendering 165
civilians
access to 108–9
civilian protection network 95
and combat 48
definition of 29
gender sub-norm 59
as gendered concept 15
Geneva Convention 2
'innocent' 75, 79, 93, 109
killing of
aerial bombing 49
male 18–19
strategies to avoid censure for 16
third party reactions 16
men as 2, 18–19, 26, 125, 166
statistics on war victims 98–9, 115–16
targeting of 47, 60–67, 115
ungendering 166–7
women and children as 2, 97–9,
106–7
clerics, civilian immunity 41

Colombia, sex-selective massacres 62
combatants
men as 2
presumptive 45
women as 18, 26, 62, 66, 121–2, 126,
165
and children as 2, 66
Commission on Security and
Cooperation in Europe (CSCE)
58–9
compulsory power 170
conscription 48, 49, 143, 173
critical theory 172
CSCE *see* Commission on Security and
Cooperation in Europe

data gathering 14, 17, 93–4
descriptive beliefs 28–9
desertion 35–6, 143, 172–3
discourse of neutrality 108
distinction principle 26, 29, 49
civilian immunity 40–42, 45
gender sub-norm 72, 167, 171
gendering of 30, 40–42
ungendering 167
double effect doctrine 60
drugs in war 63

ethnic cleansing 137–9, 151, 152, 160
ethnicity, men as carriers 61, 65
evacuations *see* humanitarian
evacuations; sex-selective
evacuations; Srebrenica,
evacuation

family violence 166
feminism
gender theory 5
international relations (IR) 5
gender analysis 163
frames 103–4
amplification 114
definition 103–4
distortion 106–8
moral ideas 113
transformation 167
French National Convention, total war
49

Index

gender 4
  civilian protection network 97–103
  international relations theory 4
  men 7–8
  norms 12–13
  and sex 11
gender analysis 6, 163
  Type 1: 7
  of war 8
gender-awareness 166
gender beliefs
  civilian immunity 20
  civilian protection 3, 163
  human rights advocacy 18–19
  humanitarian organizations 3
  influence on actors 18
  and language 13
  transnational advocacy networks 3, 163
  warping effect on norms 20
gender essentialisms 27
  analysis 39
  civilian immunity 22, 26
  data gathering 14
  evidence of 17–18
  perpetuation of 172
gender identities 168
gender-mainstreaming 91–2, 122, 166, 173
gender sub-norm 13–14, 52
  civilian immunity 42
  civilian protection 89, 145, 160
    regime norms 56
  civilians 59
  distinction principle 72, 167, 171
  humanitarian action 82
  humanitarian evacuations 148–9
  regulative role 171
  sex-selective targeting 66
gender theory 4, 5
gendercide 60–61
Gendercide Watch 60
Geneva Convention
  civilian immunity principle 10–11, 30
  civilians 2
    definition of 29
  distinction principle 26
  sex discrimination 158

  vulnerable groups 102
  war-time evacuations 137
genocide, Rwanda 75–80
Gentili, Alberico (1552-1608) 44
Greece, humanitarian aid 108
Grotius, Hugo (1583-1645) 45
guerrilla warfare 63

honor, and killing 43–4
human rights *see also* women's rights
  advocacy, gender beliefs 18–19
  civilian protection 173
Human Rights Watch 95–6
humanitarian action
  civilian protection 134
  gender sub-norm 82
humanitarian evacuations 21–2, 131 *see also* humanitarian interventions; sex-selective evacuations
  Balkan Wars 137–9, 139–43
  data gathering 16
  gender sub-norm 148–9
  prioritization by vulnerability 139–40
  Srebrenica 144–59
  strategies 154–5
humanitarian interventions 59, 72–88, 134 *see also* humanitarian evacuations
  Bosnia 74–5
  definition 73
  Iraq 73–4
  legitimization 85–7
  Rwanda 75–80
  Somalia 74
humanitarian law 113
  civilian males 8–9
  'civilized' states 168
  combatants 9
  gendering of 8
  impartiality 164
  prisoners 9
humanitarian organizations
  codes of conduct 136
  culture of 135
  discourse of neutrality 108
  donor pressures 135
  gender beliefs 3
  impartiality 134

negotiation with belligerents 134–5
neutrality 134–5
humanitarian practitioners
  interviews 16, 26
  'women and children first' norm
    21–2, 156

immunity discourse
  men 34–6
  women 32–4
immunity principle *see* civilian
    immunity
impartiality principle 134
'innocent civilians' 75, 79, 93, 109
International Committee of the Red
    Cross (ICRC)
  code of conduct 136
  as non-governmental actor 95–6
  People on War (survey) 113, 117
  Seminar on the Protection of Special
    Categories of Civilian 17
  Srebrenica 97
  statistics on war victims 116
  Vukovar evacuation 140–41
  Women and War (report) 97
  Yugoslavia 132
international norms 3, 4
  evidence of existence 14
international relations (IR)
  feminism 5
    gender analysis 163
    neo-positivism 5
    power 169–70
  gender theory 4
international security norms 4
IR *see* international relations
Iraq
  humanitarian intervention 73–4
  women and children, protection of
    169
Islam, women and children, protection
    of 42

JNA *see* Yugoslav National Army
journalists, civilian protection 110
'just war' tradition 44

Kosovo 80–88
  civilian protection 36

historical background 80–82
legitimization of intervention 85–7
NATO 81–2, 84
Racak massacre 83–4
rape 83
refugees 81, 84, 85
sex-selective massacres 82–3
women and children 83–4
Kosovo Liberation Army (KLA) 80

language and gender beliefs 13
Lebanon, sex-selective mercy 61
logic of appropriateness 145–6, 153–9

masculinity
  and citizenship 49–52
  and war 43
massacres, sex-selective *see* sex-selective
    massacres
material constraints 146, 147–9
media
  civilian protection network 109–13
  distortion 111–12
  simplification 111–12
  women and children, representation
    of 110–11
men
  as civilians 2, 26, 126, 166
    massacres 69
  as combatants 2, 45–6, 48
  ethnicity, as carriers of 61, 65
  as fathers 99, 157
  female relatives, rape of 173
  forced recruitment 172–3
  and gender 7–8
  gender-based abuse 167, 173
  immunity discourse 34–6
  mobilization of 35
  as peacemakers 100
  sexual abuse 92
  targeting of 60–61
    sex-selective 167
  as victims 123
  vulnerability 35, 101–3, 118, 125–8,
    172
  war affected 166
  war crimes 34
mercy, sex-selective 61
military, masculinity of 56, 166–7

Index 215

military culture, civilian immunity 48–52
military service, and citizenship 49–52
mobilizing structures 104–6
My Lai massacre 64, 69–72

Namibia, NATO air strikes on Serbia 86
nation-states, masculine model of 56
nationalism, civilian protection 55–7
nations, and states 106
NATO (North Atlantic Treaty Organization)
    Kosovo 81–2, 84
    Serbia, air strikes 81, 84, 86
neo-positivism 5, 6
neutrality
    humanitarian discourse 108
    humanitarian organizations 134–5
non-combatants 32
    women as 45–6
normative discourse 164
norms 5, 10
    causal effects 7, 41
    change 171
    civilian protection regime 57
    compliance 59–60
    constitutive effects 7, 11, 40–43
    as constraints 58
    entrepreneurship 44–6
    gender identities 168
    gendered 13
    implicit 164
    institutional conditions 46–8
    international 3, 4
        evidence of existence 14
    and principles 28–31
    regulative effects 11
    robustness of 11
    violation 60
        apology for 68
        excuses for 68–9
    violators'
        accounts 67–72
        justification 58, 67–8, 71–2
    warping effect 13, 20
North Atlantic Treaty Organization see NATO
nuclear weapons 72–3

OCHA see United Nations Office for the Coordination of Humanitarian Affairs
Operation Provide Comfort (Iraq) 73–4

Pakistan, sex-selective massacres 62
Peace of God movement 41
political authority, civilian immunity 47
political opportunity structures 104–5
postmodernism 12
power
    compulsory 170
    relationships 170–71
    taxonomy of 170
principled beliefs 28
principles 28–31
protection 169
    abuse of 169
    principle 30–31 see also civilian protection
public relations, civilian protection network 109–13

rape 10, 98, 173
    Balkan Wars 137
    Kosovo 83
refugees
    Kosovo 81, 84, 85
    statistics 116
    women and children as 117
regime principles 10 see also civilian immunity; civilian protection; distinction principle
rules 10–11, 27–8
Russia, NATO air strikes on Serbia 86
Rwanda
    genocide 75–80
    humanitarian intervention, failure of 75–80
    refugees 79
    sex-selective massacres 61, 78
    women and children, massacres of 63–4

Save The Children, *State of the World's Mothers* (report) 99–100
security norms 4
Serbia *see also* Balkan Wars; Yugoslavia
    NATO air strikes 81

216 *'Innocent Women and Children'*

sex and gender 12
sex discrimination, Geneva Convention
158
sex-selective evacuations *see also*
humanitarian evacuations
cognitive maps 147–52
fathers 157
logic of appropriateness 153–9
material constraints 147–9
sex-selective massacres
Bosnia-Herzegovina 65–6
Colombia 62
Kosovo 82–3
Pakistan 62
Rwanda 61
sex-selective mercy, Lebanon 61
sexual abuse
Bosnia-Herzegovina 65
young men 92
sexual violence 9–10, 83, 98
Balkan Wars 137
men 125
Sierra Leone, drugs in war 63
signifiers 104
social constraints 146
social constructivism 4–7, 11, 12–13
causal effects 7
constitutive effects 7
power 170
social facts 28
Somalia, humanitarian intervention 74
sovereignty 11, 46–7, 58, 86
Srebrenica 141
evacuation 1, 3, 68, 132–3, 141,
144–59
cognitive maps 147–52
hypotheses 145–59
logic of appropriateness 145–6,
153–9
material constraints 146, 147–9
social constraints 146
strategies 154–5
International Committee of the Red
Cross (ICRC) 97
massacre 1, 142
United Nations Protection Force
(UNPROFOR) 141, 142
states and nations 106
strategic environment 104–6

Suarez, Francisco (1548-1617) 45
symbolic technologies 106
symbols, definition 104

total war 49
transnational advocacy networks 27,
95–6
gender beliefs 3, 163
Trnopolje prisoners 92

UNAMIR (United Nations Assistance
Mission for Rwanda) 76
UNHCR *see* United Nations High
Commission for Refugees
United Nations
civilian protection 36–40
Rwanda genocide 76–80
Srebrenica 141
United Nations Assistance Mission for
Rwanda (UNAMIR) 76
United Nations High Commission for
Refugees (UNHCR) 112
Balkan Wars, humanitarian
evacuations 137–9
code of conduct 136
humanitarian assistance 137–8
needs assessment 139
relief 138
statistics on war victims 116–17
Yugoslavia 132
United Nations Office for the
Coordination of Humanitarian
Affairs (OCHA) 95
Civilian Protection Workshop (report)
102
gender-mainstreaming 91–2
Protection of Civilians (PoC) 36–7
gender essentialisms analysis 39
Reaching the Vulnerable (pamphlet)
102
United Nations Protection Force
(UNPROFOR)
Srebrenica 141, 142
Zepa 141–2
United Nations Security Council
innocent civilians 37–40
Kosovo intervention 36
Protection of Civilians debates
analysis of minutes 14–15

'women and children' 19–20
Women and Armed Conflict
  (Resolution 1325) 19–20, 123
UNPROFOR *see* United Nations
  Protection Force

Vattel, Emerich de (1714-1767) 45
Vietnam
  drugs in war 63
  male civilians, killing of 64
Vitoria, Francisco do (1486-1546) 45
Vukovar evacuation 140–41
vulnerability 9, 33, 44, 101–3
  definition 102
  men 118, 172
  reframing 125–8, 172
  women 123
    and children 165

war
  'civilized' 46
  drugs 63
  family violence 166
  guerrilla 63
  'just war' tradition 44
  and masculinity 43
  rules of 11
  sexual violence 98
  statistics on victims 98–9, 115–16
  total 49
  and women 33–4
  women and children, as victims 63–4
    statistics 98–9
war crimes trials 134
Westphalian system 47
women *see also* women and children
  as belligerents 121–2, 124–5, 126
  child protection 32
  civilian immunity 44
    discourse 32–4
  as civilians 44, 124–5

as combatants 26, 48, 62, 64, 66,
  121–2, 126, 152, 165
innocence 33–4, 44
as mothers 99–101
as non-combatants 45–6
as peacemakers 100–101, 124
rights 118–25
violence against 119
vulnerability 33, 44, 101–3, 123
and war 33–4
war crimes 34
women and children *see also* women
  aerial bombing 63
  in armed conflict 120–21
  as civilians 2, 97–9, 106–7
  as combatants 2, 66
  Kosovo 83–4
  media representation of 110–11
  non-lethal atrocities 9
  protection of 113–14, 169
    in ancient times 42
  as refugees 84, 85, 117
  Rwanda, massacres of 63–4
  targeting 99, 115
  vulnerability 9, 101–3, 125–8, 165
  war victims 18–19, 63–4
    statistics 98–9
women's network 119–22, 125
women's rights 118–25

Yugoslav National Army (JNA) 65–6
Yugoslavia *see also* Balkan Wars
  desertion 35–6
  International Committee of the Red
    Cross (ICRC) 132
  male civilians, maltreatment of 18
  United Nations High Commission
    for Refugees (UNHCR) 132

Zepa evacuation 141–2

Also published in the series:

Setting the Agenda for Global Peace
Conflict and Consensus Building
Anna C. Snyder
ISBN 0 7546 1933 8

Fashioning Inequality
The Multinational Company and Gendered
Employment in a Globalizing World
Juanita Elias
ISBN 0 7546 3698 4

Vulnerable Bodies
Gender, the UN and the Global Refugee Crisis
Erin K. Baines
ISBN 0 7546 3734 4

(Un)thinking Citizenship
Feminist Debates in Contemporary South Africa
Edited by
Amanda Gouws
ISBN 0 7546 3878 2

Turkey's Engagement with Global Women's Human Rights
Nüket Kardam
ISBN 0 7546 4168 6